Beyond the Stone Arches

An American Missionary Doctor in China, 1892–1932

Edward Bliss Jr.

John Wiley & Sons, Inc.

New York • Chichester • Weinheim • Brisbane • Singapore • Toronto

Published by John Wiley & Sons, Inc.
Published simultaneously in Canada

This publication is designed to provide accurate and authoritative information in regard to the subject matter covered. It is sold with the understanding that the publisher is not engaged in rendering professional services. If professional advice or other expert assistance is required, the services of a competent professional person should be sought.

Library of Congress Cataloging-in-Publication Data:

Bliss, Edward
    Beyond the stone arches : an American missionary doctor in China, 1892–1932 / Edward Bliss, Jr.
        p.   cm.
    ISBN 0-471-39759-8 (cloth : alk. paper)
    1. Bliss, Edward, 1865– 2. Missionaries, Medical—China—
Shao-wu hsien—Biography. 3. Medicine—China—Shao-wu hsien—
Anecdotes. 4. China—History—1861–1912—Anecdotes. 5. China—
History—Republic, 1912–1949—Anecdotes. I. Title.

    R722.32.B55 A3   2001
    610'.92—dc21
    [B]   00-033026

Printed in the United States of America

10 9 8 7 6 5 4 3 2 1

Dedicated to Lois Arnette Bliss,
who wanted so much for the story to be told

Contents

✦

Acknowledgments

I AM IN DEBT to many people. Among them are Lurton Blassingame; Mervin Block; Leona Burr; Walter Cronkite; Joseph and Margot Dembo; Bob Edwards; John K. Fairbank; Grace Funk; H. T. Huang; Walter H. Judd; Philomena Jurey; Edwin Kellogg; Robert McClure, Anne Bliss Mascolino; Edward R. Murrow; Gary Nurenberg; William L. Plante Jr.; George Shepherd; Emerson Law Stone; Julia Storrs Strode; Josephine Walker; and my sisters, Ruth Bliss Buddington and Elisabeth Bliss Dinsmore, who shared their memories.

I am grateful for the assistance of the American Board of Commissioners for Foreign Missions, the Yale University Library, and the Houghton Library at Harvard University. I am profoundly grateful to Deborah Grosvenor, my agent, and to Hana Umlauf Lane, the editor at John Wiley & Sons who gave me invaluable guidance. I appreciate the care taken by Faith Duvall in typing the manuscript.

What I owe Lois Arnette Bliss, my wife and loving primary editor, is beyond measure.

Author's Note

THIS IS THE STORY of my father in China. The life is re-created from letters and long conversations, and some from firsthand because I shared the adventure. Most of the action takes place in Fujian Province, in a walled city called Shaowu situated on a beautiful, dangerous river, the Min, which has its source in the mountains west of Shaowu and slithers southeastward across the breadth of Fujian to the sea. Until after World War II, no railroad connected Fujian with any other province. Hemmed in by mountains on three sides and facing the natural moat of the Taiwan Strait on the other, the region was able for more than a thousand years to remain proudly independent of the dynasties to the north.

China was my father's life. A predecessor to those in the Peace Corps, he healed, farmed, delivered babies, and bred cattle for the glory of God and the dignity of man. He served from the latter days of the Qing Dynasty to the early days of Mao Zedong.

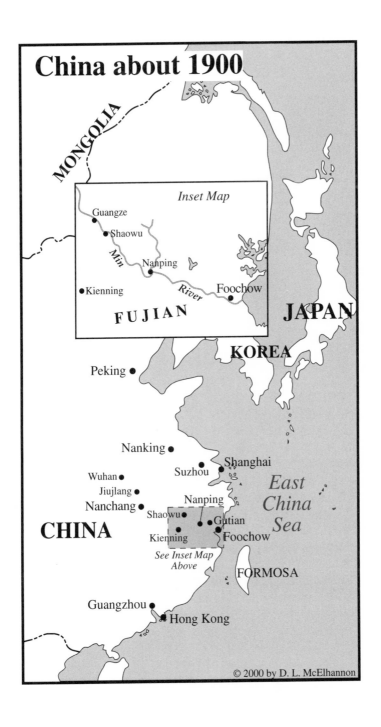

China about 1900

MONGOLIA

Inset Map

- Guangze
- Shaowu
- Min
- Nanping
- Kienning
- River
- Foochow

FUJIAN

JAPAN

KOREA

- Peking

- Nanking
- Suzhou
- Shanghai
- Wuhan
- Jiujlang
- Nanchang
- Nanping
- Shaowu
- Gutian
- Kienning
- Foochow

CHINA

East China Sea

See Inset Map Above

FORMOSA

- Guangzhou
- Hong Kong

© 2000 by D. L. McElhannon

I Feel I Have Fallen
among Friends

THE CITY WAS not yet in sight. It lay behind the hill called Monkey Head, around the great bend in the river, but the foreign doctor in the incongruous bowler hat—incongruous in the hinterlands of Fujian Province—asked the boatmen to put him ashore. He was sure he could walk faster than the river junk was being rowed.

By the Chinese calendar, Edward Bliss, M.D., had arrived in that province on the sixteenth day of the tenth moon in the eighteenth year of the reign of Emperor Guangxu. The date by Western reckoning was November 5, 1892. The coastal steamer had left Shanghai at daybreak on the fourth and had reached Fuzhou on the night of the fifth, picking its way up the intricate channel to Pagoda Anchorage in the light of a yellow moon. That same night, writing home, he described the broad harbor mouth and the encircling mountains and the warm welcome given him by the Fuzhou missionaries. He had wondered if he would feel lost among them, for they were all strangers, but he was able to say, "I feel I have fallen among friends."

He had been assigned to the mission station at Shaowu, on the upper reaches of the Min, which required a river trip that, in that time, took three weeks. He had planned to proceed there directly, but the American consul advised him to wait. The Min, with its rapids and marauding pirates, was no river to travel alone. Joseph Elkanah Walker, D.D., and his wife, Adelaide, would be making the trip in about a month and were old China hands. Walker had founded the Protestant mission at Shaowu and may have known more about China than any other "roundeye" in the province, for he made a serious study of its culture, wrote beautifully in Chinese, and was able to translate hymns. It was said that

The Bridge of Ten Thousand Ages in Fuzhou, about 1900.

he was as at home with the parables of Confucius as he was with those of Christ.

Walker's personal history captured the imagination of the children of the mission. His father, a graduate of Bangor Theological Seminary in Maine, had served as missionary to Indian tribes in Oregon Territory. The journey across the American continent from Maine took 178 days, most of them on horseback. The son enrolled at the same seminary a year before completion of the transcontinental railroad, and so to reach Bangor from Oregon Territory he had traveled by ship to Panama; by train—in a boxcar—across the isthmus; by ship to New York, and then by train the rest of the way. It was on a paddle-wheeled steamer of the Pacific Mail Line that he came to China from San Francisco in 1872.

Now with his wife he was returning from furlough in America, and the consul had no doubt they would welcome the young doctor's presence on the long, upriver trip. As it turned out, the Walkers did not reach Fuzhou for two months. Although Edward chafed at the delay, he put the time to good use at the mission hospital, treating fearsome, often unfamiliar diseases he later would have to treat by himself. (His first patient was a deaf mute who set

Dr. Joseph Walker founded the Protestant mission at Shaowu and may have known more about China than any other Westerner in the province.

forth his symptoms in unintelligible Chinese characters.) Descendants have an old photograph of Edward taken in this period. He appears in a group picture. "Oh," he said one time, recalling the occasion, "that was my first Christmas in China. The Foochow [Fuzhou] people had a celebration, and there was plum pudding and a tree." The photograph shows him wearing a mustache—the goatee came later—but he has the same alert eyes and well-shaped bald head that proves he lost his hair early.

It was not until January 19, 1893, that they started upriver. Walker superintended the loading of the two boats like a seasoned docker, shouting orders in shrill Fukienese and smiting his forehead with the palm of his hand in exasperation whenever a box was placed in the wrong boat or a crate of breakables was too rudely set down. Sacks of oranges and potatoes, flour bags wrapped in oil paper, canned dried beef, cocoa, condensed milk, and medicines were stowed under loose deck boards. Other provisions, packed in bamboo baskets, were set aside for use during the trip. Live cargo consisted of five caged chickens.

The bustle seemed out of all proportion to the business of transporting three foreigners and their worldly goods. Coolies with broad bamboo hats and flouncing queues trotted to the boats in impressive succession with the missioners' possessions while, through it all, a solitary crewman sat in the stern of the Walker boat, mending a sail. He seemed the only serene, right-minded person in the whole affair.

Their flotilla consisted of three river junks of the class called duck boats. In fact, all Min River boats were in the "fowl" class. There were duck boats and rooster boats, made of camphor wood, and super duck boats and sparrow boats. A rooster boat was twice as big as an ordinary duck boat and only a little smaller than a super duck. The so-called salt boat was a version of the super duck used to transport salt, which was a government monopoly. The sparrow boat, which reminded Edward of a whale boat, was the smallest craft on the river, measuring no more than twenty feet. With their narrow beams and V-bottoms, the little sparrows darted between rocks that would tear other boats apart. The duck boats chartered by Walker were puny compared to the great river junks of North China, which sometimes measured more than a hundred feet. The Walkers and their belongings, including a new set of dining room furniture, took up two of the boats, Edward shared his boat with a bright-faced Shaowu boy of fifteen who had been attending the middle school at Fuzhou. With a crew of nine on each boat, no one had room to spare.

It was 250 miles from Fuzhou to Shaowu, and on the first day they traveled only fourteen miles. While the patched sail fluttered dismally between an occasional breeze, Edward studied with the schoolboy Tsien, who had cheerfully agreed to teach him a few phrases in the Shaowu dialect. These lessons took place in the open bow of the boat. A large thatched canopy, or *peng*, covered the craft amidships. Edward and the boy slept in the forward cabin with a few yards of mosquito netting draped over the entrance. The large aft cabin belonged to the crew. During that first day the crewmen were strangely invisible, although their voices, low and aspirate, could be heard through the bulkhead. In the stern, the frowning helmsman stood on a raised platform, his arm on the great sweep oar, looking straight ahead, rarely moving, a graven image of purpose.

A duck boat, one of several in the "fowl" class on the Min River.

Toward noon the Walker boat pulled alongside, and Edward went aboard for a Chinese meal of mushrooms, fried red peppers, and rice. Walker said that mushrooms raised at Shaowu were famous for their tenderness and flavor. Reminiscing, he told how he and two other missionaries, Simeon Woodin and D. W. Osgood, "discovered" Shaowu on the fifteenth day of November 1873, the first Americans ever to enter the walled city. Osgood, too, was a doctor and treated such cases as presented themselves, while Woodin and Walker traipsed through the countryside, distributing tracts.

The three missionaries reconnoitered for a week, then withdrew to Fuzhou. But in 1876, Joseph Walker returned with Adelaide and stayed. During the next sixteen years they were joined by other missionary families, but the merciless climate, and malaria, forced all but two families to leave. An excitement filled Walker as he talked. Pioneering came to him naturally. He said, "I *had* to pioneer," and told how his parents had gone to Oregon Territory.

Walker said that normally they would proceed under sail as far as Shuikou, now a matter of sixty miles. If the wind died absolutely, the men would take to the oars. Shuikou marked the foot of the first rapids, where tracking would begin. To track, six men from each boat would go ashore and don their harness. Only three stayed on board—the helmsman to steer and the two others to keep the boat off the rocks with their iron-tipped poles. "In some places," Walker said, "you will see eighteen or twenty men on a single tracking line. They will pull one boat through the rapids and then go back for another. I have seen it take an hour to pull one salt boat fifty feet."

He picked up one of the lines and showed Edward how it was plaited with strands of bamboo and how each line, no matter its diameter, was composed of sixteen of these strands. If the line was heavier, each individual strand was heavier, but the number of strands was always the same magic number, sixteen. The lines were hundreds of feet long, so that they would reach several times across the river if let out their full length. And if they dipped into the current, it made no difference. They would not gain weight and encumber the trackers because bamboo does not absorb water. Walker called the river ruthless. "In four thousand years," he said, "the Chinese have built perhaps a hundred bridges between Fuzhou and Shaowu, and today not one of them stands."

As he talked, the missionary flotilla passed a village, where on the riverbank women were washing clothes. The women were kneeling. Again and again they dipped the clothes in the water, cudgeled them, and wrung them. Near the opposite shore a mandarin's caravel moved majestically downstream, propelled by fourteen oarsmen whose shafts rose and dipped rhythmically, like the oars of a Roman galley. The chant of the oarsmen came to Edward across the water, and he could make out a large dragon flag waving at the stern.

Below Nanping Are
the Worst Rapids of All

器

THE FIRST NIGHT above Fuzhou the three duck boats moored opposite another village. By the light of a kerosene lantern Edward and the boy Tsien laid mattresses on the floor of their cabin and rolled themselves in blankets. Sleep came to the accompaniment of the soft lapping of water against the side of the boat.

They awoke to the creaking of oarlocks. Not a particle of air stirred. The boatmen rowed steadily all day. The next morning, although the wind freshened, Walker refused to travel because it was the Sabbath. He held a small service and preached on the wages of sin. The boatmen spent the day gambling.

Once more, on the fourth day, they were becalmed. Again the crew took to the oars, but after two hours a breeze came up the valley behind them, wrinkling the water about them and filling their patched sails, so that they reached Shuikou at the foot of the first rapids by early afternoon. Here the masts were lowered and taken ashore to be stored until the boats returned. Now the decks were clear for the battle that lay ahead.

All that afternoon, they climbed "The Ladder." In the quieter stretches, between rapids, the men rammed their boats ahead with poles of bamboo that bent like archers' bows. With infinite patience the polers paced the gunwales, planting their poles firmly in the shallow river bottom and walking toward the stern, shoving themselves forward, boat length by boat length, until the next rapids, where they harnessed themselves and renewed the long pull onshore.

Sometimes the missionaries went ashore and walked a mile or more, then waited for the boats to catch up. "It's a good idea," Walker said, "to stretch your legs," but it was also safer onshore. Moreover, there was something uncomfortable about being warped upriver by men in harness, straining so that their hands, dangling, touched the ground. It was symbolic of the burden carried patiently by the masses of Chinese people. The missionaries could disassociate themselves from it, to a degree, by walking.

At a distance the trackers lost their identity, but all Chinese, in the beginning, looked alike to Edward. Their noses were the same. So were their eyes, their hair—it was always black—and their queues. From his arrival he was sure that sooner or later this inability to distinguish among individuals would trip him up, so now he made a study of Chinese faces. He began with the nine men on his boat. The cook, he observed, had bushy eyebrows. No other crewman approached the cook in this respect. Nor was there any mistaking the indomitable helmsman, whose walrus mustache and heavy, protruding jaw favored Grover Cleveland, who had recently been elected to a second term as president of the United States. Another member of the crew was definitely walleyed. The face of another had been ravaged by smallpox, and still another looked so much like an Irishman that all three missionaries referred to him as Pat. Thus he went through the entire crew, rejoicing in his findings. But Pat was his favorite. He cherished him not only for his physiognomy but also for the pride he took in his work; for the careful way he examined the tracking line at the end of each day; and for how, simply by looking Irish, he made him feel at home on a river junk half a world away from home.

It was a beautiful, exotic world, even in the subdued month of January. "The scenery is something grand," he wrote. "I can see, piled up in the distance, mountain peaks which in their wildness surpass imagination." Close at hand, rising from the river valley, were terraced rice paddies and hillsides covered with tea. He described the ingenuity with which the terraces were irrigated; how spring water fed into a paddy at the top was used by all the other paddies, some a thousand feet below; and how the tea shrubs, richly green, contrasted with the red earth.

On the fifth day, a raw wind came out of the north. "Most of the time," he reported, "it has been too cold to do anything except wrap myself in a blanket. When we come to a hard place, and the boat makes scarcely any progress, I pick up a pole and help a little. That sort of work soon warms me up." It was like him to help pole the boat.

Just below Nanping, the river showed its cruelty. They were waiting for a big salt boat to go up ahead of them through a rage of water and jagged rocks. Twenty trackers towing the salt boat were employing at least three hundred feet of line. Their bodies, straining, stretched almost parallel with the tracking path. But the river junk, heavy with salt, seemed not to move.

Suddenly, sounding like a pistol shot, the line snapped. At once the current snatched the boat and sent it careening down the rapids, straight toward the missionaries' boats waiting their turn. The trackers, unmoving, a frieze of dread, could only watch, but on the salt boat the helmsman fought to hold the boat in the channel. The missionaries' boatmen leaped to their poles. Perhaps they could fend off the salt boat if it did not crash them head on.

Edward saw the salt boat descending on him, yawing in the water like something drunk. Two men had climbed beside the helmsman and were working the sweep oar. If they could make the boat come down bow first, they might cheat the river. For perhaps a half minute the boat obeyed. Then came the sound of wood splintering. A rock had slit the belly of the boat. The crewmen, spilled off the helmsman's platform, scrambled for safety on the *peng,* but even as they reached it, the boat rolled over and sank.

Edward saw a boatman being swept toward him. He could not simply watch; perhaps his years of boyhood swimming had been for this. But in the seconds it took to tear off his shoes, the boatman disappeared. As far as anyone could tell, no one from the salt boat survived. This was not surprising, Walker said. Few boatmen could swim.

The rest of the voyage was an anticlimax. At Nanping, Walker made a courtesy call at the Methodist mission, and next day the tiny flotilla passed through Cheng Men Long, or City Gate Gorge, so named because the river narrowed and flowed through a defile like the gate of a walled city. In the gorge the rock face came straight down, casting a gray picture of itself on the water. Walker, who made a hobby of such things, dropped a sounding line and found a depth of fifty feet, though the river was at low stage. Often, in February and March, heavy rains sent Cheng Men Long into a torrent, forcing boats to wait days, even weeks, before they dared enter. But now, in this season, the still water made a mirror.

The foreigners' flotilla was dwarfed by cliffs towering above it like high walls. It was dark in the gorge. An eerie silence prevailed, broken only by the whisper of water at the bow and the steady, rhythmic dip of oars.

The first city above the gorge is Yangkou, which they came to on the eleventh day. Yangkou was a garrison city. Edward would always associate the place with its fortress. From his boat, on that first visit, he could see soldiers patrolling the parapets, like something from the Middle Ages. Black-tiled houses stuck their backsides over the water. Boats nudged the waterfront like hungry piglets.

The next afternoon they passed Shunchang, which forty years earlier had been made the capital of a *xian*, or county, as a reward for resisting the fanatical Taiping rebels who, in the middle of the nineteenth century, overran half of China. In the next forty years Edward would have occasion to see Cheng Men Long, Yangkou, and Shunchang many times. The river would become almost as familiar as the train rides taken back and forth from college.

Walker had said they might find pirates at a place called Rooster Fight, above the next rapids. Like Cheng Men Long, this was a bottleneck. Two rock formations, which in silhouette resembled fighting cocks, converged in the middle of the river, and as long as anyone could remember, brigands had used this geological feature to line their pockets. Robbery was so commonplace at Rooster Fight that it came to be regarded as a payment of customs. But, passing through the strait on this second day of February 1893, not a pirate was to be seen. Walker called it beginner's luck.

Four months had passed since Edward had left home to practice medicine in China. He was beginning to wonder if he would ever reach Shaowu when, on the eighth of February, Walker told him that the city lay five miles ahead, around the riverbend and waiting. It was at this point, after twenty-one days on the river and the negotiation of eighty separate rapids, that Edward left the boat to walk by himself to the place God would show to him.

The road he took on the southern bank was no more than a footpath, stone-paved in some distant dynasty. No one met him on the road. He had the way all to himself as in a dream, and

The mysterious great stone arches Edward encountered when, after getting off the riverboat, he walked toward Shaowu, the walled city where he would work for the next forty years.

when he came to a succession of great stone arches, he could stop and examine them without self-consciousness. They were very old and covered with strange inscriptions. The oldness and strangeness stirred him. He was walking toward a city he had never seen but to which he meant to devote his life, a city that was standing in the days of the Mongol conqueror Genghis Khan and where, he knew, a mission established by modern-day apostles had scarcely begun its work.

How would he do? He looked across the river to where a pagoda, high on a hilltop, guarded the southern approaches of Shaowu from evil spirits. The pagoda stood straight, seven-tiered against the winter sky with nothing close by to take from its dignity, no sign of a path on the grassy slope, no wall, no temple, no peasants' hut, but beautifully alone on the hill, by itself.

The Shaowu pagoda.

Edward quickened his step and saw Shaowu for the first time. He came around the bend of the river and saw a sprawling, black-roofed city veiled in the smoke of ten thousand supper fires.

Strange How Clearly We Remember Long Past Events

❀

IF HE HAD CHOSEN a town to be born in, it is hard to see how Edward, the China missionary, could have done better than Newburyport on the Massachusetts North Shore. It was here that Donald McKay revolutionized the design of sailing ships, enabling American clippers to wrest from slow, bluff-bowed East Indiamen the business of bringing tea from China. In 1844 Caleb Cushing of Newburyport negotiated the first treaty between China and the United States, spelling out the principle of extraterritoriality. And a Newburyport clergyman, Samuel Spring, helped found the American Board of Commissioners for Foreign Missions, along with Governor John Treadwell of Connecticut and Reverend Timothy Dwight of Yale.

Newburyport exuded history. Old Caleb Cushing, whom Edward could remember seeing in his fine carriage about the time he became minister to Spain, lived in the Federalist mansion at 98 High Street. On State Street, George Washington slept in the handsome residence built by Patrick Tracy for his son Nathaniel, who sent out the first privateer against England during the Revolutionary War. It was, someone quipped, a place famous for piety and privateering. Thomas Jefferson, John Quincy Adams, and the Marquis de Lafayette were other "big names" entertained in the Tracy mansion, which in the year Edward was born became the Newburyport Public Library.

Edward Lydston Bliss was born to the accompaniment of church bells on a Sunday morning, the tenth of December 1865. The Civil War had been over for eight months. General Grant was inspecting the Union forces still in Georgia. Napoleon III was emperor of France, and in China the Taiping Rebellion had been crushed only a few months earlier after fifteen years of fanatical strife.

Edward's father, Charles Henry Bliss.

Edward's mother, Emily Lydston Bliss.

Edward was the second child and first son of Charles Henry and Emily Lydston Bliss. Eight children were born of the union, but a daughter died in infancy. The father, a big, genial man with muttonchop whiskers, was a wholesale dealer in Eureka sewing thread and Schleicher & Sohne needles imported from Germany— "Agent for Charles Schleicher's Celebrated Needles," his business card read. He also sold silk, and remnant samples of silk ribbons, discovered unfaded in a trunk, adorned the hair of great-granddaughters sixty years after his death.

A Chinese proverb says, "The longest journey starts with the first step." Edward took his first step toward the mission field simply by being born into the family he was and at that particular time. It was a devout, almost puritanical family, which attended church twice on Sunday and in which bread was baked before sundown on Saturday so as not to desecrate the Sabbath. Church was a family affair. They walked to church in a company, and the children, toddler and teenager, endured the hour-long sermon with their parents in a family pew. Sunday school was held after the morning service. The church itself was an architectural monstrosity built in 1793, apparently by men who confused ugliness with beauty. It was a plain wooden building that but for two blunt towers could easily have been mistaken for a warehouse. It had no

Edward Lydston Bliss on his first birthday, December 10, 1866.

lawn. The building squatted on the whole plot, leaving room only for two larch trees brought from England by some colonial who had a feeling for the old country. The pastor in Edward's youth was the Reverend Randolph Campbell, a Presbyterian.

"Wasn't it peculiar," Edward was once asked, "a Presbyterian tending a Congregationalist flock?"

There was reproach in Edward's face, as though the question were somehow out of order. "Not at all," he said. "Campbell was a good man." It was as simple as that.

Charles Henry Bliss was a staunch supporter of the church, serving as deacon and superintendent of the Sunday school. Emily helped on the missionary committee. It raised money for missions, arranged for speakers, and there was the business of the annual missionary barrel. This was the wooden barrel that women of the church filled with baby clothes, quilts, doilies, ironing board covers—anything conceivably useful to a missionary family. Once a month, on Missionary Sunday, letters from missionaries were read in church. One letter told of cannibalism. As a boy, Edward reckoned it the best.

On rare occasions the congregation saw, and heard, a missionary in the flesh. Among these "live" apostles visiting Newburyport was his father's second cousin Edwin Bliss, who had served as a missionary in Turkey. The two times he came to Newburyport he stayed at the Bliss house, and chances are these were pleasant occasions. Charles Bliss was a cheerful man, and in his book *Leavening the Levant,* the Reverend Joseph Greene describes Edwin Bliss as "a man of broad mind, sound judgment, and sweet humor, a delightful companion." Like Charles, he was a native of Vermont. Another second cousin, Isaac Bliss, represented the American Bible Society in Egypt and Turkey, where he supervised the distribution of an estimated two million Bibles. He never came to Newburyport, but Edward heard him speak during his freshman year at Yale. Daniel Bliss, founder of the American University in Beirut, was a distant cousin whom the family never met.

Another family tie is cause for speculation. The Blisses of Newburyport were also related by marriage to Ralph Waldo Emerson, whom Charles greatly admired, and it may be that Edward received his name from one of the essayist's four brothers, Edward Bliss Emerson. When the brother died young in 1834, Emerson wrote in an "In Memoriam" that "[h]e could not frame a word unfit, an act unworthy to be done," qualities Charles would want in his firstborn son.

One influence came in an odd, roundabout way. While Edward was in high school, General Adolphus Greely, who lived practically next door, set out on the first of his daring expeditions to the Arctic. This so fired the teenager's imagination that he read all the books on exploration he could find. One was Henry Stanley's story of David Livingstone in Africa. The account of his search for the medical missionary made an impression so deep that one day it would determine Edward's lifework. But his ambition at that time was to be a minister, respected and beloved like the Reverend Campbell. Neither he, nor his parents, could think of a higher calling.

Early evidences of this ambition are fragmentary. One Sunday morning Edward was found on a tree stump, posturing like a preacher and appealing in a shrill, childish treble, "Will 'ou, oh will 'ou be dood." The rapt audience being implored to sin no more consisted of one gray cat. Edward was four at the time. Two years later, at Sunday school, his teacher presented him with a small card. On one side appears his name and the date—June 24, 1871. On the other side is printed the Bible quotation "Teach me to do Thy will." A larger card bears Edward's signature and the words "I, the undersigned, hope I have found Jesus to be my precious Saviour, and I promise with his help to live as His loving child and faithful servant all my life."

He would live as God's servant in the ministry, and from books on exploration and novels by Sir Walter Scott—"I loved Scott"—he turned to the Bible. For exercise he spoke frequently at young peoples' Christian Endeavor meetings and occasionally at services attended by adults. People told him, "You touched our hearts," so he believed he had indeed received the Call, until gradually, to his dismay, he found his own heart was not in it, that what he was saying was forced, that speaking of redemption had become, for reasons he could not understand, an agony. Perhaps it was from a sense of unfitness that he felt so painfully ill at ease. Who was he to tell others how to conduct themselves? For a while he thought that if he persevered, and prayed hard enough, he could overcome this feeling. But no matter how often he tried or how hard he prayed, it was wrong for him. So he gave up. And it didn't feel so bad. If God had meant him to preach, surely it would have gone better. With all he had heard of missions, the thought of becoming a missionary must have occurred to him, but apparently he was not then ready for so big a step. He decided if he could not preach, he would teach.

He had in his disillusionment the comfort of family. It seemed so safe and permanent, the white, green-shuttered house at 18 Allen Street, with its monumental picket fence and the name C. H. Bliss in German silver on the door. The house, originally quite humble, had grown with the family. At its southwestern corner, where a pear tree was growing, a new dining room was added with another bedroom above it, and the old dining room became the living room—sitting room, they called it. Then a bay window was added to the parlor to make space for the grand piano Charles bought in a burst of extravagance for his girls.

"I think," he explained, "that every young woman should know and appreciate music."

But none of the girls ever really learned to play, and for years the huge instrument stood in virtual silence, stranded, serving no useful purpose until the grandchildren started coming. Then its lid was used, ignominiously, as a shelf for family photographs, until finally it was crowded with the pictures of grandchildren and great-grandchildren taken by photographers ranging from Bachrach of Boston to Platz of Los Angeles. The final addition, architecturally, came at about the turn of the century, when an uncovered porch was built along the southern side of the house. In the floor of the porch was placed, for no reason known today, a slab of thick glass, roughly two feet by three feet, through which small children peeked because of green things growing mysteriously underneath. Throughout these alterations some things did not change. One was the closeness of the family. Another was the large sampler over the fireplace in the living room that read, "God Bless Our Home." It was put there when Charles and Emily married and was still there at the end.

The next-to-youngest baby died of diphtheria at ten months. Edward almost died of scarlet fever at eight months, and Will came down with tuberculosis of the spine and never stood straight again. All the children had assigned chores. As eldest son, it was Edward's responsibility to get up first in the morning and light the fire. He would also cook the oatmeal. He told of standing by the stove on frosty mornings with a Latin grammar in one hand, a wooden spoon in the other, and the family tomcat on his shoulder.

It was one of those rare nineteenth-century families in which daughters as well as sons attended college. Clara, the oldest girl, went to Mount Holyoke. So did Marian, and Mary, the youngest, graduated Phi Beta Kappa from Wellesley, where she became a professor of botany. Marian was said to be the first woman to practice medicine in Beverly, Massachusetts; Clara taught chemistry at Wells College in upstate New York. In fact, when it came to education, the girls did better than the boys. Edward graduated from Yale and George from the Massachusetts Institute of Technology, but young Charles had only a year at Harvard, and Will never went beyond high school.

Still, the white frame house on Allen Street was the place they all came back to down through the years—Edward from China; George from Idaho, where he worked as a geologist; Clara, professor of chemistry at Wells College; Mary from Wellesley; and

Marian from Philadelphia, where she studied medicine, and then from Beverly, which was close enough for commuting on the Boston and Maine. Will spent much of his time at home, and Charles lived only three blocks away, on High Street. None of the girls married, which was surprising because, with the exception of Mary, they seemed the marrying type. Mary, it's said, had "an austere look."

Among relics discovered in the Allen Street attic after Edward's death were his slingshot, whittled from a forked stick; sundry clay marbles; and a battered wooden top, a toy that as a boy he loved to spin. His chums were Sam Mulliken, George Woods, and Arthur Noyes. When Edward founded a hospital in Shaowu, the first contribution from outside the family—twenty dollars—came from Woods, although he was at that time a low-salaried clerk. Both Mulliken and Noyes went into teaching. Mulliken taught organic chemistry at MIT. From 1907 to 1909, Noyes, whose field was also chemistry, served as acting president of MIT. He then moved to Caltech, where with astrophysicist George Ellery Hale and Nobel laureate Robert A. Millikan he led that institution to preeminence in the field of chemistry and physics.

To hear Edward tell it, he and his friends had incomparable fun. On May Day they would clamber up Oldtown Hill and hide their picnic baskets in a thicket until they got hungry, or hike out to Plum Island Point or down to Ipswich Bluffs. One Fourth of July Edward and Sam walked to Rye Beach and back, a distance of some twenty miles. For boating they had Parker River or the Merrimack, which took you up past Chain Bridge, the first chain bridge in America, or down Plum Island River to Ipswich. You didn't take your rowboat out to the sea side of Plum Island—no outboard motors then—but negotiated the inland river with fine calculation to make use of the tides. In these waters, in the summertime, boys frolicked like porpoises—and not only there but in the ocean itself.

Yes, the ocean. In that day, Melville's phrase "spires of the port" applied doubly to Newburyport. Then the steeples of the churches were matched by a harborful of masts. It was a shipbuilder's town for two hundred years, echoing with the sound of broadaxes and caulking mallets. Oak and pine logs were floated down the Merrimack from New Hampshire and axed and whipsawed into ships' lumber. Masts, spars, pumps, windlasses—even

19

figureheads—were Newburyport-made. And many of them tasted salt from the China Sea.

At age twelve, Edward made what he jokingly called his first voyage. It was aboard a schooner, newly launched, that was sent around Cape Ann to Boston, a log of thirty-nine nautical miles. He went on a Saturday with thirteen schoolmates, and he recalled, long afterward, how sweet the sea air smelled that day, how blue the water in the Basin, and how the sun danced on the sails of a dozen other ships—sloops, schooners, barks, and brigs—putting out after the violent squall of the previous afternoon. He would describe how the new schooner moved gingerly into the middle of the river, then along with the tide past the Water Street wharves, down past the clam diggers' shanties and the Basin, twixt the dunes and stone jetties to the open ocean. It had excited him the way the ship came alive, feeling the cold Labrador current along its keel, shivering at the first shock, then rearing and plunging between the troughs, discovering spray and obedience to the helmsman as the wind freshened and the spires of Newburyport receded and all was made fast by the skeleton crew.

Looking back, he thought he saw the two chimneys of his grandmother's house on Madison Street. He could not be sure. Then, quickly, he ran to the foremost part of the ship and, standing in the bow, pretended he was making the long voyage to Cathay.

The Most Fool Thing I Ever Did

EDWARD BLISS EMERSON went to Harvard. Edward Bliss of Newburyport applied to Yale because it was beyond Boston and because he heard that teachers graduated from Yale were in demand. He had not heard of Mrs. E. M. Poteat's statement "I would rather send my son to hell than to Yale," although the prominent preacher's wife was still living at the time. One doubts if it would have made any difference. He knew what he wanted.

During his freshman year Edward waited on tables at the Vermont Dining Rooms, which were in a boardinghouse on Temple Street, next door to the old Mory's. Its proprietress, Mrs. Cogston, a kindly soul, took a shine to Edward and hid cream pies for him because she knew he liked them. Indeed, he spent his first Thanksgiving away from home with Mrs. Cogston as her guest. He did not go home because the round-trip train fare would have cost nine dollars and fifty-six cents. Long afterward he would recall how good the dinner was. "There were just three of us at the table with all that turkey—Mrs. Cogston, another boy who was stuck in New Haven, and myself."

A letter he wrote in late September 1883 shows how it was with him as he entered upon college life. "Every day," he said, "I am becoming more and more acquainted with boys in my class, also in classes above me. Perhaps that's why I haven't been hazed yet! At any rate, I expect to have some good times. This afternoon I went to Lake Whitney, which is about three miles off. I had there a very good row for an hour." He described "two steep, rocky cliffs, one on each side of the city, from which eminences there are grand views of the surrounding country." He did not report his rash attempt to scale the sheer face of East Rock. Halfway up he became stranded, unable to find another foothold, and succeeded only after the greatest difficulty to reach the top.

"It was," he said in his ninety-fifth year, "the most fool thing I ever did."

At Yale Edward studied under such legendary educators as Noah Porter; the renowned mineralogist Edward S. Dana; and William Graham Sumner, the economist turned sociologist who has been called the founder of anthropology. Porter taught moral philosophy and served as president of the university at the same time. It was, as someone said, a period when the fruits of Adam's fall weighed heavily on the minds of regulation makers. It was against regulations to entertain a young lady in your room—at that time Yale had not even dared to employ a female secretary! Attendance at daily chapel was compulsory. No plumbing existed above the basement, and the only bath, for which twenty-five cents was charged, was to be found in the college gymnasium.

Classical courses abounded. Edward studied extensively in Latin and Greek but also took courses in physics and chemistry, which later would help him in medical school. A classmate, William Lyon Phelps, remembered him as a scholar of the first rank. "We were both deeply interested in religion. A prayer meeting was held immediately after the Sunday morning service, and another prayer meeting was held every Wednesday evening. He and I always attended both of them." In sophomore year, Edward joined the Pundits, a literary society in which Phelps, who would become one of Yale's preeminent teachers, was a leading light.

Aside from the stylized plays performed in Chinese temples, Edward in his lifetime attended theater only once, in junior year, when he paid fifty cents to see *The Mikado*. The operetta, Edward allowed, had some "fine catchy singing," but he had to apportion his spending. A ticket to a baseball game also cost fifty cents and, given this choice, he rated Amos Alonzo Stagg's performance on the pitcher's mound over "Three Little Maids from School." Stagg, an all-round athlete, also played football, and in the late 1940s would be the dean of college football coaches.

Half the money sent to Edward from home was in the form of a long-term, interest-free loan, so he kept accounts. For four years every expenditure—the price of every shoelace and bottle of ink—was entered in a small leather notebook that reveals what goods and services were required, and what luxuries could be afforded, by a none-too-affluent Yale student in the 1880s. Haircuts, which went from twenty to twenty-five cents after freshman year, were indulged in once every six weeks. Occasionally ten cents was spent for a new chimney for an oil lamp. The average life of one of these fragile glass chimneys in academic surroundings appears, on the basis of Edward's accounting, to have been about nine months. For the trip from the New Haven railroad station the hack driver charged fifty cents, but the fare by horsecar was only six cents. Shoe blacking cost five cents.

It has been said that you can tell a lot about a man by how he spends his money. The account book shows that Edward, as an undergraduate, contributed regularly to religious activities, that he kept fresh fruit in his room, and that he was obsessed by baseball. In four years he bought seven baseballs, two books on baseball, a baseball bat, and attended every baseball game Yale played on its own grounds. On balmy spring evenings, before dark, he would set up a game of scrub baseball on the Old Campus near where the statue of Nathan Hale now stands. In sophomore year, while fading back for a high foul, he stumbled into a catch basin and dislocated his right shoulder. He had almost forgotten the incident until, sixty-seven years later, he fell from a stepladder. The fall caused a new dislocation of the same shoulder, and he spoke laughingly of his "old wound."

Next to baseball his chief extracurricular interest was football. If he couldn't make the team—"Alongside those fellows I was pretty puny"—he could attend the games. And at least twice a week, in season, he went out to the practice field to watch scrimmages. He studied the battling, unpadded players, and the players he studied were immortals like Pudge Heffelfinger, Charley Gill, and, of course, Stagg. Gill, who later went to China as a missionary, was on the first All-America football team.

The football game that stood out in memory was a sad one played in junior year. Edward told the story over and over again. It was always the same, his eyes brightening, hands gesturing, his voice rising. "I was standing on the sideline," he would say, "near the Princeton goal. We were ahead five to nothing, only seconds left, when this Princeton man got the ball. We went for him. He sidestepped one rusher, twisted free from another, and another, got clean away, and ran the whole length of the field. I can see it now. Peters, the Yale captain, just threw himself on the ground, face down, and hammered the ground with his fists." The final score: Yale five, Princeton six.

He liked to walk. He walked to classes, to Hamilton Field, for this was before the Yale Bowl, to East Rock and West Rock and to Lake Whitney, where he skated in winter and rowed in the spring. It was almost as though he knew he was going to wind up in a part of China where about the only way to get around was to walk. The account book shows that in four years as an undergraduate he bought twelve pairs of shoes, not counting gym slippers, and that he had these shoes repaired thirteen times.

The most enigmatic item appears under the date June 2, 1886. The item as entered is "Celebration, 10 cents." One wonders what kind of celebration it could have been. Had he, flushed with success in some enterprise, possibly an exam, bought a beer? In senior year he did show signs of profligacy. He began going to a barber to be shaved, at fifteen cents a shave. On January 25, 1887, he had his shoes shined for the first time by a bootblack *and* got a shave. He bought a silk top hat for seven dollars. Another dollar went for a cane. There is something touching about this spree by the young, happy scholar on the eve of graduation. Never again in his long life would he spend money on himself in this fashion. Never after he left Yale did he feel he could afford the services of a bootblack. He never owned another top hat, or another cane, until he was seventy; he had fallen off a roof and broken his right foot. He never again allowed himself the luxury of being shaved. Yet his life, he felt, was rich.

Altogether, his was an exquisite commencement. The sun was shining. Yale had won the boat race, beating Harvard. And, better still in Edward's view, it had defeated Harvard for the baseball championship. The game was played in Cambridge, but as soon as he heard the score he ran out and helped build a bonfire.

"My appointment is high orations," he had wired home, sending his first telegram in the flush of baccalaureate excitement. "Now you will have to hear me make a speech." In truth, Edward's oration was rather dull. How could a discussion of the philosophy of Horace be otherwise? The star of the show was a Chinese student from Kwangtung Province, now Guangdong Province. To quote the *Yale Daily News*, "The orations were all good, but that of Mr. Yan Phou Lee was probably the most popular. He was applauded throughout, and his witty remarks were frequently the cause of much laughter among the audience." Unfortunately we are not

Edward's graduation picture, Yale Class of 1887.

told what Yan Phou Lee said. However, the remarks of Thomas Curtis, the valedictorian, are recorded. "Our body," he said, "may have its representatives in every station of life. Only let us remember to be useful."

Edward planned that June day to be useful as a schoolteacher. He never dreamed of being useful in the celestial land of Yan Phou Lee.

I Found a Lifetime of Teaching Dead Languages Would Be Exceedingly Dull

ARMED WITH a Bachelor of Arts degree and a letter of reference from Noah Porter, Edward sallied forth to teach. He landed in the Massachusetts hamlet of Granby, in the Connecticut River Valley. He was principal of the high school there—and its sole teacher and janitor. The custodial duties did not discourage him, but he had not imagined how it would be giving instruction to one small group of students and leaving thirty others to make mischief. Nothing was more distasteful to Edward than exacting discipline. "I find it painful," he wrote, "to punish a boy for what amounts, in the last analysis, to exuberance of spirit."

It did not enhance his experience at Granby to learn on arriving that he would receive no pay until December. He had earned money during the summer peddling an encyclopedic tome called *The Museum of Antiquity,* but by October this was spent and he sent an SOS to brother Charles. "How much will you lend me until Christmas at six percent? Let me know what you can do as soon as possible, for I don't want to ask Father." He already owed his father four hundred dollars for college expenses. He was supposed to be repaying that debt, not increasing it. Young Charles floated a loan. The amount is not recorded.

But there were compensations. Townspeople liked him, and since Granby was near Mount Holyoke, he could occasionally see Clara. He also took comfort in the local Congregational church. When one Sunday he was asked to speak, the old hobgoblin presented itself. He was tempted to flee, but the subject assigned him was "Cheer, Not Fear." All right, he would not be afraid. And this time, miraculously, the words came to him. After writing of the compliments on his performance, he said, "Perhaps the above seems a little vainglorious, but it was not meant so. I am merely glad that it is becoming easier for me to think on my feet."

In college, Edward had majored in Latin and Greek. At Granby he got a glimpse of himself as a teacher of those languages, and the outlook, for him, was unsatisfying. He felt no enthusiasm, no inner fire. He recalled the adventures of Livingstone in Africa and the stories of missionary enterprise he had heard firsthand from his father's cousins. They challenged him, these missionaries. He resolved to follow in their train.

But he would not be a preaching missionary; he would not inflict on the heathen what he could not bring himself to inflict on his own. "As soon as it was settled in my mind to become a missionary, I asked myself in what way I could best serve. The answer, I thought, was to become a doctor." His fascination with physics and chemistry convinced him that he would take readily to medical science.

Of course, it meant starting over again. He would have to go back to Yale and earn a medical degree. And, before that, the debt to his father had to be repaid. So he registered with a teachers' agency and got an appointment in Chicago, teaching at the Harvard School for Boys, described by him as "a private academy for young swells." The position would pay a thousand dollars a year, twice what he made at Granby, with a promise of an additional two hundred dollars the next year if he stayed. He wrote his parents, "It looks as though I am fixed for next year." But he said nothing of his plans to enter medicine. Nor, when he announced his intention a few months later, did he say anything about becoming a foreign missionary.

He spent the summer in Virginia peddling his *Museum of Antiquity*. In his ninety-fifth year, shortly before his death, Edward laughed at the recollection of something that happened that summer. "I asked this man if I might show off my four-pound illustrated history, and he said go ahead; so for perhaps forty minutes I went through my spiel, telling him what a wonderful offer I was making. He listened closely. I thought he was going to bite, but when I got through he said, 'Not a bad talk you give. I used to sell that book myself.' All he wanted was just to listen to my line!"

In early September, Edward said good-bye to Allen Street and took the train for Chicago. He had time before classes started to visit the famous stockyards. "It was very interesting, but I don't think you would care to see them, or have them described." He also reported a new fad. "There is a firm here which makes what they call 'chewing gum.' I doubt it will last."

He found nothing in his experience at the Harvard School for Boys to make him regret his decision to become a missionary, and when the year was up he returned to New Haven in high spirits, ready to grapple with whatever might come. There is a buoyancy, a joy in the letters now that never appeared before. "What a wonderful day this has been!" he would exclaim. Or, "Now I am getting down to the really important work." It was, one senses, what he had been waiting for. He did his utmost because he was determined to finish the three-year course in two years. Often he was bone tired. But the theme recurring triumphantly throughout his correspondence was: "Everything is going first-rate." He might be down with a cold, or short of sleep, or down to ten cents, but everything was first-rate. He wrote his father, "Do you remember you tried to frighten me out of studying medicine by telling me about the terrible sights, sores, etc., that I would meet? Well, I have seen a good many such things now and, far from being repulsive, they are very interesting."

Edward was beginning his second year of medical study when a man came into the New Haven dispensary saying that his daughter, eighteen days old, was dying of a gastric disorder. Edward wrote, "The case was assigned to me. I went over and saw the child, and found it about as near dead as could be and get better—extremities cold and blue, eyes rolling up into her head. Couldn't make her cry if you tried.

"Well, I poured whiskey and aromatic spirits of ammonia down her throat, kept her wrapped in hot cloths, and finally put her into a bowl of hot water just as hot as she could stand. She came around under this treatment, and it gave me great pleasure. She has been getting better ever since." The next day he took a cinder out of the eye of the president of the Winchester Rifle Company. That gave him pleasure, too.

In this period, Edward still took long walks and still attended Sunday services on the Yale campus. He wrote of going to Sunday vespers at Trinity Church on the Green. He said, "They have by far the best music of all the New Haven churches." He spoke once of having to be at a YMCA meeting "because I have the honor of being vice president for the Medical School." Another time he wrote, "Oh, dear me. I have to lead a prayer meeting for postgraduate students on Wednesday and have got no farther in my preparation than to select a subject." He had gone to the library for source material but became so absorbed in a book on China that he never got around to the research.

The young medical student caught the attention of Dr. Herbert Smith, the dean of medicine, who asked him to become his assistant. Smith was chemist for the state Board of Health, as well as professor of chemistry. He put Edward on the state payroll in return for a series of tests on the purity of New Haven drinking water. Occasionally an entire day would be occupied with water analysis, but Edward's scholarship does not appear to have suffered. He received his degree of Doctor of Medicine in June 1891, with the second-highest standing in his class, completing the three-year course, as he had hoped, in two years.

Here the presence of romance in his life is revealed for the first time. In the midst of final examinations he slipped away to New York to see a young woman, Elizabeth Wilkinson. There were members of his family who were sure that if it had not been for this truancy, he would have graduated at the head of his class. Edward himself regarded the matter as of small consequence. He claimed never to have studied for grades.

On the twenty-third of April 1891, Edward wrote a letter informing his parents of the decision he had made three years before. He said, "About the time I began teaching, I became interested in the work of medical missionaries and the thought came to me, 'Here is what you are fitted for. You have always had a natural bent toward medicine. What is to prevent your giving yourself to this work?' The more I thought of the subject, the more firmly I became convinced that this was the work for me. So I gave up teaching, resolving that if the way should be opened, I would be a medical missionary." He had kept silent, he said, because he wished to save them as long as possible from the dread of parting. "But now," he explained, "the time is come when I must apply to the American Board."

Two days later he wrote to the mission board, asking how he should apply. The letter was addressed to E. K. Alden, D.D., secretary of the American Board of Commissioners for Foreign Missions, 14 Beacon Street, Boston. Edward wrote, "Last August I consulted you in regard to foreign missionary work, though it is not likely that you, meeting and corresponding with so many, will remember my name. . . . The more study and thought I give to the subject, the grander it appears, and I pray that God may honor me by using me in this service."

Even as Edward was writing this letter at Mrs. Cogston's boardinghouse in New Haven, his mother, in Newburyport, was composing the most important letter she would ever write. The letter said:

My dear Son:

Your welcome letter has been received and read and reread by Father and myself. The subject you wrote about was not wholly unexpected to me. I was in a measure prepared for it. During the past year I have been deeply impressed by the thought that perhaps God would call you to this very work which you have now chosen. At first I could not bear to entertain the thought of your leaving us to go to heathen lands, even to carry the blessed Gospel. I reasoned with myself that you were needed here as much as anywhere. There is so much sin and suffering all around us, and I felt that duty could not call you away.

But I can see now how selfish I am. I was willing to send others but wished to keep my own. When you were so sick in infancy, and there was little hope of your recovery, did I not earnestly pray that the Lord would spare your life that you might live for His glory? And now if in His infinite love and mercy He has called you to this great and glorious work, how can I hold back and place any obstacle in your path? Truly we can say as a family, "The Lord hath done great things for us, whereof we are glad."

I don't know of a nobler, grander work than a medical missionary could do, and I think that you are eminently fitted for such a work. May God bless and keep you in all your ways. And may your life be very precious in His sight. All unite in sending love to you, and want to see you very much.

Your loving
Mother

The way was now clear for him to make formal application to the mission board, "endeavoring to state without reserve all facts regarding myself which can aid you in deciding upon my fitness."

He said, "The words of David Livingstone express my feelings better than any words of my own, 'God had an only Son, and He was a missionary and a physician.' A poor, poor imitation of Him I am, or hope to be. In this service I hope to live; in it I wish to die."

And at just about this time, in the American Board magazine *Missionary Herald*, a small article appeared with a fortuitous title: WANTED: A PHYSICIAN FOR SHAOWU.

I Think I Always Have Been One to Get Off the Beaten Track

❖

EDWARD SAILED from San Francisco on September 27, 1892, aboard the SS *China,* after crossing the country leisurely in twelve days. His father had accompanied him in a dark downpour as far as Georgetown, a pitiable seven miles, delaying the inevitable parting by twenty minutes. Whereas the mother had accepted her son's decision, painful as it was for her, the father tried to change Edward's mind, reciting the dangers he might encounter and pointing out that he already had made twice the salary he would earn as a missionary. No, Edward argued, that was not quite right. As a missionary he would receive free lodging, which should be reckoned in. Basic needs would be provided, and he asked, "Isn't that all I have any right to expect?" He did not mention the Yale professor who called him a fool for going to China, or others who, less bluntly, said he was scuttling a promising medical career.

Edward had impressed doctors at New Haven Hospital from the first week of his internship. A patient was suffering from a urethral malfunction. Medicine was prescribed, and an incision was made for a rubber tube to drain his bladder. Still, his condition deteriorated. He babbled incoherently and began having seizures. Nurses reported an almost complete loss of appetite. In days, it was feared, he might die.

The case baffled the doctors until Edward, making a routine urine test, discovered traces of iodoform, an insoluble antiseptic. Although it was Sunday, he left the hospital and hurried across the New Haven green, through crowds of afternoon strollers, to the home of the dean of medicine, carrying unabashedly, almost proudly, in his right hand the test tube of urine that, he was confident, could make the difference between life and death.

From the Newburyport Daily News, *1891.*

The maid ushered a somewhat breathless young man into the
presence of Dean Smith. Producing the precious urine sample,
Edward explained his theory of what had happened. A salve made
up of iodoform powder and Vaseline had been applied constantly,
over a period of two weeks, at the point where the rubber tube
entered the patient's body. It was Edward's conviction that enough
iodoform had been absorbed into the bloodstream to cause lethal
poisoning.

"I think you're absolutely right," Smith said. "But why come
to me?"

"I thought it might be better if *you* told the doctors."

The dean understood. "You're only an intern," he said.
"Yes."

Application of iodoform was discontinued, and the man's life was saved. What Edward did not know until later was that the dean gave him full credit. And for his tact in requesting anonymity he made a hit with the hospital staff. Patients liked him, too. He seemed caring. Sometimes he brought them small bouquets of violets picked during his walks. He was, as Dean Smith wrote the mission board, highly esteemed.

He was able because of his reputation to earn as he studied. Dr. Henry L. Swain, who lectured at the medical school, had a large private practice, and he asked the young intern to assist him in surgery. Edward, at the same time, was earning money as assistant instructor in physiological chemistry. He not only paid his own expenses during the year of internship and repaid the sizable debt to his father, but saved a hundred dollars besides.

Edward asked to be sent to China "in view of the probability that, at no distant day, it will occupy the position of supreme influence among nations of the East." He expressed this conviction in his letter of application to the mission board in 1891. China also claimed his interest, he said, because a Christian nation, England, had foisted upon it the curse of opium. From the beginning he was pro-China. One of his early letters excoriated Congress for passing the Chinese Exclusion Act. Also, he shared with the Chinese their love of family. No family in Newburyport was more closely knit than his.

He was barely settled on the train, after leaving his father at Georgetown, before he took a prescription blank from his pocket and penciled what was tantamount to a cry of pain. "Perhaps it isn't hard to be going off so all alone!" Then upon reflection he wrote, "But I know it is terribly hard for you to have me go. I say to myself that it won't be for so very long after all, not nearly so long as it seems."

It would be six years. He would not see his father again. On the train window the raindrops ran down like tears.

Two hours later he was writing, "I will get ready to mail you another note at Albany. I had to finish the one mailed in Springfield in a great hurry. Did you receive it all right? I gave it to a man to put in the box for me, as I didn't have time to hunt for it. It is dark as a pocket outside, but we left the storm behind us

34

at Springfield. I don't mind it raining when we are on the cars." Evidently his mother had given him a final message to read on the train, for the note ends with his saying, "I thank you, Mother, for your loving letter. If I am anything, or ever accomplish anything, it is all due to your and Father's teaching."

His train passed through the Appalachians and the Great Plains only sixteen years after the Battle of the Little Bighorn. Each day he wrote a letter home, reporting his experiences. He told of crossing the Mississippi and seeing prairie dogs—"cute little fellows"—and grand mountains in the distance. To save money he rode in coaches in the daytime and entered the Pull-mans only at night.

On the SS *China,* crossing the Pacific, he prepared himself for his China adventure. He was studying a book Marian had given him just before he left home. She said, "It may give you some information." This seemed an understatement, since the book proclaimed on its title page that it contained all there was to know about China—"A Description of the Country and Its Inhabitants, Its Civilization and Form of Government, Its Religious and Social Institutions, Its Intercourse with Other Nations, and Its Present Conditions and Prospects." The author suggested that a sea voyage was good preparation for the work of a missionary. "In the vacuum between two worlds, the wanderer of the wide waste of waters might estimate aright his function, undistracted by the bustle of the society whence he came." But the author had not reckoned with the most elementary, most absorbing of all distractions for a man—a pretty woman.

Edward had heard of her from other passengers. They would ask mischievously, "Have you met the other Dr. Bliss?," for her name also was Dr. Bliss—Dr. Ruth Bliss—and she, too, was going out to China as a medical missionary. They did not meet at once. As Edward reported from Honolulu, "There was a big sea on, and very few were they who did not succumb to the fell sickness." But on the fourth day he met her. The seas had subsided. He had gone to the top deck and found an empty chair under a canvas awning, sheltered from the sun. He was writing a letter, but occasionally he stopped writing and looked out over the ocean, which was a beautiful green-blue. He was watching flying fish, and was surprised they could fly so far. The ocean air stimulated him. He was aboard no Newburyport clipper with bare-bosomed figurehead and white sails burgeoning in a twenty-knot breeze. The SS *China* was a black iron ship. It belched soot and throbbed with great internal engines. But to Edward it was marvelous all the same. It was a seagoing thing. Its wake spread to the horizon. Its bells rang clear, and its saloons were elegant, everything ornamented in Victorian style. "A palace," he wrote. "This is only her fifteenth voyage, so you see she is almost new."

He looked up from his letter and beheld the one who must surely be the princess of the palace. She was accompanied by an older woman who introduced them but who, almost at once, recalled something she must attend to. "Besides," she said, smiling the absurd smile common to amateur matchmakers, "I know you two doctors have a great deal to discuss."

The young woman was not embarrassed. She settled easily in the chair next to Edward and asked in a friendly way where he had taken his degree. She herself had graduated from the Women's Medical School in Philadelphia. Looking at her, Edward could think only of the picture of Athene in his Greek grammar. She had the same goddess face.

Twenty-eight other missionaries were aboard, bound for the Far East, but the star attraction was the couple they called simply "the Blisses," who walked the decks together for exercise, who played shuffleboard together, and who seemed interestingly happy.

Edward did enjoy the company of Ruth Bliss. "I found her," he wrote, "not only a pretty and vivacious young woman, but also very intelligent. I don't think Marian would call her goody-goody."

Yet nothing came of it. There had been Elizabeth Wilkinson, whom he had hoped to marry before starting for China. She was still much on his mind—and perhaps in his heart. He had counted on her to be the companion in his adventure. In applying to the mission board he had written, "The woman whom I am to marry is in full sympathy with me in love for the work."

That was the only sentence in his nine-page letter of application that aroused doubt in the minds of American Board officials. It was one thing to approve the appointment of a candidate when you had all the particulars; it was another thing to take such a step not knowing who would accompany the applicant to the mission field as his wife. So they demanded that the lady be identified.

Edward politely refused. "I am not at liberty at present to give you her name," he said. "I have not yet requested her parents' consent." He hoped to obtain that consent soon. And so board officials might rest easier in the meantime, he unintentionally dropped a small bombshell. His future wife, he said, had already been appointed by them for missionary work. One can picture board secretaries scurrying through their files to find the name of a recently appointed missionary, female and marriageable, who might be assigned to Africa, for all they knew, while her fiancé wanted to go to China. By the process of elimination they may, indeed, have discovered the young lady's identity. No one today knows.

Later, in July 1891, a subdued Edward wrote the mission board, "I have delayed so long because there has been nothing definite to write, but now I must inform you that it has been decided best that the engagement be broken off. I, therefore, expect to enter the mission field unmarried when the way shall be open."

It had been this crisis of decision that caused Edward, in the midst of final examinations at medical school, to rush off to New York. Little is known of this meeting with Elizabeth Wilkinson, only that they luncheoned in New York and then took an afternoon train as far as Bridgeport, where they parted. She went on to Hartford to visit an aunt, and he returned to New Haven. The romance had ended.

"She could sing and was good-looking," Edward recalled when he was ninety. "Everybody liked her."

What came between them? Edward never said. Perhaps he came to realize that, despite real affection, the element of love was lacking. At least, years later, he told the woman he married that he had loved no one else. It is also possible that Elizabeth Wilkinson enjoyed receiving the young medical student's attention but shied from marriage. In a letter to Marian, who had been a close friend at Mount Holyoke, she wrote, "The mistakes of my life have been many. Oh, Marian dear, don't ever flirt!"

It took him a long time to get over Elizabeth Wilkinson. On the SS *China,* when he met Ruth Bliss, the experience was still fresh and he did not allow his heart to become involved. Moreover, the girl with the goddess face was going to a different part of China—to the Presbyterian mission in Canton. He knew that in China, so far as they were concerned, the eight hundred miles between them might as well be eight thousand. But he found her a delightful shipboard companion.

At Night We Crawl into Our Cages

☸

SHAOWU LAY about a mile ahead, the smoke from supper fires hanging over it like a shroud, the black tile roofs clustered within and without the city walls. The scent of woodsmoke from a nearby farmer's house made Edward think, in some inexplicable way, of Old Newbury on an Indian summer night. But nothing else was familiar, and he waited for the boatmen to catch up with him. He did not quite know how to enter the city by himself.

The impact of Shaowu was immediate. The moment the newcomer stepped from his boat among the drying fishnets and began walking up the damp, stone-paved alley to East Gate Street, he was assaulted by the sights, sounds, and smells of a city transplanted from the Middle Ages. Writing later, he called the filth indescribable. No sewage system existed. Men carried human feces, stored to a ripe putrescence, out to the fields in wooden buckets. Other slop was emptied into the streets, which were without sidewalks. And walking with the Walkers from the landing, Edward found himself, like them, stepping gingerly to avoid the excrement of pigs. As they turned into East Gate Street he heard a cry almost at his feet. Startled, he saw a toothless old man, squatted on the ground, caressing a snake.

"Perform a good act!" the beggar entreated.

Walker explained, "He means that by giving him a coin you incur favor in the eyes of the gods."

A few yards farther on, a leper cried out to them. He wore rags and pleaded with rotting stumps of arms. It was hard for Edward to realize that this street, fewer than twenty-five feet wide, was the city's main thoroughfare. Fish shops, pawnshops, rice shops, every kind of shop jostled each other for streetfront space. Everywhere there was a chattering that in the narrow street took on a kind of resonance, bouncing back and forth between

East Gate Street more than one hundred years later, no longer crowded and busy, as it was in 1892.

the buildings and off the smooth, flat paving stones into the foreigners' ears.

Carriers of firewood labored by with high, backbreaking loads. The missionaries passed other coolies bearing vegetables in bamboo baskets and squeaking wheelbarrows weighted with sacks of rice. Some trading was going on in the shops, but most were shuttered for the night. The street was full of men who seemed simply to be taking an evening stroll. No women were visible. It was all very strange, but at the entrance to the mission compound, a gray-striped cat devouring a fishhead looked like any cat at home.

Most of the people of Shaowu, in the beginning, had been hostile to foreigners. The first doctor to come to the city, Dr. Philip Osgood, had a spear thrust through his foot—he later died of sunstroke—and another early missionary took a bullet in the shoulder. It was two years before any Chinese would sell the first missionaries land on which to build. This original plot measured only a few hundred square feet and was surrounded by an earthen wall. On one side of the compound, facing the busy street, was the shop where Bibles were distributed. Religious tracts sold for ten cash, or about two-thirds of a cent. It was explained to Edward that if the Chinese had to buy the literature, they would read it.

Inside the compound a two-story frame house had been built, and it was where Edward would live for the next six years. He shared the house with the Gardners, a young married couple who, ten months earlier, had come to Shaowu with their small son. The Walkers did not live in the city at that time but maintained a separate residence four miles downriver, near a village called Tungsang. Walker named his home site Crystal Hill, because of the numerous quartz crystals he found there. The Gardners owned a cottage at Crystal Hill, which they occupied in summer. After Osgood's death, no missionary risked spending a summer in the city, and it was to avoid this moving every spring and fall that the Walkers decided to stay on the hilltop year-round. Since the evangelist did so much touring—the jurisdiction of the mission station extended over eight thousand square miles—whether he lived in Shaowu was of small importance.

The Gardners took pity on the newcomer and invited him to take meals with them. Edward accepted gladly, on condition that he share the expense. Years later he said, "They made me almost one of the family." He recalled Mary Gardner as a small, agreeable woman of high intelligence. She had straight brown hair and brown eyes. He found Milton Gardner to be a student of the Bible, well equipped for his principal work, which was training Chinese preachers. The striking thing about Gardner's appearance was his set of side whiskers, which hung down over his jowls like Spanish moss.

Incidentally, Edward no longer shaved. It had seemed a propitious time, traveling on the river, to stop using the straight razor his father bought for him on his seventeenth birthday. By wearing a beard he could save a lot of time. For forty years his small chin and dimple were concealed, first by the full beard, then by a goatee.

THAT FIRST EVENING at Shaowu, everyone had supper at the Gardners. Walker wanted to know all that had been happening. It seemed there was trouble about a Chinese Christian who refused to donate money for an idol ceremony. The collector of donations had threatened to tear down the believer's tea shop, and Walker was going to have to see the city magistrate about it. Things had been going well at the boys' school. Mrs. Gardner was again teaching English, now that the baby was old enough to be left with a Chinese amah. The selling of tracts had been going well, too.

Edward listened with fascination. He was actually in a foreign mission, hearing a report of the work as it was happening. This was not at all like a missionary meeting at the Prospect Street Church.

Gardner turned to him.

"I know you want to get started with the language," he said. "Will it be Mandarin or Shaowu?"

This was something Edward had talked over with Walker on the river. His predecessor had spoken Mandarin, the language used universally by the educated class, but he had decided to learn the local dialect, feeling that way he could work more effectively with patients, most of whom would be uneducated. Walker, who spoke both Mandarin and the local earth words, as the Chinese called them, seconded his choice.

Gardner spoke only Shaowu and heartily approved. "I have a teacher," he said, "who is a fine literary man, though no Christian. If you like, I'll ask him about starting with you next week."

Edward said that would be first-rate. Everything was still first-rate. But when Gardner asked him if he had a Chinese name yet, he blushed.

"Oh, we gave him a name in Fuzhou," Walker said. "His name is Fu Yihua."

Gardner was delighted. "Fu is perfect. It means happiness, which certainly is bliss. Yihua." He turned to Edward. "That's 'benefiting China.' Bliss benefiting China. You have a name to live up to."

Edward kept his "name to live up to." "I never tried to change it," he said. "It reminded me of what I was in China for." He once asked, almost as though musing aloud, whether it might not be possible that communism never would have taken hold in China if the so-called Christian nations had done more—much more—to lift the people out of their poverty. He spoke at a time when everyone was talking about the Marshall Plan. He wished there had been something like it for China. He was loyal to the Chinese all his life.

His Chinese name was Fu Yihua—the handsome characters, inscribed on red paper, hang framed in his son's home—but he often was addressed as Fu Xiansheng. Xiansheng is a term generally applied to persons of learning and can be roughly translated as "teacher." He was Fu Xiansheng. His Chinese tutor was Shi Xiansheng, and the helper at the boys school was Yuan Xiansheng. They were all teachers.

Edward had his own two rooms with a separate entrance. He had come to Shaowu with no furniture, but for thirty-six dollars he bought the furnishings left by the last occupants, Dr. and Mrs. Henry Whitney, who dared not stay for reasons of health. If it occurred to him that Shaowu was a singularly unhealthy place, he gave no hint of it. On the contrary, his first letters from China were full of enthusiasm. He could not foresee the future. It is unlikely he would have fled, but he might have felt dismay.

That first night at Shaowu, after crawling under the *wen zhang,* or netting, that would guard him from mosquitoes, he considered how God had protected him on his long journey. As he fell asleep, the last sound he heard was the distant rumble of temple drums. It was a strangely satisfying sound. He knew he had come to the right place.

Just Imagine That!

DURING THAT FIRST NIGHT, a marauding bear was discovered in a field outside the city. Farmers armed themselves with spears and killed him. At daybreak, two mauled, bleeding men appeared at the compound gate and asked for the new foreign doctor. The shoulder muscles of one of them had been shredded by the bear's claws, and all Edward could do was pour iodine over the raw mass and bind it with gauze. The other man's face had been torn so that a flap of skin lay open, exposing his teeth. The bear had made a clean tear, and the cheek was neatly sewed up.

Edward was so thankful for his first patients that he did not think of charging for his services. But he was disappointed when Gardner said the bear's carcass had been sold, not for food, but for the purchase of what he regarded as useless medicines. One of the hardest battles Edward waged during those first years at Shaowu was the battle against the practitioners of native medicine. He had heard that the Chinese discovered iodine and that, centuries before any European, they had practiced a form of inoculation for smallpox. Yet he found Chinese "doctors" treating cancer by puncturing the skin with gold and silver needles. They prescribed bile from the gallbladders of bears for eye sores, uncooked pears for malarial fever, snake meat for rheumatism, and the ginseng root for almost every ailment known. A woman treated by Edward for an abscessed ear had spent fifteen dollars—her family's entire income for three months—for prayers to idols and some powder made from beetle wings. Edward never did appreciate how effective some Chinese practices such as acupuncture could be.

There was an irony in his competition with the remedies of the Chinese. An early memory was of American medicine men, dressed as Kickapoo Indians, who came to Newburyport and sold Kickapoo Indian snake oil for rheumatism and Kickapoo Indian Sagwa for ailments of the stomach and liver. At age five he would come running when he heard their war whoops and watch wonder-eyed as "Injuns" sold their elixirs to the unsuspecting white man.

For any doctor the first year of practice is difficult. Having assumed responsibility for human life, he must demonstrate his competence, not only to his patients and to the community, but also to himself. And he must adjust to the fact that, under a given set of circumstances, death will not be put off. In America, a young doctor could go to an older, more experienced colleague for advice. But Edward was alone. And if he failed in the foreign place, it was more than a defeat for himself. It was a defeat for Western medicine and a victory, he felt, for fear and superstition. And a defeat for Christianity, for he had come to China as a representative of the Christian faith. His faith would be judged by his performance.

Edward knew when he went to Shaowu that the nearest hospital was more than 150 miles away. He did not know that the mission station lacked even a dispensary. His predecessors had carried their "dispensaries" about with them in little black bags. He was not content with that. If he was going to introduce Western medicine at Shaowu, he meant to found a modern hospital and, with God's help, get to the masses. He would give such a demonstration of Western medical practice, and its benefits, that the Chinese would adopt it as their own.

But first he had to learn the language. His teacher, Shi Xiansheng, was a broad-faced, broad-shouldered young scholar who spoke English and had passed the provincial examinations. Twice a week, on Tuesday and Thursday, they sat down together at nine o'clock in the morning and studied until one. In the afternoon they met from two until four-thirty, when the cook would serve tea. On other days, Edward studied by himself, doing the assignments Shi Xiansheng outlined for him. Occasionally he was interrupted by a Chinese who wanted treatment, either for himself or for a member of his family. One day a tinsmith wanted him to see his twelve-year-old wife, who was suffering from "spitting of blood." A partially blind man on whom he had operated for glaucoma said apologetically that he could not pay. He already had mortgaged his wife for six dollars!

Edward had been studying for a month when he wrote, "It will be a long, long time before I can understand what people say,

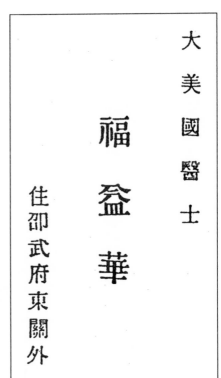

Edward's calling card.

or make people understand me, still I can catch a good many words. So I guess I won't decide to be discouraged yet."

What made it hard was that a Chinese word had so many meanings. His own surname, *fu,* could mean prefecture—the Shaowu prefecture, composed of five *xians,* or counties, was Shaowu Fu. It also could mean home, or dose of medicine, or man, or happiness, or summer heat. The trick was to learn the different intonations, since they, as well as context, determined what the word meant. *Fu* with a low, even tone meant summer heat; with a high tone it meant man. For other tones the modulation rose or fell, or fell at first and then rose. The tone that fell and didn't rise was called the receding or departing tone. It seemed to trail off in the distance. Mastering this medley of intonations was a formidable task. So that he might study six and a half hours a day and still have time for treating patients and compiling financial reports—he was also treasurer for the station—Edward began getting up every morning at six o'clock.

On Sunday afternoons, for recreation, he took walks around the city wall. The earthen ramparts, faced with brick and, at the base, massive blocks of hewn stone, rose thirty feet. Four arched gateways opened to the four points of the compass. Each day, at sunset, was heard the blare of a trumpet, followed by a signal gun. Three hours later two guns were fired and all gates closed for the night. The wall had last been battle-tested during the Taiping Rebellion, thirty—perhaps forty—years before Edward's arrival. His children liked to hear him tell the story.

"The wall was no good," he said, "not because the people were not brave but because somebody was dishonest. You know that hill outside the West Gate? Well, centuries ago, when the wall was built, it was supposed to take in that high ground, but the official in charge of the work built a smaller wall so he'd have money left over for himself. The Taipings set up cannons on that hill and pounded the city into surrender. They poured in, screaming, and put thousands of people to the sword. Old pastor Kueh remembers what happened. His mother hid him under a washtub and, peeking out, he saw both his parents killed."

On walks on top of the wall Edward discovered, half hidden in the earth, some of the cannons used by the hapless defenders, and within the walls he could see a large area where no houses stood, only weeds and the crumbling foundations of houses that had been destroyed. Boys, he noticed, had found the space a good place for flying kites.

Edward had not been in Shaowu long before he bought a fractious little mule, which he named Jacqueline. He explained in a letter to his father, "Since I will have to do a good deal of traveling about, and as walking is out of the question much of the time because of the climate, I have to choose between a sedan chair and horseback. I abominate sedan riding. The mere thought of being carried on men's shoulders disgusts me, and you know how fond I am of horseflesh, so I naturally chose to own this admirable steed."

There was no question, he said, that Jacqueline was superior to any of the horses in those parts. "For they are a sorry lot, very small and inflicted with a most disagreeable gait. As for Jacqueline, she is the fastest-walking animal I ever saw. She will walk

Edward on the fractious little mule he called Jacqueline.

pretty nearly as fast as most Chinese horses trot, and when she trots she can leave them out of sight."

This remarkable piece of horseflesh cost thirty dollars. "So," he said, "I can well afford to let you laugh."

Jacqueline had one fault: She loved the independent life. Occasionally she bolted, and once Edward did not recover her until the next day. Another time she refused to stop when the saddle began slipping, and the Yankee doctor ended up in the dust. Gardner owned a mule of somewhat less spirit. For years, to Chinese farmers, the two missionaries astride their mules presented a familiar quixotic sight.

It Is Good to Feel Needed

NOT UNTIL MID-MARCH, in the Season of Excited Insects, was Edward called to help a Chinese woman in childbirth. He had wondered when he would receive this first call. The attendance of a male physician on a woman in labor was frowned upon. It was against tradition; delivering babies was the business of midwives. But Edward was to find through the years that if complications arose, and if the midwives did not succeed, he would be summoned to try again. Consequently, most of the women he attended were near dying.

As it happened, he was studying with Shi Xiansheng when the husband came to him. The wife, overdue with child, was in extreme suffering. A thousand pardons, but would the foreign doctor come at once? The man led them across the city to a crumbing house of earth near the West Gate. At first when they entered the windowless chamber they could hardly see. Shi Xiansheng called for light, and the first son brought a lamp consisting of a tiny wick floating in a saucer of vegetable oil.

"That won't do," Edward said, and this time the husband brought a blazing pine faggot. The air was nauseating. It seemed that somewhere an animal was decomposing, and the woman, who had hemorrhaged, had not been bathed. She lay half conscious on boards placed across two sawhorses. The first thing Edward did was remove a snakeskin a midwife had wrapped about the woman's abdomen.

The unborn child was hydrocephalic, its head so grotesquely large that normal birth was impossible. The only way to save the mother was to collapse the skull of the infant, doomed in any case, and relieve her of her unbearable burden.

As Shi Xiansheng translated his dire prognosis, Edward saw for the first time the small crowd of men, women, and children in the doorway, watching. Some at the back of the crowd leaped to catch a better glimpse. What an awful demonstration, he thought, for his medicine. For he knew what he must do, and it would be ugly. He could not order them away. The Western doctor, they would say, is afraid for us to witness his strange practices.

The husband nodded his assent. Edward perforated and drained the fetal head. Then with forceps he crushed the skull and delivered the dead man-child. Shi Xiansheng took the lifeless, brainless baby and wrapped it tenderly in a swathe of blue cloth.

When Edward had finished, and put away his instruments, he stood up and faced the family. They had said nothing during the operation, but now the husband's father, acting as spokesman, expressed regret that the foreign doctor could not be paid adequately for saving life. He wanted to make a small presentation of tea. Nothing was said of the life the foreigner destroyed.

As Edward stepped toward the door, the crowd parted and, to his astonishment, bowed in reverence. "They knew," he said later, with a trace of incredulity still in his voice, "that except for what I did the woman would have died. I knew in that moment something of the compensation that comes to a doctor practicing in such a place."

Two days later—it was a Sunday—he and Shi Xiansheng were with the Walkers at Crystal Hill when a toothless old peasant wearing clothes covered with patches called at the door.

"It is my daughter," the man said. "If you do not come, she will surely pluck the flower of life."

"Where does the daughter lie?" asked Walker.

"In her husband's house, near Tse-tsin."

This was a village seven miles away. Edward had gone there twice with Gardner. He said, "Tell him I'll go. But first I have to get my instruments at Shaowu."

It was decided that Shi Xiansheng should go on with the farmer to Tse-tsin. The doctor would meet them there.

By the time Edward started from Shaowu on Jacqueline it was midafternoon. He had been delayed by a man who wanted worm medicine. Now it was like cavalry coming to the rescue. The mule covered the ground with a sense of mission. She traveled at her best pace and suffered no distractions. When small boys shouted "Foreign devil!" and "Barbarian spider!" she looked neither right nor left but pricked her ears forward, intent on the road ahead.

Edward must have presented a ludicrous picture. Though it was not raining, it was the season for rain, and in his left hand he carried a folded Chinese umbrella, the sort made of bamboo ribs and paper waterproofed with tung oil. The reins and a small whip, which he had no need for, were in his right hand. A bag crammed with obstetrical instruments and medicines, slung over his shoulder with a leather strap, bounced merrily in time with Jacqueline's trot. And he wore his favorite straw hat because, after all, it was Sunday.

At Tse-tsin, he was met only by the old peasant. Shi Xiansheng, it seemed, had gone ahead, believing he might be able to make the woman more comfortable. After proceeding some distance beyond Tse-tsin, with the peasant leading the way, Edward supposed they were near their destination. So he was surprised, and a little dismayed, when the old man stopped at a roadside shop to buy candles for his lantern.

"How far?" Edward asked, using one of the few Chinese phrases he knew.

"Eleven li," the ancient one said, adding that soon they would be overtaken by darkness.

"I think I've been in the dark for some time," the doctor said in English. They had gone nine miles, and eleven li meant they had nearly four miles to go. It was supposed, altogether, to have been a trip of seven or eight miles. He had not spoken loudly, or unpleasantly, but the Chinese turned around with an anxious expression on his face. To show he bore no ill will, Edward used a polite phrase to inquire about the old man's age.

"I have lived vainly for seventy-one years," the man said. For a Chinese peasant, Edward thought, this was old indeed. Few peasants survived their sixties.

"Would you ride?"

"I dare not," the peasant said, wagging his head. Edward was relieved. While he felt that because of his years the man should be the one to ride, he was not sure how the mule would act. And he saw rugged country ahead.

It became dark. Rocks strewed the path, and the mule settled down to a slow walk, picking her steps while the old man led with the lantern. They reached a gap in the mountains that closed in the valley. Here the narrow path, gouged from the mountainside, was steep. Far below, Edward could hear a stream. The sound

Transplanting rice in the fields around Shaowu.

came up to him as from a pit. He dismounted and began leading the mule. It was lucky he did. They had just crossed the divide and were descending on the other side when he heard a wild scramble behind him and, looking back, saw Jacqueline scrambling with her hindquarters over the edge.

It was fantastic to think of a mule clinging to anything, but Jacqueline clung, braying for dear life, while Edward pulled the bridle. In seconds she managed to catch a foothold and clamber onto the path. She had suffered a deep cut in her right hind leg but could still walk.

After another hour, Edward again asked how far they must go.

"*Bu jiu,*" the old man said.

"How many li?"

"*Bu jiu.*" That was all he would say. "Not long time."

Edward felt put upon, but the fellow was desperate to help his daughter. Perhaps if the situation were reversed, he would do the same.

Two miles farther on, they saw a light ahead. Surely this is the place, Edward told himself. But it proved to be only Shi Xiansheng with a lantern. The house, his teacher said cheerfully, was just a half-hour walk. The mule's leg began bleeding. Edward bound it, but the animal limped so badly that when they came to Kai-tung, the next village, he made arrangements to quarter her there for the night.

When the doctor finally reached his destination he was greeted by a chorus of dogs. The woman's husband, carrying a pine torch, ran about, silencing them with much shouting. It was a poor two-room house. The patient lay in a small, windowless room on a bed of straw, next to a large wooden chest in which was stored the family's rice. On top of the chest lay four children, sprawled in sleep. Cobwebs hung about the ceiling, but the floor of hard-packed earth was swept clean.

The birth was complicated because the baby was trying to enter the world feet first. Shi Xiansheng oversaw the boiling of instruments—he was to become a doctor one day—as Edward thought of what he must do and asked God's help.

The woman had grown weak. The uterine contractions after forty-eight hours were inappreciable. In mercy, Edward administered chloroform. He wore no gloves. (Surgeon's gloves did not come into general use until after William Halstead of Johns Hopkins introduced them in 1898.) Neighbor women pressed inside the doorway for a good look. Gradually, by hand and instrument, the fetus was brought around to a shoulder position, then into normal position, with the head down. Inside his clothes, the doctor could feel the sweat running. Soon the baby would be delivered. It would not come easily, for it was a large baby with a large head. If only there could be a breath of fresh air! Then at last the baby was with them, glistening with womb wetness. And Edward said to himself it is a boy, let him be spanked. And he was spanked, and he made a loud cry, and Edward thanked God for it.

Later, after the placenta also was delivered and the parts irrigated, and the woman had fallen into natural sleep, Edward looked at his watch and saw that it was long past midnight. In his letter home he said, "They found a place for me to lie down."

"What kind of place?" his father asked in his next letter. Letters from Newburyport were full of such questions.

"A clean place," he replied, "but it was next to the pigsty, so I didn't get much sleep."

Three weeks after the boy was delivered, an old peasant wearing clothes with many patches appeared in Shaowu with a beautiful fat duck for the foreign doctor, and because the old man had walked all the way from his village, and because the duck represented so great a sacrifice, the foreign doctor was deeply touched.

And he accepted it because that was what the old man wanted.

A Strange Thing Happened on the Way to the Dispensary

器

EDWARD OPENED a dispensary on East Gate Street, taking over a room in the small, ramshackle building where Bibles were distributed. The only daylight came through the doorway. Half the floorboards were missing. Edward had carpenters install a new floor. They put in shelves for medicines. An operating table of camphor wood was set up in the back, shielded by a bamboo screen. He set two benches against the wall for prospective patients, and Gardner brought in three chairs. When all was in readiness, Shi Xiansheng posted a notice announcing in large Chinese characters that the clinic would be open each day, except Sunday, from ten o'clock in the morning until noon.

The project disrupted Edward's schedule of language study, but he frequently had time—too much time—to study at the dispensary. Sometimes in an entire morning he would have only one patient—at most five or six—and he spent his free time, when not putting up medicines, increasing his Chinese vocabulary. It was a sort of game. On one side of a small card he wrote the word in Chinese, and on the other side in English. Then he would shuffle the cards to see if he could go through the deck without having to turn a card over for the translation.

He never forgot his first patient at the dispensary, a frightened Chinese girl, about fifteen, who slipped in, her eyes full of desperation. He was by himself, practicing his vocabulary, and he was startled. She approached him and shyly, without a word, held out her left hand. At first he saw nothing wrong. There was no sore, no sign of infection. In fact, it was a lovely, exquisitely proportioned hand, decorated on the third finger by a silver ring. But when he turned the hand over he discovered that skin had grown partially over the ring and was badly inflamed.

During this examination the girl had looked at him solemnly, never taking her eyes off his face. When he was finished, she begged him to remove the ring. Her voice was soft, almost a whisper. Edward had studied the language only three months, but it was clear what she wanted.

"Your parents know?" he asked, choosing the words from his small vocabulary one at a time.

She nodded. Not convincingly.

"Why are they not with you?"

"I am a most humble and imperfect child."

"What is your name?"

"Ka-mei."

Edward performed the slight operation against his better judgment. He was sure the girl had come without permission. But how could he refuse? She was trusting. His patients were so few. She sat very still as he made the incision, filed off the ring, and bathed the cut with a solution of mercury perchloride. Then he bound the finger. He tied the bandage with sewing thread because adhesive tape was always in short supply.

"How is that?" he asked.

The girl, whose name meant Beautiful Little Sister, did not speak. Instead, she stared at her bandaged finger, then at the ring that Edward had given back to her. He looked at her questioningly. She smiled. Her smile said she was grateful.

IT WAS ALMOST SUMMER. Edward was walking to the dispensary from North Gate, sidestepping exploding firecrackers, wheelbarrows, chickens, noodle peddlers, and pigs. He was fascinated by this street of exotic sights, where the small shops, behind which the shopkeepers' families lived, displayed everything conceivable, from red candles and dried fish maws to brass warming baskets and scrolls. He was remarking to himself how all food in China seemed covered with flies when he heard the fierce barking of dogs. By the time he reached the scene, the barking had turned to bloodshed.

"Ai!" a man cried. "The dogs are doing each other to death."

Two huge dogs were locked in battle under a rice shop, and several Chinese were trying to break up the fight by throwing stones. It looked hopeless.

North Gate today.

In China, dogs are highly valued guardians of property. And here was a struggle that looked as though it would cost the life of at least one watchdog. Ferocious sounds conjuring up visions of severed jugulars emanated from under the rice shop as the doctor ran to his dispensary. He returned with a long bamboo pole swathed at one end with rags. From a small bottle, while the crowd watched, he soaked the rags with spirits of ammonia. Then he poked the pole under the shop. The snarling stopped, and the two dogs took off in opposite directions, as though pursued by devils.

From that day forward the dispensary did more business. Edward had demonstrated the efficacy of his medicine. It could even stop dog fights. For years, he kept in his medicine bag a copy of the poem by William Cowper that reads in part:

> God moves in a mysterious way
> His wonders to perform.

There Must Be Some Peculiarity in the Atmosphere

IN MAY, Edward moved up to Crystal Hill to escape the heat. Again and again during his years in China he would comment on the harsh, mysterious properties of the climate. Shaowu missionaries not only talked about the weather but also became amateur meteorologists. Setting up their own primitive weather station, they kept daily records of maximum and minimum temperatures, barometric pressure, wind direction, and rainfall. They lacked apparatus for measuring humidity, and perhaps this was merciful. Living on low ground by the river, surrounded by rice paddies, they knew the humidity was high. Perhaps it was better, psychologically, not to know how high.

"I do not know what it is," Edward wrote early that summer. "The thermometer never registers over a hundred in the shade, but the least exertion brings out the sweat. In the winter, it's the other way around. It seldom goes below freezing, but the cold pierces you to the bone."

Sometimes temperatures did exceed one hundred degrees in the shade, as he would discover. And often the thermometer registered in the nineties for seven, eight, or nine consecutive days, and this, with the humidity, could have murderous cumulative effect. Or the temperature would reach ninety degrees one day and plummet to fifty-five degrees the next. Or hailstones as big as kumquats might fall in bright sunshine and smash the tiles on the houses.

Shaowu is at roughly the same latitude as West Palm Beach, Florida. Banana trees grew in the mission compound while Edward lived there, although their fruit was inedible, and two palm trees stood outside his front door. Indian summer came in December. It was also the month when you could expect the first frost. When the temperature fell below freezing, you set out tubs of water, and if you were lucky, the water froze over like a big, round pane of window glass. You could shatter this and use it to make ice cream. Every missionary family owned an old-fashioned freezer cranked by hand. The rainy season began in February and continued through March. It might rain steadily for fifteen days. Food would mold. Clothes became mildewed, and books had to be put away carefully in boxes so as not to spoil.

The city was built on the edge of a small plain. The North Gate opened onto the river and a pontoon bridge made of sparrow boats. Beyond the river lay a long, barren hill and the road leading up across the divide to Jiangxi. A mandarin's grave marked the middle of the hill like a navel.

To the west lay the foothills of the Wuyi Shan. But to the east and south stretched fertile vegetable plots and rice paddies and fallow fields, which in the springtime rippled with the yellow-blossomed rape used for forage. Scattered about this landscape were waterwheels and shrines and high-arched stone bridges and groves of bamboo, with paths running through them like wrinkles on the back of an old man's hand.

As a backdrop in the distance—north, east, south, and west—rose a panorama of mountains.

CRYSTAL HILL was a Gibraltar-shaped hummock rising a thousand feet above the village of Tung-sang, on the southern bank of the river. The two missionary cottages stood on a plateau below the summit, facing south to catch as much as possible of the prevailing breeze and, at the same time, receive a minimum of sun. The hill did not give the missionaries full asylum. It frequently was stifling there, too. But its temperature averaged seven degrees lower than on the plain, and the air was purer. "You can't imagine," wrote Edward, who took a spare room at the Walker cottage, "the odors of a Chinese city in midsummer."

Despite the odors and debilitating heat, he continued to work at the clinic two hours every forenoon. Jacqueline—"You will be glad to know that she has now fully recovered from her unhappy experience"—made the four-mile trip into the city in forty minutes, which was excellent time considering the path. A century, perhaps two centuries earlier, it had been paved with cobblestones, but with the passage of time the paving had deteriorated to such a degree that the stones were, as Edward said, an awful nuisance. Some were loose. Many were broken, and all were uneven. Walking on them bruised your feet. They could be cruel to the hoofs of animals, treacherous when made slippery by rain.

It was something of a puzzle to know what to do with the mules that summer. No suitable quarters existed on the hill. In the nearby village, he and Gardner, inquiring together, had found a place that they rented for the season for three dollars. But when they went to take possession, the owner changed his mind; now he wanted five dollars. In Shaowu the mules had been stabled for much less, so the missionaries rode off, leaving the owner to repent his avarice.

The next day they rented a vacant, earthen-walled house for only a dollar. They were delighted with the bargain, but the mule boy had a fear of the house. He dared not sleep there by himself.

"Don't worry," Edward said. "U Chin will stay with you."

But U Chin, Edward's house servant, protested that every person who had ever lived in the house had met a mysterious death. Eerie sounds were heard emanating from the house. He could never spend the night there. The place was possessed.

It was impossible to convince either the mule boy or U Chin that their fears were unfounded. Everyone knew the house was haunted, except the missionaries. So finally Edward said he would spend a night alone in the house. If any spooks appeared, he promised to let U Chin know. He brought his bedding down and fixed a place to sleep on top of an old grain chest.

Obviously no one had lived in the house for years. Dust lay over everything. Twice during the night the missionary was awakened by bats, but he neither saw nor heard anything remotely resembling spirits. The mule boy was reassured, and U Chin's services as companion to the lad were not required. The ghost of Tung-sang was laid to rest.

Thus Edward began the summer riding into the city each day on his beloved mule. He was happy on several counts. On the hill he could study without interruption. It seemed that, at last, he was getting the "feel" of the language. And he took heart in the growing acceptance of Western medicine. Instead of treating no more than five or six patients a day, he was now treating more than twenty. They were coming to him with their boils and remittent fevers and intestinal worms, and he had a sense of accomplishment.

He was gratified, too, by a proposal Shi Xiansheng made to him and that he immediately accepted. It was that in exchange for his instruction, Edward would teach him the fundamentals of medicine. It was more than winning a medical disciple; Edward liked him personally. The man's family was wealthy. He had distinguished himself in the imperial examinations. But he was not too proud to bandage the toe of a peasant.

Edward did not press Shi Xiansheng on the subject of religion. There was his old aversion to instructing people in religious matters, an aversion contradictory to his life's endeavor. But the subject came up naturally one day. Edward was struggling with the Chinese translation of a New Testament passage when Shi Xiansheng, in a quiet way, praised Christ's denunciation of hypocrisy. Edward looked up, and the Chinese, smiling, quickly added, "But I am still a Buddhist."

"I think," Edward said, "you are a good Buddhist."

The inadequacy of the dispensary was proved that first summer. Flies came in and swarmed over the open sores, for summer was the season for sores. The smells of the street were compounded with the stench of suppuration. Onlookers crowded into the small room and had to be asked to leave. Sometimes a chicken got underfoot.

"You should see me," wrote Edward, "holding a clinic amid these inquisitive chickens."

Men came with their leg ulcers, scabies, erysipelas, and consumption. Women still hesitated to come, but they brought their babies, ill-nourished and diarrhetic, many covered with boils. A surprise to Edward was the few patients with heart trouble, a fact now attributed to the relatively little meat in the Chinese diet. Almost all of his patients had malaria. He wrote, "I feel like a quack dispensing quinine to everyone. Often I never see the patient again and for so many the end result is death." Soon he himself would be ravaged by it.

(Edward would have been interested that the Chinese canon of medicine, the Neijing, described the mosquito-transmitted disease in 2700 B.C. While other peoples turned to quinine extracted from the bark of the cinchona tree of South America, Chinese physicians used their own drug, *qing hao su,* prepared from a plant related to the thistle family. During World War II, Western scientists developed chloroquine, which showed promise until the malaria parasite, after building resistance, counterattacked and reduced its effectiveness. The same happened with mefloquine, a synthetic analog of quinine. In Southeast Asia and in other parts of the world, as in Africa, malaria still is a mass murderer, inflicting at least two million deaths a year.)

Before opening the dispensary in the morning, Edward would spend an hour—sometimes two hours—preparing tinctures and pills. His son remembers seeing him, years later, use a mold to "manufacture" the little white pills he swore by for ridding patients of worms. Shi Xiansheng often came to the dispensary to observe. His class in *materia medica,* they called it. Each morning Edward would set out for Shaowu on his mule and each evening arrive back on the hill, wearing his incongruous straw hat (later exchanged for a pith helmet) and soaked with sweat. From then until suppertime he studied.

"Better ease up," Walker warned. "This is your first summer."

"I'm first-rate," Edward said.

But in a letter home he confessed, "This going to and fro leaves a man a little tired at the end of the day. In the evening it is hard work to read or write because swarms of mosquitoes, moths and flies of one kind or another surround the lamp, darting into my face and tickling my hands. Perhaps crawling up my arm until they make me so nervous that I have to give up reading. Happily, I have gotten rid of most of my fleas."

In this letter Edward's handwriting, normally bold and free-flowing, appears as a child's scrawl. He had become host to another, more dangerous parasite than fleas. He was felled by such a severe case of malaria that during three days of paroxysms he lay on his bed. Then a week later, when he was strong enough to walk, the Gardners persuaded him to journey with them to Nishitu Mountain for a rest. They would stay, the Gardners said, in an ancient temple.

A Great Way to Take a Tonic

器

THERE WAS no grander, more picturesque scenery in all of Fujian, yet the name given the region could not have been more prosaic, for Nishitu meant, simply, Twentieth District. The rugged massif rose slightly more than twenty miles from Shaowu, to the west. Joseph Walker had first visited it on an evangelistic tour in 1887. No Westerner had ever climbed the high passes before him, and he came back after four days with a glowing account of a mountain paradise full of wildflowers, waterfalls, *songmu* (pine), and giant bamboo. Walker reported peaks more than a mile high. The mountains had been heaved up in all manner of fantastic shapes. And in the recesses of the valleys, he said, were friendly, idolatrous folk who had never heard the Word of God.

In intervening years, Walker returned to Nishitu many times and made many converts. Nowhere had the Gospel been received more eagerly than at U Shi Piang, a small, white-walled village perched on a high divide. The first convert was run out of town and told that he would be killed if he returned. He came back to see his family, and the villagers forgot their threat. That was the beginning of the conversion of others, until now the village was equally divided between idolaters and Christians.

In summertime the climate at Nishitu was immensely more invigorating than at Crystal Hill, so Walker made a point to come in the warmest season. And often, when he came, he stayed at an old temple at the top of the final climb. He and Adelaide Walker were at the temple when in August 1893 the Gardners prevailed on Edward to go with them to the mountain retreat.

They set out on a Friday morning after getting up before daylight to have breakfast and pack the few things that could not be loaded the night before. For several miles their route lay on the plain, winding between parched rice fields. If it did not rain soon,

Nishitu. The white patches are bamboo pulp placed on the mountainside to bleach before being made into paper.

the crop would be lost. Gardner led the caravan. Jacqueline hankered to take the lead, but Edward held her back. It would be wrong, he reasoned, for a "greenie" to take command.

Because of the early start, it was cool for the first hour. Then the sun beat down on them, and the south wind swept over the baked paddies, filling the air with dust. Edward thought unhappily of the night soil he had seen poured on the fields; with each breath he was taking powdered human feces into his lungs. He marveled how the coolies, bearing hundred-pound loads, managed to keep their steady pace. Their backs, burned copper, glistened with perspiration, and their carrying poles bent rhythmically with the loads. These, thought Edward, are incredible people. So hardworking, so full of self-respect.

For several miles after the first ridge it was fairly level. The path took them through a meadow full of tiger lilies, then into a valley and alongside a half-dry stream full of boulders. It reminded Edward of a New England trout stream, only it was bordered by groves of bamboo. They ate their noon meal at a rice tavern, surrounded by a crowd that marveled to see the foreign devils take food to their mouths by means of strange metallic instruments. Occasionally a man or a woman—children were too shy—reached out and touched the sleeve of one of these odd people who had white faces and round eyes.

The proprietor of the tavern said his second son had the trembling sickness, and Edward could see that the boy's condition was serious. The child, about twelve, weighed no more than fifty pounds. He looked up from his mat with immense dark eyes.

"Can you cure?"

The father had asked the unanswerable question. The malarial fever was far advanced. The boy's strength might give out before quinine could take hold. Edward must explain. And so he said, "Your son is very sick. I do not know whether my medicine can save him. I will give the medicine if you wish." The father said it was his wish, and Edward gave the child twenty grains of quinine by mouth. The more effective method of injecting quinine hydrochloride had not been introduced. The heavy initial dose was to break up the fever. The doctor could only hope it would work.

The caravan resumed its journey. Edward wrote, "The grasses and ferns make quite a jungle in places. We found red day lilies, purple asters, white hyacinths, mountain peas closely resembling your perennial sweet peas, wisteria and even begonias just like the ones you have at Newburyport. And, of course, the mountainsides are covered with bamboo, each looking like a magnificent plume."

In midafternoon they came upon the Shan Kou. The letters of missionaries describe this dramatic cleft between the mountains variously as "wild," "magnificent," and "wonderful." "You emerge from the bamboo forest and there, before you, loom these great frowning rock masses for which you can never psychologically be quite prepared." The missionaries dismounted. The trail, hewn from the mountainside, meandered upward and out of sight. A stumble on the narrow rock shelf could be fatal. They climbed steadily for an hour. By the time they reached the top they had, to their right, a drop of almost a thousand feet. From this point, in whatever direction they looked, they saw cadences of mountains. Above them, crags of granite stood dark against white, billowy clouds, and in the chasm, beyond hearing, tumbled the small river they had followed since climbing the first ridge.

Now, striking down into a new valley, they came to a village where Mrs. Gardner's chair bearers stopped to rest. Terraced rice paddies seemed to overhang the village, they rose so steeply. It looked as though with the first heavy rain they would slide down the mountainside in an avalanche of mud.

They began the final ascent in the shadow of Nishitu Mountain. It was like going upstairs. The weary traveler climbed seven hundred feet in less than a mile, ascending stone steps worn smooth by the sandaled feet of Chinese who lived centuries ago. As he trod these steps with his Western-style leather shoes, Edward tried to picture the generations of woodsmen, itinerant peddlers, imperial messengers, and bearers of heavy burdens who had come that way long before the discovery of the New World, the world from which he had come. He tried to picture them, but the toilers of his vision were no more real than the cloud pictures he saw up ahead in the sky—less real, perhaps. He himself felt unreal. How came he here?

But when he reached the saddle of the mountain, there were the Walkers to greet him. And there stood the old temple in a clearing among the *songmu.*

THE TEMPLE WAS a place of worship, but as common property of surrounding villages it also was used for feasts, for presenting classical dramas, for manufacturing bamboo bird cages, for storing empty coffins, and for lodging. Walker, after securing permission, had set carpenters to work fitting up five anterooms for their use—at a cost of eight dollars. This small expenditure was accepted as full payment of rent.

Edward was tired, but a good night's sleep and the bracing air, acting as a tonic, made him robust again. At the morning prayer service—in the Buddhist temple!—Gardner read from Psalms, "Thy righteousness is like the great mountains. O Lord, they preservest man and beast." Even as they prayed, the morning mist lifted and ranges of mountains became visible, the farthest fifty miles away, inside the neighboring province of Jiangxi.

That day Edward wandered on mountain paths under the bamboo. These were not ordinary bamboo but giant, cathedral grasses whose shafts rose like grenadier lances forty and fifty feet high, pennons rustling in the breeze. No wood served the Chinese as faithfully in so many ways. From bamboo came myriad products ranging from drinking mugs to back scratchers. There was a saying, "As the bamboo is hollow and empty, so a humble man is not filled with his own importance." Perhaps that is why, in time, the Chinese took Edward to themselves.

But now he was exploring. He sighted a green tree toad, observed the abundance of spring water and the red earth. He came upon pits filled with lengths of bamboo. The bamboo was soaking in water and quicklime, and he learned that the chief industry of the region was the manufacture of paper from bamboo. He saw he was closeted with mountains, but the mountain he kept coming back to in memory as an old man was the peak called Lion's Head, which raised itself proudly to the southeast. Lion's Head stood alone in grandeur, noble like the king of beasts. From its summit you could see halfway to the Pacific Ocean, all the way to the mountain range at Nanping.

The closest rivals to Lion's Head were Long Mountain and the mountain called the Fishnet. Long Mountain lay three miles to the southwest and was the site of a Buddhist monastery. It boasted no sheer precipices, no dramatic peak, and was not set off. The mundane-sounding Fishnet, on the other hand, was truly monumental. Its silhouette—viewed across a great valley—had the long, graceful lines of a net that has been cast and not yet struck water. This net seemed cast by a god intent on enveloping half the earth.

"It is a majestic mountain," Edward wrote. "On the summit there is nothing but grass, beautifully smooth and green. It asks you to come walking, and I think I will."

That summer Edward did not climb the Fishnet. He did not have time. After his day of recreation the sick discovered him, as he intended they should, and the temple became a clinic. "Not quite the way things were at the New Haven Hospital!" he reported. In five days, Edward treated eighty patients. Besides the usual malarial cases and skin eruptions, he performed two operations for cataracts, pulled eleven teeth, delivered three babies, and removed the infected lower right jaw of a young rice farmer. He missed the assistance of Shi Xiansheng. His general handyman, U Chin, did what he could but it consisted mostly of fetching bandages and filling and emptying washbasins. He spoke little English, and his knowledge of medicine was nil.

ON HIS WAY BACK to Shaowu, Edward learned to his surprise, and relief, that the second son of the tavern proprietor was recovering. The boy still needed quinine, and Edward left a fresh supply.

Henceforth, on the long trail to Nishitu, which he was to climb a hundred times, the foreign doctor never lacked for friends. He liked to recall how the boy, grown to manhood, once insisted that he take along an umbrella from the inn when the sky was threatening. The native New Englander, laboring in the remote vastnesses of Fujian, never hesitated to set out on such a journey alone.

When he got back to Crystal Hill, Edward felt stronger, but he was by no means in good health. The letter he wrote on the twentieth of August reporting his Nishitu adventure was composed again in a childish scrawl. The letter betrayed the toll the malaria had taken. In no letter did he mention being ill.

The lesson that he could not spend himself recklessly had been learned. Reluctantly he resolved in summer not to go into the city more than four times a week. He made no more twelve-mile "house calls" like his excursion with Jacqueline to the village that was supposed to be near Tse-tsin. He had a choice: He could scurry about the countryside sapping his strength, or he could pace himself and stay the distance.

Events proved the rightness of his decision. No other American served in that place as long as he did and lived to come home again. But the decision to ration his energy, and survive, rankled in him. The next summer he spoke self-accusingly of the patients he could not see "because of all this taking time out." Ten years later he was writing, "I am here at Crystal Hill for a rest today and Sunday. Perhaps I should get more good from it if I didn't feel somewhat as though I had run away from duty."

There Is No One to Consult, Only the Great Physician

THE YEARS IN CHINA caused an evolution in Edward. They taught him moderation, and they taught him understanding. In letters he stopped referring to "the heathen." It was not that he no longer cared whether China became a Christian nation. Indeed, as China's role in the world became apparent, it seemed to him doubly important that China, as well as the other powers, be guided by Christian principles. It was, rather, that he had acquired so much respect for the Chinese that he could not call them heathen. The term stuck in his throat. They became, instead, Taoist, Buddhist, or Mohammedan. He had respect for them, first of all, as individuals. He healed them, delivered their babies—or lost them—one at a time. Each Chinese colleague is referred to in his letters as So-and-so Xian, or Mr. So-and-so. He simply could have used their surnames. He never did.

His sympathies were with them. In writing home he voiced concern for China more often than for the United States. This was not for lack of patriotism. It was just that, working where he was, he saw more in China to be concerned about. He wanted China's rights respected, not just Westerners' rights, so he protested the sellout of China to Japan after World War I. And he cringed when on a train going from Shanghai to Nanjing he saw a white man slap an obviously educated Chinese. He cringed in shame and for the hatred sown, and for what he feared would be the harvest. He saw in the avarice of Westerners the betrayal of Christian endeavor. He was naturally an internationalist. Missionaries, he used to say, were the first anti-isolationists. Like every missionary he knew, he was for the League of Nations.

But it was a mad, impossible thing he was trying to do. How does one doctor care for medical needs in an area where there are two million people? And on a budget of $350 a year? The questions themselves were absurd. You only make a beginning.

A man can be tormented by lesser questions. That patient with the infected leg. Had he made a right judgment? Should he have tried to amputate? And that peasant woman with pneumonia. Had he done all he could? We find him writing, "It is a very fine thing being a physician when you can save people's lives, or relieve suffering, but there are other times when it is not a very fine thing at all."

He resolved, finally, not to allow cankers to grow in him if he could say afterward, "I did my best." That was the philosophy that saved him. He did his best and then put the experience behind him, except for the lesson learned from it. Without faith he would have been lost. It was faith that sustained him after seeing his small edifices, erected after so much striving, demolished repeatedly by flood, plague, and civil war. He was building all the time, looking ahead. His letters occasionally reflect disappointment. But there is no suggestion in them of self-pity or remorse.

The Chinese philosopher Lao-tze said, "Dig your well before you are thirsty." At Shaowu, if Edward needed something from America, he had to order it months ahead of time. This was true of both medicines and household supplies. Shipments were made twice a year by the mission board, which received a discount on its purchases. Orders for the December shipment had to be sent the first week of September. Orders for June had to be sent in March. But often the December shipment arrived in April and the June shipment in October!

Invariably, at ordering time, Edward asked the family in Newburyport to make personal purchases for him. All goods would then be crated by the mission board and shipped out together. These were the "blessed Boston boxes." The list Edward sent home in 1893, for the first December shipment, read as follows:

2 pr. low shoes, good and durable No. 7 1/2–4, or No. 7 1/2 E.
1 pr. rubbers. No. 8 1/2.
1 Exeter cookbook.
2 tooth brushes (about 25 cents apiece).
1 ball strong twine (like the smaller size that comes around Father's silk bundles).
2 small bread tins (for baking loaves).
2 doz. sheets assorted sandpaper
1 small milk pitcher

1 key ring

2 fine combs (for fleas).

Edward made up this list on September 2. A week later he wrote,

I have thought of a few more things for the December shipment. Please include:

2 nurse bottles (with nipples and so shaped that milk tends toward mouth of bottle when it is lying down).

2 extra nipples.

1 picture called "Thoroughbred" with a pretty girl, a magnificent horse and a dog. This is my favorite engraving and I'd like to have you send it, if you can find it in Newburyport.

The nursing bottles and nipples were needed because the Gardners had told him, after he sent off the first list, that a baby was on the way. The picture was needed because life was austere and he needed something like that to look at.

The following March, for the June shipment, he was telling his father, "I need some Christmas presents for Ray Gardner, who will be three and a half. Suppose you buy a Jack-in-the-box to fly up when you open the lid and a nice-sounding trumpet with a mouth piece of something other than brass. Besides these, I should like you to select a few other things suitable for a boy of that age. He has no playmates and deserves some toys." Then he asked, "Can Seaver, Foster and Bowman thread be washed a number of times without fading? (A nice question to put to the regional sales representative of that company.) If the scarlet, navy blue and medium dark green can stand washing, I'd like you to send me a spool of each. The Chinese use a good deal of silk for embroidery, and these would make a small gift. You might also send 40 papers of needles, Nos. 5–10, and some rubber toys for a baby nine or ten months old." The March list included:

1 Noah's ark.

This ordering business was quite a chore. Edward would send his parents money, and the cost of personal items would be deducted from this. Also he would be billed by the mission board for what they bought, plus freight charges. This entailed bookkeeping. He abominated red tape—it kept him from his real business—

and he was always remembering things he needed after the order went off.

He wrote, "Mother suggests keeping a list and adding to it as items come to mind. I have done that, but still things often come to mind after the list has gone which you don't want to wait a whole year for. You can't imagine how hard it is to look ahead and plan for things a year in advance, for that is what it amounts to. With medicines, that can be serious."

In the beginning he ordered medicines through the board, but in about 1900 he started buying directly from the big pharmaceutical houses in England and Germany. His favorite British company was Burroughs-Welcome. During World War I he resumed buying medicines in the United States. The American firm on which he relied most was Parke-Davis. He had to be prepared to cope with any one of a dozen plagues, including smallpox, typhus, and cholera. A ton of quinine may have been dispensed during his years in Shaowu. He ordered chloroform instead of ether because chloroform took less room to store.

His other staples—how he hated taking inventory!—were ammonium chloride or muriate (for sore throats); santonine pills (for worms); paregoric (for babies' tummies); zinc oxide and sulfur ointment, which he made by mixing powdered sulfur and lard, because lard was cheaper than Vaseline (for scabies); tincture of iodine and carbolic acid (for cuts and abrasions); Dover's powder (for Chinese who wanted to break the opium habit); and potassium chlorate (for ulcerated tongues, mouth sores, etc.). He did not use the potassium chlorate in tablet form but dissolved it in water to use as a mouthwash.

Forty years later, when his wife complained that her tongue was sore, Edward said, "Try some potassium chlorate solution. It worked for hundreds of Chinese."

His old reliable, besides quinine, was bismuth ointment, which he made by mixing bismuth powder with Vaseline. He used it for infections to which he wanted to give special treatment, since it was more expensive than the zinc oxide or sulfur. Yet it was the zinc oxide that, of all salves, proved most popular.

BY APRIL 1894 Edward was treating fifty patients a day, and he appealed to Boston for money to build a new, larger dispensary, one that would have a waiting room and windows. Such a building, he argued, was essential for the expanding work of the mission. He begged for two hundred dollars.

His appeal could not have been more badly timed. Donations to charities, including foreign missions, had all but dried up. The United States was going through an economic depression following the Panic of 1893. Instead of appropriating more money for medical work, the board slashed the already inadequate allotment. But this had no effect on the demand. Edward was busier than ever. "I have given up trying to write a journal," he wrote. "My hands are full of work."

Four days after he wrote that, a son was born to a rice farmer in Hunan Province. The world would know the infant as Mao Zedong.

We Are Safe Here

"I HAVE SOME NEWS this time. A week ago, the Gardners had another son added to their family. Both mother and babe are doing well."

Edward had grown attached to Milton and Mary Gardner. They could have gotten on each other's nerves, seeing each other continually. Instead, they became fast friends. Baby Leon, who would become an army surgeon, was the first of many missionary babies Edward delivered. Missionaries, as Pearl Buck said, are a fecund breed.

But the big news in the summer of 1894 was that China and Japan had gone to war. The issue was control of Korea. China did not realize it had become a paper dragon, whereas Japan had modernized its army and navy and was ready for a test of arms. Her forces swept through Korea into Manchuria, and in the peace treaty signed on April 17, 1895, China had to give up the island of Formosa, now Taiwan, and a slice of southern Manchuria. It was the start of Japan's expansionist program, culminating half a century later in World War II.

At Shaowu, life went on as usual except that a good many letters from Edward to his parents never arrived. His first knowledge of this came with an anxious letter from Newburyport saying that no word had been received from him in seven weeks. Edward wrote back, "If you don't hear from me regularly, don't worry but attribute it to a suspicious government and bad mail facilities. We are safe here. You must remember that Shaowu people are different from many of the Chinese in their attitude toward foreigners. Never since I came here have I seen any indication that the people don't wish us here."

He spent the summer in the Walker cottage on Crystal Hill, next door to the Gardners, and again tried to take things easier. "I am trying to get a rest from patients," he wrote. "By resting, I mean studying the language and reading the medical literature which has piled up in the last six months." The opportunities for exercise, he concluded, were inadequate. In hot weather, a walk into the city was too strenuous, as was the climb to their cottages, two-thirds of the way up Crystal Hill. So with the help of two hired men he dug a rambling path to the summit. "Now," he exclaimed, "we have a chance to get a little gentle exercise befitting the climate!" Several times that summer, he wrote, "I have been out digging." It was a form of exercise, like walking, of which he never tired. When he was an old man, neighbors would see him in the backyard digging great pits. He would fill these pits with raked leaves and make an emulsion for his vegetable garden. When he was ninety, his wife told him it was time to stop. But he didn't.

Edward was glad to get back to Shaowu from the hill. "Now for work in earnest," he wrote. "I think I always feel best if I am a little rushed." He began dispensing medicines an extra hour a day and added a new wrinkle—selling soap. He sold the soap at less than cost and made up the difference out of his own pocket. "A lot of misery," he said, "especially these skin eruptions, comes from just not being clean."

The Dongzhi, or winter solstice, heralded the coming of Christmas, which saw the five missionaries gathered at the Gardners' to feast on the goose a wealthy patient had given Edward in return for professional services. The doctor joked about the goose. "That I should have been presented with a goose," he wrote, "does not necessarily suggest the patient's estimate of my mentality."

On Christmas Eve they decorated a tree in the mission chapel. "The tree looked pretty with its presents and candles. The gifts for the Chinese children were toys and candy, for the women a half-paper of needles apiece, and for the men, paper lanterns having on them the sentence 'The true light illumines all.' The needles Father sent were just the thing for the women. I thought it wasteful to give each a whole paper, as a half-paper will last for years. So you see, Father's needles made many women happy."

From his family Edward received a russet-colored pair of slippers and a set of china to use when he would no longer be eating with the Gardners. His gift to the Gardners was a set of novels by Sir Walter Scott.

And the boy Ray, Leon's brother, received a most magnificent Jack-in-the-box and trumpet.

I Have Realized That Any Mail Might Bring Me News of Some Sorrow

THE PART OF MANCHURIA that China was to surrender to Japan was the Liaodong Peninsula, including Port Arthur, but France, Germany, and Russia protested, and Japan forewent this taste of Manchurian pie for the time being. The European powers then presented their bill for getting Japan to back down. France won concessions, economic and territorial, on the border of Annam. And all three powers tightened their stranglehold in the form of new loans. These loans were forced on China, and antiforeign feeling grew as a consequence. On August 1, 1895, several missionaries at Gutian, less than two hundred miles from Shaowu, were massacred. Shaowu missionaries were advised by the American consul at Fuzhou to come down to the treaty port for safety.

Edward, judging by his letters, enjoyed the change. He was able to take charge of the large hospital at Fuzhou for two weeks while its director got a much-needed rest. He reveled in having a real hospital in which to work — "this is something like it"—and then he took a vacation himself on the coast near Fuzhou, at a place called Sharp Peak, where the missionaries had a small sanitorium. It was also the site of an overseas cable station. Edward played tennis with British workers who ran the installation. "They can beat me," he said, "but we have some good games. And we benefit from the exercise." He was always speaking of "the benefits of exercise."

Two months later, he was back at Shaowu. Everything was quiet. He told his family, "It is peaceful here. I have received the box which you sent last June, and thank you all very much. The paintings by Marian are very pretty. They're very natural and will often remind me of the river and the marshes and the Amesbury hills." He was a little homesick, and on Christmas Day 1895 he wrote, "I wish you all a Merry Christmas. I think of you gathered at Allen Street to spend the day together. How I would like to be with you!"

It was the last letter the father would receive from his son in China. The patriarch of No. 18 Allen Street died of a heart attack in Concord, New Hampshire, on February 3, 1896. "He was a citizen," the Newburyport *Daily News* said, "we can ill afford to lose."

Word of his father's death, at age fifty-seven, did not reach Edward until three months after the event. For some unknown reason the mail, so slow in coming up the river under ideal circumstances, was further delayed. In the meantime, the mission was saddened by another death. Adelaide Walker, the small, stout-hearted, fragile woman of fair countenance, was taken by an abdominal cancer. Edward was her doctor until the end. "We were thankful that, so long as she must have that disease, it ran such a rapid course. Mr. Walker," he wrote, "has stood the whole trial wonderfully. He seems full of faith."

Walker buried his helpmate in the foreign cemetery at Fuzhou, overlooking the picturesque river they both loved. He wrote sadly, "The triangle is broken. [The third member was Josie, his daughter, away studying in America.] Never again can we three work and play and joy and sorrow together. With the majestic mountains, beautiful valleys and winding river, little need has she of a tombstone. Her name, her memory, is engraved on a hundred lovely scenes and holds a unique place in many a grateful heart."

He buried his wife and went home alone to Oregon on furlough.

On April 22, Edward learned of his own bereavement. The letter came from his brother Charles. It had been placed in an envelope addressed to Gardner, so the preacher could choose the time to deliver the message and perhaps soften the blow. When the young doctor came down to breakfast that morning, he saw several letters on the table and knew that foreign mail had arrived. But, as far as he could see, no letter was from home.

Edward was crestfallen. "I remarked to Mr. Gardner that it was a long time since I received a home letter. He said nothing. After breakfast he motioned for me to follow him and led the way to my room. I was puzzled but saw that he wished to speak to me in private. When we had entered my room and closed the door, Mr. Gardner put his hand on my shoulder and said he had some sad news to tell me—my father was dead. He held me until the first shock was over and left me alone.

"Here, so many thousands of miles from home, I have realized that any mail might bring me news of some sorrow. God in his love arranged that Charles' letter and yours and Marian's all came close together. So some way I didn't feel so much alone. And then God heard your prayers for me. He was, and is, present to help me."

For months, Edward's mind was filled with memories of his father, the big, genial man who had tried to dissuade him from going so far from home. "I often think of Father as I saw him last, standing on the platform of the train when I parted from him at Georgetown. The picture is impressed very vividly on my memory. He could hardly keep the tears back. Dear Father, he loved me far more than I can ever deserve."

Edward received the news of the death of his father and went back to doctoring, prepared at any time to receive another such message. Yet a quarter century passed before a black-bordered letter came reporting the death of brother Charles. The angel of death spared the large family that long a time.

One Building Here Must Have a Lot of Patience

※

BY EARLY 1896 the Chinese were flocking to Edward's cubbyhole of a dispensary from as far as six days' journey away. They came over the mountains on foot from Jianning and Chukow, and Lichuan and Guangze, and from innumerable towns beyond and between. To treat seventy patients a day was not uncommon, but the conditions made Edward sick at heart. The dispensary was pathetically small for thirty patients, let alone seventy. Many who came should have been hospitalized. There was no hospital, so they were given medicine and sent into the street. Some tarried in the homes of relatives; others might die on the road home.

As summer approached and he thought of the stifling heat inside the dispensary, the pitiful humanity and chickens underfoot, and the lack of facilities for inpatients, he resolved to call a halt to that kind of medical practice. "I have waited for the board to do something as long as I can," he wrote. "I must have some suitable quarters for my work, so I am beginning to build."

From the start, Edward had begged for money for a proper dispensary. A few hundred dollars would have been enough. In 1893 he thought he might be able to build "in a year or two." But the financial depression was still being felt. The mission board, faced with global demands on its meager reserves, was granting higher priority to projects elsewhere. It didn't have money for a new dispensary at the remote Shaowu station. So now he would build with his own money, "together with fifty dollars or so that friends out here have contributed." The board had purchased the site directly across from the compound on East Gate Street. He was spared that expense.

Edward stayed up at night drawing plans, and during the day, when he could snatch time, he measured off distances and drove in stakes where foundations would be laid. There was a new gleam in his eye. He was not just drawing plans for a larger dispensary but for a whole new hospital. The dispensary would be built first, to be sure, but in such a way that hospital wards could be added as funds became available.

After a year of hard work, only two rooms of the dispensary—the storeroom and the dispensing room—were completed. In April 1897 he wrote, "You may wonder at the long time required for building a little affair, but this is China. There are no sawmills here, or door and window factories. Everything has to be done by hand. Then the workmen are not used to this kind of thing and make mistakes." He had to contract for both labor and materials. This in itself was no small chore. Nothing had a set price; the cost of foundation stones, lumber, bricks, nails, tiles, and lime could be determined only by endless haggling, at which the Chinese were expert. There was enough of the Yankee trader in Edward to enjoy this bargaining up to a point. The catch was that the Chinese seemed to have all day to dicker and he didn't!

No agreement seemed possible on the price of foundation stones, but Edward told workers to start digging anyway. Perhaps if he ignored the stone merchants, they would drop their fantastic demands and talk sense. As it turned out, he got the foundation stones for nothing. Before the coolies had dug three feet they came to the foundations of a wall that had stood hundreds of years before. And a few feet deeper, they found the stones of a still more ancient structure. The student of antiquities in Edward became excited over these discoveries. "The present Shaowu," he wrote, "apparently is built on the site of several buried cities. Digging here, there is no telling what you will find." But he found no artifacts—only the stones for his hospital. That was enough. The Chinese came to respect this foreigner for his shrewdness in business as well as for his medicine. The mission recognized Edward's talent for contracting, and henceforth, as long as he stayed at Shaowu, he was the supervisor of construction.

Financial help came from an unexpected quarter. The First and Second Congregational Churches of Waterbury, Connecticut, sent $180 for the hospital. He told Marian, "I am going to try to write the best letter I can. Perhaps by it their interest in missions in general may be increased." The hospital would have been finished sooner if Gardner had not decided, at the same time, to

East Gate Church about 1910.

build a church. Certainly the small chapel on East Gate Street had been outgrown. It held scarcely a hundred worshipers. But it was unfortunate that the two projects came together. There was a shortage of skilled labor—Shaowu was unused to such building activity—and the city boasted only one brick kiln. In October 1897, when it became obvious that both projects could not go forward simultaneously, Edward suspended work on the hospital. It seemed important that the new East Gate church be ready for the annual meeting of the mission in December.

Shaowu had never seen anything like the East Gate Congregational Church. Gardner, who was his own architect, knew the ancient superstition concerning the height of buildings. According to the principle of *feng shui,* a man gained advantage over his neighbor by having a loftier house. He remembered how the Chinese in Ningbo had been alarmed by the erection of a Christian church there. As the edifice rose, surpassing all other buildings, apprehension increased among the people. But when a weathercock finally was mounted on the steeple, they were horrorstruck. Until that time the highest structure had been the bell tower at the end of what was called Centipede Street. The bell tower represented the uplifted head of the centipede, and everyone knew that cocks devour insects, including centipedes. The Chinese appealed

East Gate Hospital was renamed Shaowu Christian Hospital in about 1947, when missionaries returned after World War II.

to the foreigners to remove the predatory rooster. The appeal was ignored, and soon afterward the esteemed bell tower was destroyed in a fire, whereupon a Chinese soothsayer made a proposal. "Cocks may eat centipedes," he said, "but wildcats prey upon the cock. Let a picture of a wildcat be painted on the wall opposite the foreign church." This was done, and when the whole facade of the church crumbled, tumbling the steeple to the ground, the foreigners blamed the accident on bricks that had been insufficiently fired. But the people of Ningbo knew better.

The steepleless church at Shaowu was a tasteful blending of East and West. The corners of the roof curled in Oriental fashion, but the arched front door was unmistakably Gothic, and so were the windows. Another innovation was the elimination of supporting pillars in the middle of the auditorium. According to Chinese architectural planning, it was almost impossible to build an unobstructed room more than thirty feet wide. Gardner showed the Chinese how to put a roof on Western-style rafters, eliminating the supports, only to discover that fir timbers sagged under the weight of tile. There was nothing to do but wait for delivery of stronger timbers of oak. Meanwhile, the operator of the kiln ruined two batches of special brick for the front of the church—"Of course, we wish good-looking bricks for this"—and all hope of holding the annual meeting in the new building had to be abandoned. Instead, the sessions were held in a rented hall used for firing and boxing tea.

Work on the hospital resumed in January 1898. Edward took heart. But in February, with arrival of the rainy season, it became apparent that the roof would have to be done over. It had been made too flat. Water did not run off the tiles fast enough, causing multitudinous leaks.

When the hospital finally was finished, he wrote, "This is a start. I have got a good deal of experience which will be useful when I come to build again." Already he was thinking of building a girls' boarding school. It bothered him that, with few exceptions, Chinese girls were not taught to read.

To his mother's surprise, Edward's next letter was written in Fuzhou. He was coming home.

How Good to Think
of Being Home!

"I HAVE SOME NEWS which I think will make you happy," Edward wrote in his surprise letter. "The Gardners are starting home on furlough, and since there will be no missionary family in Shaowu for a year or more, the mission has decided that I am better spared now than later." He would make the long journey with the Gardners, who had engaged passage by way of Suez. The cost, he explained, was not appreciably greater than for the Pacific route.

There was a postscript: "I was late in receiving Father's portrait, but I can't tell you how proud I am of it. It was a help to look at it from time to time and think of what he would like me to be and do." Edward had difficulty realizing that when he returned to Allen Street, his father would not be there.

In leaving China after six years, he was gratified by how the Chinese had taken to Western medicine. By sheer pressure from them, arising from their need, he had built a hospital, just as Gardner had been compelled by the growing acceptance of Christianity—the good Buddhist Shi Xiansheng was a convert at last—to build a new church. The church and hospital bore witness to the people's response.

Shi Xiansheng would carry on at the hospital. It was not orthodox, this going off and leaving a Chinese in charge. But to deny the sick simply because of his absence, Edward felt, would be criminal. The quinine and santonine were there. They were to be used. So he appointed Shi Xiansheng hospital druggist with full authority to prescribe and dispense.

And he sold Jacqueline, his faithful mule.

THE MISSIONARIES SAILED from Fuzhou on April 8, 1898, and promptly ran into rough weather. Writing from Hong Kong, Edward confessed that the storm caused him "some discomfort." This is the only time he was ever seasick, and he made fourteen voyages in all.

After being isolated so long, he felt almost lost in the British crown colony. "It is," he said, "a strange mixture of Occident and Orient, and the people are a medley of all the nations of the earth." Everything seemed expensive. He had "a time" finding a suitable hotel because of the "exorbitant rates." Globetrotters and free-spending sailors, he guessed, kept prices up. But he thoroughly enjoyed the view from Victoria Peak, which reminded him of the wild vistas around Fuzhou. If it surpassed the beauty of Fuzhou, he would not confess it. In Singapore he made a point to visit the botanical gardens. He was still an amateur botanist. And when the steamer put in at Penang, on the western coast of Malaya, it was the stately palm trees that impressed him most. Everywhere he went he took long walks.

Colombo, the capital of Ceylon, now Sri Lanka, was supposed to be an overnight stop. Instead, they stayed six weeks. All four Gardner children had come down with whooping cough and were quarantined. Edward wrote, "I can't say that I am glad for this enforced stay in Ceylon, and yet it is a beautiful place. Some consider it the loveliest spot on earth." He remarked that, after tea and coconuts, one of the chief products of the island was cinchona bark, from which quinine was made. He made a deep bow to the cinchona tree.

They did not get away from Ceylon until the tenth of June. Edward wrote his last letter of the voyage as they crossed the Bay of Biscay. Three months had passed since they left Fuzhou. "We expect to arrive in Plymouth tomorrow morning," he said, "and then another day's run will bring us to London. As a letter mailed from Plymouth will probably catch an earlier mail steamer, I will write tonight, especially as it is your birthday." He told how they had encountered a fierce storm in the Indian Ocean. "Spray dashed high above the ship. The pitching became so violent that at meal times we had to hold onto our victuals to keep them from being tossed on the floor." The storm delayed the ship for two days, and plans for a side trip to Jerusalem were canceled. He concluded, "The Bay of Biscay has a reputation for being very rough, but it is treating us gently tonight. I thank God that He has brought us over the greater part of our journey in safety and trust that He will soon bring me home."

He was in London for two days, then sailed on the *Boadicea*, a relatively new vessel that made the New York run in eleven days. Its owners advertised "superior accommodations for saloon passengers and elegant music." No such blandishment was needed to persuade Edward to book passage. The *Boadicea* was the first ship leaving for New York. That was persuasion enough. We know nothing of the transatlantic crossing except that the steamer reached New York a day early—on Sunday, July 17. Edward was greeted by headlines proclaiming the capture of Santiago de Cuba and imminent peace with Spain. He parted with his good friends and took the noon train to Boston.

It was exciting, that last lap of the journey along the cozy southern shore of Connecticut, up through Providence and into Boston's South Station. As the train passed through New Haven, he could see none of the college buildings, although East Rock stood out plainly enough. It seemed a lifetime since student days. Could it have been only seven years? So much had happened since he had last seen these salt marshes and inlets and gray rock masses, so much since he had seen the beloved house on Allen Street and his mother and brothers and sisters and uncles and aunts. In a few hours, he kept telling himself, I'll be home. It was almost beyond belief.

I Have Come Home!

TEARS WET his mother's face. They were tears of joy. The family made a small crowd on the station platform. They could all rally there because it was summer. Mary, a senior at Wellesley, was home for vacation. So were Clara, the teacher of chemistry, and Marian—nicknamed Green Eyes—who had somehow become a physical education instructor at a girls' school. George had just graduated from MIT. Charles was beginning to make a name for himself in the shoe business, and Will, after making a stab at raising poultry, had decided to sell insurance.

Only one was absent.

How good to be home again, to smell the sweet roast in the oven and taste fresh bread and see "God Bless Our Home" above the fireplace and grasp old friends' hands and hear family laughter and church bells and walk down High Road to where you look east to the sand dunes and the sea. They had picnics and shore dinners and old-fashioned drives in the country. Edward hired the horse and carriage from Greenough's Livery Stable, as his father had done before him, and took his mother and sisters on the old Byfield road through cool, dark woods and sunny meadows, or over to Salisbury, or up to the Pines. Sometimes only she accompanied him. As they rode, he would try to answer all her questions.

His chums Sam Mulliken and Arthur Noyes were back from Leipzig and studying at MIT. Their manual, *Laboratory Experiments on the Identification of Organic Substances*, had just been published, and they proudly gave him a copy. Recalling their boyhood excursions, they hatched plans for an eight-day cruise on Mulliken's new motorboat. And they carried out their scheme, venturing along the Maine coast as far as Mount Desert, catching up on each other's lives, and hopes, and browning themselves in the August sun.

By September the vacation was over. Edward enrolled at Harvard for postgraduate work in obstetrics. He could not learn too much about abnormal childbirth. Almost all his cases involved premature separation of the placenta, inversion of the uterus, or any one of a dozen other complications. At the same time, he took a course in eye surgery. Among the maladies of the Chinese, Edward found trachoma one of the most prevalent. Chronic inflammation caused eyelashes to turn in upon the cornea, setting up a constant irritation that produced ulcers and eventual blindness. He learned how, in advanced cases, to remove the offending lashes and how to make new pupils for eyes blinded by scar tissue. If part of the cornea was clear, you made an incision, drew out a bit of the iris, and, separating it, created a substitute pupil that would serve. A Jiangxi man on whom he performed this miracle carried a small mirror so he could see and exult in the wondrous thing that had been done for him.

It was almost time to return to China when Edward came down with a severe attack of malaria. During the period of paroxysms he lay on the couch in the living room with hardly enough strength to raise his hands. After two weeks the family physician, who had never attended a malaria patient before, pronounced him well enough to go outdoors. That day he walked as far as Parsons Street—just one block—and the next day was seized with dysentery. He belittled its seriousness, saying it was only his bowels again, but doctors advised that his departure for China be delayed. They feared that dysentery, coming before full recovery from the malarial attack, might have lowered his resistance dangerously.

Edward decided to stay home another year. It was not entirely a matter of health. Ocean travel agreed with him. He had no doubt he would be recovered by the time he reached Shanghai. Edward asked the mission board for permission to remain with his family because he felt, after weighing his responsibilities, that he should stay. His mother needed him. She depended on his counsel. Marian wanted to study medicine. Did he think a woman ought to enter that profession? What should Mary do, now that she was finishing college? Will could not seem to find his niche in life. His poor, twisted back was paining him dreadfully. Should he stop taking the exercises? Should George go to work for the government? He was such a good civil engineer, they said. And Charles had been working much too hard at the shoe factory.

Would he speak to him and try to make him see reason? She herself was depressed. She still grieved for her husband and was having spells.

It was not as though, medically, he were leaving the mission uncovered. The American Board had assigned a woman doctor to Shaowu. She would be there shortly. Nor were there missionary children to care for. Gardner's health had deteriorated. He would not be returning for another year, and when he did return, the board was sending him to Fuzhou, where he would be under less strain. And—oh, yes—Mrs. Gardner was having another baby. For a change, she said, it would be born in the United States. Edward promised to visit them after the baby came; he felt a sort of proprietary interest in Gardner babies.

That next year Edward studied in New York and Philadelphia. The purpose, he said, was to brush up on general medicine, although it is not clear why he went to both cities. He did feel an urgent need to "brush up." At Shaowu he seldom found time to read the medical journals and learn new procedures. In Philadelphia he studied at what was called the Polyclinic, and, while there, he looked into entrance requirements for the Medical School for Women. It was there, he remembered, that the young woman doctor on the SS *China* had received her training. Evidently he was satisfied with what he found, for he advised Marian to enroll. "Don't feel you *must* finish the course," he said. "Anything you learn is bound to be useful in physical education." He attended lectures at the Postgraduate Medical School in New York while Clara was studying for her master's degree in chemistry at Columbia. Twice, to give his legs a workout, he walked uptown from his rooming house on Twenty-third Street to the university, a distance of a hundred blocks. On the southwestern corner of Twenty-third Street and Fourth Avenue stood the first YMCA to be equipped with a gymnasium. Edward discovered it and exercised there, just as he had at Yale. He wanted to be in shape for whatever lay ahead.

ONE AFTERNOON in late June 1900, Edward heard a newsboy shouting that China had declared war. He bought a paper. It was true. The thing had begun with bands of antiforeign agitators, the so-called Boxers, pillaging mission property. Railroad shops employing foreign technicians were burned. Then on June 9 the rail line to Beijing was ruptured, isolating the foreign legations. Two days later, scores of Chinese Christians in Beijing were massacred along with several missionaries. The foreign missions in Tientsin, now called Tianjin, were sacked at almost the same time.

Protests proved futile. Instead of acting to suppress the Boxers, the Imperial Court encouraged the movement. It was tired of foreign encroachment. An international expedition of two thousand men set out from Tientsin for the Chinese capital. To protect the rear of this column, a naval force, including elements of the U.S. fleet, knocked out a series of forts guarding the approaches to Tientsin. It was this action that brought the declaration of war on the Western powers.

Today it would be called a brushfire war. Nonetheless, it was ugly. The imperial government offered a bounty on the heads of all foreigners, young and old. The head of a child brought thirty taels, or about twenty-two dollars. Adult heads were worth slightly more. From June 20 to August 14, the legations in Beijing were under siege, relieved finally by a motley force of British, Russian, American, Japanese, French, Austrian, and Italian troops. In Shanxi Province more than two hundred missionaries were slain.

Fujian Province, by all reports, was relatively quiet. But then came word that many buildings of the Shaowu station had been destroyed. As soon as he could secure passage, Edward sailed for China. He had to see what had befallen his beloved hospital.

There Is Still Hope!

WHEN EDWARD RETURNED to China in 1900, he found himself on the same ship with Josie Walker. The sunny-dispositioned young woman had graduated from Oberlin College and now, her formal education complete, was going back to work with her father at Shaowu. Edward had met her once before, in 1892, when he stopped in Oberlin on his way to the West Coast. Josie was then a blond, freckled girl just entering high school; now she was a blond, freckled woman. She had her father's mischievous blue eyes. Her heavy, honey-colored tresses were piled on her head Gibson girl style, but even with that she stood a good two inches shorter than the missionary doctor.

It is strange that he should have been thrown in this way with Josie, for the two thoughts uppermost in his mind as he boarded the SS *Coptic,* or, for that matter, during his whole long train ride across the continent, had concerned the fate of his hospital and the need of taking unto himself a wife. He had resolved that *this* time in Fuzhou he would keep a sharp lookout for someone to marry. Invariably, eligible young women were stationed there. One might be his bride, though past experience had not made him optimistic on that score. He remembered how, in 1892, he had no sooner appeared in Fuzhou than older missionaries had tried to marry him off to "that fat, jolly nurse from the Methodist Hospital." Everything had been so obvious, not like that nurse in New Haven—"She was pretty, too"—who had made him a proposal by way of a bouquet of maiden-hair fern and bachelor buttons.

It would be understatement to say that Edward did not look forward to another seven years of bachelorhood at Shaowu; he dreaded it. Perhaps until this time he had not entirely given up Elizabeth Wilkinson, who jilted him so long ago. He was not one to transfer affection easily, and certainly during the first Shaowu period there had been no other woman in his life, except possibly the pretty girl in the "Thoroughbred" engraving. But now Elizabeth Wilkinson had married, and the last chance of reconciliation was gone. Pretty, talented Ruth Bliss, whom he met during that first voyage, also had married, he heard. Everyone was getting married. And if he was to find a bride within the next seven years, he would have to find her soon, before he was shut off from eligible American womanhood in the mountain fortresses of Fujian.

So here, on a ship one day out of San Francisco, he met the one woman in the world whom he would be able to court after arriving in Shaowu. It seemed almost as though Fate had intended them for each other. Josie was good-dispositioned, young, and intelligent. She was well nerved. The third day out, with the *Coptic* wallowing like an iron pig, she and Edward were the only couple who showed up for dinner. She seemed interested in everything he was interested in; she was even fond of walking, and the way they promenaded, you knew it. She walked, he said, like a trooper. Perhaps that was the trouble. For all her blond tresses and upturned nose and appreciable bosom, she lacked femininity. She was resourceful and, one suspected, self-sufficient. No man could imagine her running to him in any difficulty. Perhaps this was why Edward felt nothing except a sense of good fellowship. He himself never spoke of it. He did remark once that Walker, soon after the ocean crossing, asked him point-blank, "Are you interested in my daughter?" And he had to answer, less directly, that he was not. He and Josie were coworkers for many years after that. But the question of what might have been was buried.

A year earlier—that is, in December 1898—another woman, completely feminine, had sailed from San Francisco on the SS *Gaelic,* bound for Fuzhou. She was a missionary, too, but in a delightful way, without artifice, she made men feel important. As a girl she had marveled at what boys could do; now she felt the same way about men. Men appreciated this attitude. Nor were they oblivious to her physical assets, the warm brown eyes, flawless complexion, and fine hourglass figure.

It is intriguing to read the letters recommending her to the American Board. These letters, now in the Houghton Library at Harvard, lauded her teaching ability, declared her devout, not easily discouraged, and then, invariably, commented on her good looks. One writer suggested she might be too voluptuous for the business of saving souls. The secretary of the Saline County

Minnie May Bortz, left, as she looked when she sailed for China. Below: Evelyn and Simon Bortz at their farm on Military Road, Irvington, Nebraska.

Sunday School Association said, "I shall be frank. Miss Bortz is well-built."

Minnie May Bortz, who was called May, was the fifth of six children born to Simon and Evelyn Bortz, a couple who shortly before the Civil War had come down the Ohio River and settled on a piece of rich farmland near Omaha. Of Pennsylvania Dutch stock, they had farmed in the community of Greensburg, near Pittsburgh, and fared well, but Simon, unable to resist the promise of cheap land when the Nebraska country was opened up, brought his family into the new territory. They traveled by flat-boat down the Ohio, past Cincinnati, Louisville, and Paducah to Cairo, where they transferred to a stern-wheeler that, fighting the dark currents of the Mississippi and the Missouri, carried them to Omaha. In recalling her mother's account of the trip, May told more than once how on the Ohio a great windstorm struck the overloaded flatboat, sending waves over the gunwales so it seemed all would be lost.

Once arrived in Nebraska, Simon Bortz bought a hundred acres along what is called Military Road because it was the route frequently traveled by army forces going out to put down Indian uprisings. One summer day, when she was a pinafored girl of five, May saw a company of General Custer's 7th Cavalry ride by, never to return. Years later—in her eighty-sixth year, to be exact—she cut out a newspaper clipping reporting the death of Chief Iron Hail, one of the last survivors of the Battle of the Little Bighorn. On the edge of the clipping she wrote in her still bold, graceful hand, "He was a Sioux, but in Nebraska the American Board sent missionaries to the Pawnees." It was like her to tie in Custer's Last Stand with the missionary movement.

She was born, like Edward, on a Sunday, although late at night instead of in the morning. "Father and Mother," she said, "spent the evening singing hymns. He had a fine baritone voice, and she was a soprano. A good one. They didn't have the little organ then but sat side by side on the sofa, using an old Lutheran hymnal they brought from the East. They sang for two hours, Mother said, and then he got the doctor."

Simon, a great admirer of Robert E. Lee, raised the usual corn, barley, and wheat, but his specialty was livestock. He knew and loved horses, and his great Belgian mares—he once owned five of them—were real beauties. May rode bareback. She was thrown the first time she attempted it, but she got back on and never fell off again. Her older brother Harry read cowboy stories in *The Youth's Companion*, then acted them out. "Once he and George Knight, a neighbor boy, pretended to be 'Wild Bill' and 'Bloody Jack' and shot it out in the chicken house." May laughed. " 'Bloody Jack' lost his balance and sat down on two nests of eggs!"

The father was a broad-shouldered man with a prophet's beard. His idea of fun in wintertime was bundling the whole family in the sleigh and taking them for a dash through the snow. At night, after supper, he liked to sit and read aloud from Longfellow. The mother, who often did mending as she listened, treasured these evenings. She was a small, hardworking, frugal, straight-haired woman who raised six children with tenderness. She died in May's arms. Simon already was dead.

They were Lutheran, but the only church in the vicinity was Congregational, so May was brought up in that denomination. Otherwise, she never would have met Edward. One of the deacons was S. C. Brewster, whose maternal grandfather, Reuben Gaylord, founded the first Congregational church in Nebraska Territory. Everyone looked up to the Brewsters, and when Deacon Brewster's daughter Hattie decided to become a missionary, it made a deep impression on May, who already taught Sunday school and was interested in religious work. The thought of becoming a missionary grew in her. She entered Yankton College in South Dakota in 1892 and noticed the words

Christ for the world we ring;
The world to Christ we bring

inscribed on the chapel bell. She recalled the words seventy years later and said, "Every time I heard the bell I asked myself: Is it ringing for me?"

In the fall of 1893, she transferred to Doane College. She spent the year after graduation teaching mathematics at Doane Academy and the next year as mistress of a one-room country school. "Then all of a sudden," she said, "I remembered the chapel bell. I applied to the American Board and was assigned to a teaching position at Pagoda Anchorage, ten or twelve miles below Fuzhou."

Hattie Brewster, the girl who inspired her, got married and never became a missionary.

LATE IN 1898, the man idolized by American womanhood was a young naval officer by the name of Richmond Hobson. As a lieutenant in the Spanish-American War, Hobson was credited with bottling up the enemy fleet at Santiago de Cuba. Everyone knew how the handsome officer, with seven volunteers, ran the dismantled navy collier *Merrimac* into the harbor entrance and sank it amid a hail of gunfire. He was captured in the water, but as the Associated Press reported, "So audacious was the feat that it excited even the admiration of the Spanish commander, Admiral Cervera, and the whole world."

The fact that the "bottling" proved ineffectual and that Hobson had company in his heroism did not keep him from being singled out for adulation. The country would see nothing like it again until Lindbergh. Young mothers ambushed Hobson so their babies might touch his uniform; men dragged him off trains in the middle of the night to make speeches. Small wonder that Hobson breathed freer when, on Christmas Eve 1898, he sailed for the Philippines on the SS *Gaelic*. Most females on board were proper missionary ladies. They might be titillated by his presence—they were human—but they did not run after him screaming or embrace him on sight.

For her part, May Bortz was thrilled to be China-bound on the same ship with a national hero. She was almost, as events proved, thrilled beyond words. "We were never introduced," she recalled, "but he spoke to me at a taffy pull, and I was just foolish like a school-girl. He asked if he might pull taffy with me. I wanted to, but you know how you can be when you meet someone you think a lot of. I could hardly say a word, and then I said no. He bowed and turned to Frances Bement. *She said yes!*"

Frances Bement and her older sister Lucy were among a group of new missionaries appointed to Shaowu. Christian preachers, doctors, and educators were being dispatched to the four corners of the earth as never before in history. The goal was nothing less than that inscribed on the Yankton chapel bell, "Christ for the world." The whole world. This was not a vague thing. There were missionaries who expected, in decades, to see the Christianization of all nations.

Lucy Bement was a physician who, by sheer coincidence, had served her internship in Newburyport. She was not pretty—her features were strictly utilitarian—but she was courageous and capable. Once, single-handedly, she routed a passel of river pirates by whacking their heads, and buttocks, with an oar. They were flabbergasted by this fierce woman and fled. Her sister Frances had dark, flashing eyes—Lucy's were cold gray—and Frances was companionable. She pulled taffy with Lieutenant Hobson, but he did not, as they used to say, cultivate her acquaintance. Instead, he tried again to get through to the strange girl who refused him, the pretty, shy one the steward had told him was Miss Bortz.

Operators of ocean liners feel a compulsion to put on games for the entertainment of passengers. This was especially true before the advent of motion pictures. No lotteries or other games of chance were conducted aboard the *Gaelic*—too many missionaries on board—but there were shuffleboard and deck tennis, and quite early in the voyage the captain persuaded Lieutenant Hobson, hero of Santiago de Cuba, to organize a game of drop the handkerchief. It was in the course of this game that Hobson, possessing the handkerchief, made his move.

"There were a lot of us," May recalled with more than a touch of pride. "It was a large circle, and he dropped the handkerchief first behind me. He did it twice." Asked if she caught him, she replied, "Gracious no!"

It was a strange romance, even for shipboard, and a little sad. "That evening," she said, "I found him standing by me. I found him near me many times, and I was very flattered." But he did not speak until the steamer reached Shanghai, and, of course, according to the rules, May could never speak first to him. As they were docking he met her outside her cabin—was it accidentally?—and asked if he could help with her luggage. She had two heavy bags, and he carried them for her down the gangplank. After he left her, she had to look back. She said he was looking back, too. They never saw each other after that.

A POSTSCRIPT TO THE CROSSING: A winter storm caught the SS *Gaelic* off the coast of Japan. For twenty-four hours waves broke over the ship, threatening to pound it to pieces. Few passengers dared leave their staterooms; none was so foolhardy as to venture on deck. At the height of the storm the captain asked those who believed in the mercy of God to pray for deliverance. The ship did not sink. But the storm deserves mention because it conditioned May against ocean travel for the rest of her life.

I Believe Now in Falling in Love

EDWARD DISCOVERED MAY on the seventh day of the Twelfth Moon in the fourth year of the Third Regency of Tzu-hsi, which was the elaborate Chinese way of giving the date of January 26, 1901. May had come up from Pagoda Anchorage to attend the annual business meeting at Ponasang, a Fuzhou suburb, and she and a bevy of other women, all unmarried, had rushed onto the terrace in front of the American Board Female College as the young bachelor doctor was coming up the walk. Everyone had heard, of course, of the arrival of the coastal steamer from Shanghai; it was one of the great excitements—a real happening—to see the new missionaries from America and greet old friends.

Edward was not alone. He came up from the landing with Josie Walker and her father and Lyman Peet, head of the boys' boarding school. Peet had known Edward at Yale—they both boarded at Mrs. Cogston's—and had gone down to the anchorage in a houseboat to meet them. His wife, Carrie, had been a friend of Clara's at Mount Holyoke, and when Edward first arrived in China, before he had gone up to Shaowu, they sort of adopted him. Now Peet led Edward and Josie onto the terrace and introduced them to the young single ladies—Ella Newton, Elsie Garretson, Jean Brown, Frances and Lucy Bement, and May Bortz. He and May had quite a time fifty years later trying to remember just who was in that lineup.

"That's the funny part of it," he said with a laugh. "They were lined in a row!"

He said nothing about being "taken" with May, but the fact is that, writing home, he mentioned only the Bement sisters and "a Miss Bortz, who has charge of the girls' boarding school at Pagoda Anchorage." It's easy to see why he spoke of the Bements; he would be working with them at Shaowu. But he had no reason, except that he was impressed, for mentioning only May among the four other eligible women he met that day.

As for May, she said, "I was curious. Ever since I arrived in China I had heard about the fine young doctor who had been at Shaowu. I was interested in meeting him, but, you know, there must have been something wrong with me—I didn't think of the possibility of marrying him. There were a lot of other girls there. I just wondered what he was like."

"How did he strike you?"

"He was carrying a suitcase, I remember. He came through the gate and looked up and smiled. When we met I was struck by his manner. He was modest and genteel."

During the annual business meeting, Edward saw George Hubbard, another Yale alumnus, who preached among the villages scattered below Fuzhou, near the Min River mouth. He got about the parish in his own sampan. His house was at Pagoda Anchorage, and as soon as he saw Edward, he invited him down for a visit.

"Come on along," he said. "You've got nothing special to do."

It was true. For days Walker had been urging the American consul, C. P. Gracey, to let them go upriver for a firsthand assessment of damage to the Shaowu property during the Boxer Rebellion. The consul refused permission until the imperial viceroy at Fuzhou guaranteed their safety. The viceroy hesitated to do this. During the bloodbath in North China he had held antiforeign elements in the province in check, but he still was not sure of the temper of the people. Let harm befall a few Americans now as negotiations with the major powers were in progress, and China would again be punished. So while he waited, Edward went down to Pagoda Anchorage as Hubbard's guest.

That very first evening the Hubbards had May over for supper. "She was wearing a pretty dress," Edward recalled, "about the color of chocolate. There must have been eight of us at the table—four of the seven Hubbard children were still in China—and Mrs. Hubbard had spice cake for dessert." After supper they sang songs, including rounds for the children, and Edward began entertaining thoughts of walking the pretty teacher home. This was not to be. Shortly after nine o'clock a coolie showed up with a lantern to take her back.

Edward, here with several of his pupils, had just returned from furlough and so appears rested.

"She didn't trust me!" Edward exclaimed on their fiftieth wedding anniversary. Disappointment showed in his voice after all those years. But he wasn't discouraged. "I asked the Hubbards if they thought she would object to my going over to her house for tennis. There was a court right alongside the house. They said 'Of course not,' so I went over with the two older Hubbard children, and we played doubles. The next day she and I played alone." They played only one set. "Her game was good for a girl, I thought, but the thing that really impressed me were her heavy braids of brown hair. And she didn't get mad when I beat."

In a letter written at that time to his mother, Edward said, "I am not much at describing people so will simply say that Miss Bortz is a young lady whom all of you would like." Lest the folks back home get the notion he had gone overboard, he hastened to add, "In fact, all the young ladies who have come out during my furlough are very pleasant people and very valuable additions to our force."

There Was Plenty of Ventilation

❈

IT WAS A MONTH after the tennis match with the dark-eyed girl from Nebraska that Edward and his coworkers finally started upriver. He had no fear; neither did Walker. Shaowu, geographically isolated, did not know gunboats. It knew only missionaries who taught the Jesus doctrine and healed.

Edward found the East Gate house that he had shared with the Gardners an empty shell. Every movable thing, every piece of furniture, every personal article, including the prized photograph of his father, had been carried off.

"It was raining," Edward wrote. "We came over to the house to see how much was left of it and found all the doors and window frames gone. About two-thirds of the floor boards were torn up. The plaster had been ripped off the ceilings, along with a good many slats. And the plastering, dirt and lime, lay deep on what was left of the floor."

The new church, which was Gardner's dream, had fared no better. All the doors and windows stood gaping. The pulpit and entire floor were gone, even some of the heavy, handhewn supporting timbers. But for Edward the saddest sight was the hospital. A March wind moaned through ugly holes that once were windows. How much he had wanted fresh air and light! The two waiting rooms were a shambles. Not only the doors but also the door frames had been removed, so great was the hunger for wood. And because the front door had been stolen and there was nothing to deny free passage, chickens roosted on the floor beams, which were still intact. The place smelled like the inside of a henhouse. The walls he had done over, so they would be smooth and washable with antiseptic, had been broken up as if by sledges. But, surprisingly, the door into the dispensary proper remained on its hinges, and two windows in that room were still in place. It seemed almost as though the mob, reaching the inner sanctum, reconsidered. But the store of medicines had disappeared; so had his precious microscope.

Edward's work, the one permanent thing established in six years of labor, had been despoiled. The permanent thing's impermanence had been cruelly demonstrated. Still, his first letter after returning to Shaowu shows no trace of bitterness. "Everyone," he said, "appears friendly. I can't see any reason to believe that the trouble here was due to any special ill-feeling. They thought their country was at war with us and they would get what plunder they could."

Shi Xiansheng and other Shaowu Christians had been powerless. They were "secondary foreign devils"; if they had lived in another part of China, they might have been killed. Even the civil magistrate, when he tried to reason with the mob, had been beaten and his sedan chair smashed while the military magistrate, either from fear or principle, holed up at his headquarters with a handful of opium-eating troops.

Because the cottages at Crystal Hill had been sacked, the Walkers—father and daughter—camped with Edward and the Bements in the house by the East Gate. Shi Xiansheng invited the missionaries to his home inside the city wall, but they demurred because of their number and began living in the wrecked mission residence from the first night, after scraping out most of the debris with hoes.

The missionaries stayed in Shaowu only three months before returning to Fuzhou for the summer, but it is remarkable what they accomplished. Within two days, forty workmen were busy putting in new floors, windows, and doors. "It is my business to oversee the workmen," Edward wrote, "and to tell them what is to be done and in what order. A carpenter had many windows all made, so that we had simply to fit them and set the glass. It does seem as though God got things ready for us."

Edward had brought an emergency supply of medicines, but it was soon obvious that, despite the good progress made, the hospital would not be ready until fall. All patients that spring were treated at Edward's house. Inside the city, by the North Gate, two acres of land were purchased for the women's work of the mission. A separate women's dispensary would be erected on this tract, along with a girls' boarding school and a residence for Frances and Lucy Bement.

The girls' boarding school near North Gate shortly after the school was completed.

From Allen Street, in the midst of this activity, came two photographs of Edward taken during his furlough. "They are," he said, "as good as I could expect." He gave one of the photographs to Walker. Frances Bement asked for the other one. But it was neither Frances nor Lucy whom Edward was thinking of. He thought of the petite brunette at Pagoda Anchorage who was very shy but who played a good game of tennis for a girl and had great braids of brown hair.

I Had to Move Warily to Avoid Gossip

✤

THE WATER WAS GOOD, about the right height for fast work on the river, and the missionaries reached Fuzhou in five days. After calling on the consul, they repaired to Kuliang, two thousand feet above the Fuzhou plain. Cottages of foreign tea merchants, steamship agents, postal commissioners, customs men, and missionaries—Anglican, Methodist, and Congregational—nestled below the highest ridge. Each stone cottage, like a small fortress, was shielded on the north and east by eight-foot-high typhoon walls, for here you caught the full force of raging storms as well as fine breezes.

Miss Bortz had bought one of these bungalows. "I don't know what got into my head," she said, "but I wanted a house of my own. Of course, it cost only four hundred dollars, and I had saved a little money. But still I have to wonder. I was the only single lady, I think, who did such a thing."

Edward had planned to stay at Shaowu that summer of 1901. His honest opinion was that most trips to Fuzhou were unnecessary. As a summer sanctuary, Crystal Hill was inadequate, but Nishitu met every requirement if they would only buy land among those lovely mountains and build. He suspected that the main reason for Kuliang's popularity was social. There one could attend teas and religious conferences and, most important, see new faces. After eight months of sharing everything from diarrhea to prayers with the same few people, however knowledgeable, you were ready for a change.

Edward could rationalize that he was going to Fuzhou this time because his supply of medicines was low and because there would be need at Kuliang for another doctor. But the real reason he was going, he knew, was to see Miss Bortz. And he had a plan of attack. He would build a tennis court at her doorstep. He wrote

The bungalows at Kuliang, one of which was bought by May Bortz.

afterward, "You see, Kuliang is a little summer community, and everybody knows everybody else's business. It is impossible to do anything without it being talked about, so I had to move warily to avoid gossip which would be unpleasant for her. She is extremely sensitive." In such matters, so was he. He was at a loss to know how to go about winning this woman until he hit upon the idea of the tennis court. "I knew she enjoyed tennis and hoped it would be the means of bringing us together." If all went well, he would take her back to Shaowu that fall as his bride.

Edward was spending the summer with Willard and Ellen Beard of the Fuzhou mission. Beard, who had charge of the theological seminary at Ponasang, was a tall, athletic man who loved a good game of tennis. Edward lacked money for the court—it would have to be dug out of the mountainside by coolie labor—but he had no trouble persuading Beard to buy a share in the enterprise. Frances and Lucy Bement; an Englishman named Bland; Jean Brown, the poetess of the Fuzhou mission; and May Bortz purchased the five other equal shares at four dollars and fifty cents a share. Because each investor had the same last initial, it was called the "B" project. Edward found the Chinese owner of the land and leased a tract, 60 feet by 110 feet, for twenty-five years for ten dollars. If he could not make a conquest in twenty-five years, he would quit!

Work got under way on the twenty-third of June. Edward superintended the excavation from morning to night, lamenting each wasted rainy day, frequently swinging a mattock alongside the coolies, setting a killing pace because as the days, then weeks, slipped past, the fear grew in him that the court would not be finished in time to win the girl he was now entirely satisfied he loved. This was courtship with a court. He could not bring himself simply to go calling; he was no good at making conversation. They would have to *do* something together.

At last, on July 16, the court was finished. Edward marked it off with lime. Then, when all was in readiness, when he was about to enjoy the fruits of his labor and Miss Bortz told him, "I do think it will be pleasant," he was taken out of action for two weeks with an attack of dysentery. So he returned to Shaowu without a bride. In the few weeks left of the summer he had been able to play only two games with her. The weather was terrible, and he had been busy getting medical supplies together for the upriver trip. He also bought some household effects, including a handsome potbellied stove so that if he married, life at Shaowu would not seem too austere. He would come up to the mountain after a long day in Fuzhou tending to this business, and sometimes, looking across the ravine, catch a glimpse of his beloved tending flowers. On the last evening the Beards, taking pity, invited the object of his affection for supper.

"I remember," she said, "how quiet he was during the meal. Afterward he walked me home."

"Did he say anything special?"

"No, just good-bye. He was very serious."

A year later, he wrote, "I felt we had not become well enough acquainted to speak out, so I went back to Shaowu, intending to stay for two years. I must say I went with a heavy heart." He was not even sure that the young schoolteacher liked him. "I ought to say that the first few times I met her she was cordial, but later she became very reserved. It seems that the Bement sisters, who are very intimate with her, had begun to plague her about me. As she is very proud, she was determined no one should say she led me on."

For Edward, the next eight months were the longest, most painful he spent in China. They were months that, under normal circumstances, would have given him a pleasurable sense of achievement. The woman's dispensary was finished. Work had started for a residence for the Walkers in a new compound outside the East Gate. Plans were approved for a new boys' school, and the first financial contribution for the school had come from none other than Shi Xiansheng. Edward's onetime Buddhist mentor now owned the first modern drugstore in Shaowu and was well-to-do. Edward was gratified but not cheered by these developments. As he attended the sick, straightened accounts, superintended carpenters and masons, slept, walked, ate, and prayed, he was haunted by the possibility of losing the young woman with lovely brown eyes and braids. He did not even dare write to her. And all the time he remained silent, fearful of rejection, May was worshiping him from a distance. Because she was shy and proud, she had given no sign of her love.

"Oh, Mother," a daughter was to exclaim one day, "how could you be so foolish? Don't you see you almost lost him?"

"Yes," she said. "I suppose I stood in reverence of him."

In two years they had seen each other perhaps a dozen times. What, Edward asked himself, if they *never* became well enough acquainted? What if he returned to Fuzhou to find her engaged to someone else? The thought tortured him. The eldest son in a large family, he yearned for the pretty teacher and a family of his own. He could no longer enjoy family life vicariously with the Gardners; they were now stationed in Fuzhou. He was thirty-six years old. He was lonely. He longed for May.

Edward had not meant to return to Fuzhou for two years as a matter of principle, but the self-exile was intolerable. When on the first day of June 1902 a letter came from Newburyport announcing Charles's engagement, Edward realized he could not endure another year of uncertainty. So when a flotilla of sparrow boats left Shaowu that month, he was on board. He never imagined that in another boat Walker, too, was thinking of marriage and that the woman in their thoughts was the same.

... Announce the Marriage
of Their Daughter

號

WALKER HAD DECIDED to ask the schoolteacher for her hand because, like Edward, he could scarcely stand the loneliness. Six years had passed since his wife's death, and because it had been a good marriage, and she had been loving, he found a widower's life painfully empty. But when he reached Fuzhou and went up on the mountain, he was even more tongue-tied than the doctor.

This was because he felt ridiculous. At fifty-eight, he was old enough to be the woman's father. In a few years people would be calling him "old Dr. Walker." His diary suggests the inner torment. He speaks of seeing Miss Bortz sitting next to another man at prayer meeting, of not being able to sleep at night—"I get the blues"—and of disappointment with himself for "lack of self-command."

Then one night under cover of darkness, the tortured, self-reproaching, lonely, kindly man slipped over to the Bortz cottage and pushed a note through the lady's bedroom window declaring his love. The struggle within himself that preceded this indignity can only be guessed at. There was no need, he wrote, for her to reply. He would know the next time he saw her, from her very glance. Long afterward she said, "I respected him, and I just went on treating him as a friend."

It was his only attempt.

Edward pressed his campaign on the tennis court, unaware of the pitiful drama that had taken place. To get in his quota of games with Miss Bortz, he often had to play with other owners of the "B" court. So did the pretty schoolteacher. One day, recalling together those extraneous matches, May said, "It's queer. We had all those games, but I remember, Edward, only playing with you."

"Not strange," he teased. "You were paying no attention to the others. You were out to get *me*!"

On the twenty-third of July 1902, May Bortz was in the west room of her cottage studying Chinese. It was a dark, rainy day with a definite chill in the air, and only a few minutes earlier Dr. Emily Smith, who shared the cottage that summer, had put on her raincoat and gone out to attend to a patient. When a knock came on the door, May assumed that it was someone to see Dr. Smith on a medical matter. Most calls were for the doctor.

"Oh," she said, when she saw it was Edward. "I'm sorry, Dr. Smith just went out."

"I didn't come to see Dr. Smith," he said. "I came to see you."

He looked very solemn as he entered. His business, thought May, must be fairly important. But she couldn't think what it might be.

"Will you have some tea?" she feinted. "I can get it in a minute."

"No, thank you," he said. "I came to ask you something." He was not going to waste words. Yet he seemed to be taking an interminable time.

She waited, and suddenly a touch of pink came on her cheeks. But it couldn't be *that*! If he made a proposal to anyone, it would be to one of the young woman physicians.

Edward spoke with difficulty. "I came to ask if you would marry me." He hesitated a moment, then went on determinedly. "I must go back to Shaowu and if I waited another year, we would not know each other any better. I would be there, and you would be here."

It *had* happened. She was full of gratitude, excitement, and surprise. And no words. Finally, in her confusion she managed to say, "Of course, I admire you." There was another awkward silence. "I have to go back in two months," he said. "I hope you will come back with me, but . . . "

He could not finish. He looked so serious May knew she had to say something, and it had to be more than an empty phrase. "I will let you know tomorrow," she said.

Tomorrow! Had she said that? She must be out of her mind. It was not time enough for such a decision. But she had said tomorrow, and she would abide by it.

"Thank you," he said. His voice was husky. But he had done what he set out to do, and he sat down.

May insisted on preparing tea because, she said, there was such a chill in the air. She went into the kitchen with a pounding heart.

The next afternoon she sent a coolie to him with her reply—the one word, "Yes" on a sheet of paper in a small white envelope. He must have been waiting. In minutes he was at her door. And this time she was not studying. She was ready for the man she would marry. And until that day he had never called her anything but Miss Bortz!

Their romance no longer was confined to the tennis court. Persons having business with Edward soon learned to look for him first at the Bortz cottage, for the engaged couple was trying to make up for lost time. Twice they took the long trail to the Gushan monastery and its pool of sacred goldfish, and once they made an all-day excursion to Pagoda Anchorage, returning after dark in the moonlight. When she was an old lady, May remembered Edward carrying a lantern to discourage tigers that always were on the prowl at night in that region.

The wedding was announced for the twenty-second of September. During the last week of August the prospective groom went up to Shanghai. He needed a Prince Albert coat and, more importantly, he wanted May to have engagement and wedding rings that matched. So Edward purchased two rings in Shanghai, a plain gold wedding band and another of equal weight, set with a small ruby. Never in all their fifty-eight years of life together did May voice her suspicion that the ruby ring, so large and handsome, was designed for a man's finger. She accepted it and wore it proudly.

The wedding took place in the Gardner cottage because, as Edward oversimplified, "Milton Gardner and I used to traipse around together, and he wanted to give us a wedding." It was gratitude, of course, that made Gardner want to do it, thankfulness for the young doctor's care of his family, as well as affection. So it was a Gardner production. Milton Gardner, solemn in his side whiskers, pronounced them man and wife, and lively, diminutive, indefatigable Mary Gardner arranged the wedding supper. Food was served buffet-style on the veranda by the light

May Bliss on her wedding day.

of Japanese lanterns, for the day was dark. As pageboy, Ray Gardner, now ten, bore the wedding ring in its tiny, velvet-lined box. Ruth Peet, as flower girl, held a bouquet of snapdragons. She was a sad little girl. In swift, brutal succession, four brothers and sisters had died.

A dozen missionary ladies, superintended by Mary Gardner, had labored to transform the small cottage of blasted rock into an elysian bower. Tall vases of white chrysanthemums, red, blue, and purple asters, as well as tuberoses and tiger lilies stood in every corner. The walls were garlanded with ferns, and in the bay window, where the vows were exchanged, bamboo fronds were entwined to form a leafy arch.

The guest of honor was C. P. Gracey, a Methodist preacher turned U.S. consul, who came with his wife. Gracey's presence was functional to some extent, for the marriage, strictly speaking, should have been performed at the consulate. The American consul lent the affair an air of official dignity with his title, substantial waistline, and punctilious dress. He was, Edward said, a sort of worldly fellow whom everyone liked.

At seven o'clock, the three-room cottage was filled with guests. A quartet sang "O Promise Me!" Joseph Walker was a member of the quartet. He loved to sing, but today he looked tired. Mary Gardner played the wedding march on the pump organ, and the bride and groom emerged arm in arm from the bedroom, such were the exigencies of the occasion. On their golden wedding anniversary, May recalled that an "Oh!" of delight escaped from the ladies assembled as they made their entrance. She was wearing, she said, a floor-length dress of brocaded satin. In her free hand she carried a bouquet of white tuberoses. She wore no veil.

"Don't ever tell anyone that," she warned. "Most people wouldn't feel married without a veil."

Edward remembered a remark the consul made: "I never witnessed the wedding of a finer-looking couple."

Edward's eyes shone.

At Home after November the First, Shaowu, China

THEIR HONEYMOON was the trip home, up the beautiful Min, and they shared it with Walker and his daughter, although the Walkers, to be sure, traveled in a separate boat. A third boat was loaded with supplies. The trip began auspiciously, in bright sunshine. A south wind caught the dark, patched sails of the three duck boats and sped them forty miles by nightfall. The next day a short nine-hour run brought them to the foot of the rapids at Suikou.

The fine weather never deserted them. Fog shrouded the river each morning but soon disappeared. The river stood at precisely the right stage. On the fourth day, Walker saw strange bubbles coming up beside his boat, almost as though the water were boiling. Edward collected a sample of the mysterious gas in a glass tumbler and found that it burned freely with a blue flame. The flotilla pushed on.

This was the height of the season for shipping lumber down to Fuzhou. Timber was cut in the spring, when the sap was rising and bark could easily be peeled. Logs were left to dry during the summer, so they would be lighter for handling, and then the raft-makers went to work, composing rafts no more than ten feet wide, because of the rapids, and sometimes a hundred feet long. By October, when floodwaters had receded, the great fir rafts were launched. It was exciting to see the raft people come down the river and, with their long oars, pass through seemingly impossible places. On the fifth day, the honeymooners counted ninety-six rafts.

May was enjoying everything. She did not, Edward noticed, seem offended by the lack of privacy. With eight Chinese boatmen, in quarters smaller than a boxcar, they read, ate, slept, prayed, performed their natural functions, and made love. Only a thin bulkhead separated passengers and crew. Edward had expected her to be game. It was a spirit that endeared her to him. He gave it prominence in his description of her in his letters.

The accident occurred on the sixth day. Edward was reading aloud from *Jane Eyre*. May was lying on their cotton mattress, listening, and Edward was sitting next to her, propped against a bamboo basket full of groceries. He had just read Charlotte Brontë's melodramatic line "How sad to be lying now on a sick bed and be in danger of dying!" when they heard loud cries. Edward hurried on deck. A lumber raft was out of control, bearing down on their boat from a distance of fewer than fifty feet. In another moment the raft struck them a glancing blow, spun, and snapped one of its oars.

At the end of his life, Edward said, "What happened next gave me my worst fright." A deadly sliver of oar, three feet long, was sent flying through the boat's bamboo-woven covering, or *peng*, burying itself completely into the place where he had left May. No sound came from inside. He ran and looked. May was sitting up, her face drained of color. Less than a foot from her head, and at precisely the same level, the sharp oar fragment had impaled the basket of groceries against which Edward had been leaning.

It was a strange thing. The only narrow escapes on the river came on their first trips, Edward's in 1893 and hers nine years later. It was as though the river had said, "I'll teach them respect. I'll scare them, show what I can do, and then, from that day forth, having taught them not to take me for granted, bear them faithfully, and safely, as long as they like."

On the twenty-fourth of October, which was the first day of the Frost's Descent, they reached Shaowu, and May was "at home." Sixteen days had passed since they left Fuzhou. Edward wrote that it was, by two days, the fastest trip he ever made upriver, and the least irksome. "After all," he said, "I have had very congenial company."

Joseph Walker and his daughter moved into the east side of the house where the Gardners had lived, and the newlyweds took Edward's old duplex. "May likes the house much better than I had dared hope," he reported. Then he listed the new furniture they had brought: "One dining room table, six high-backed chairs, one large rocking chair, three wicker chairs, a wicker table, a parlor bookcase, a bureau with a large mirror, a desk much like Father's, except that it is not roller-top. Also a Morris chair." This furniture replaced the pieces lost during the Boxer Rebellion.

"The surgical instruments," he added, "arrived in good condition. Please thank Charles for attending to them."

The honeymoon was over. They knew it the next day when Edward found sixty patients waiting at the dispensary. How, he wondered, did word get around so fast? While resuming his medical work Edward contracted for construction of the new boys' boarding school. It would be known as Han Mei Academy, with Han standing for China and Mei for America. China and America. Partners. Edward hoped to have the foundations in before the rainy season. The Bement sisters were living in their new residence by the North Gate, but the girls' boarding school was not finished. Neither was the Walker house. All these projects had to be supervised. Her husband, May said, was doing two men's work.

She began studying the Shaowu dialect with a fine young scholar named Chao, who, after the Republic was established, turned up in North China as a mining engineer. May was proud of his accomplishment. She also started teaching English in the boys' day school. It met in the gallery of a former teahouse. The downstairs rooms were occupied by seven Chinese families; sometimes the gallery would be filled with smoke from their kitchen fires.

"She was so interested in her girls' boarding school," wrote Edward, "I did not know but she would be homesick for that work. But the boys seem to have taken the place of the girls, and I think the boys like her very much."

It was true May loved the girls at Pagoda Anchorage. Her special interest had been getting them to unbind their feet, and she appeared so distressed, and implored with such earnestness, that few could resist. The story was that they removed their bindings so *she* would be more comfortable. But now that she was at Shaowu, her pet project was teaching Chinese boys, for the first time in their lives, to sing. Their voices competing in "Three Blind Mice" and other rounds filled the old teahouse. And let one of them show the least aptitude for music and he would be wheedled into taking free lessons on the reed organ she had brought up from Fuzhou. Music was her first love.

114

Yes, I Played a Cornet

※

EDWARD SUFFERED a malarial attack before he had been back at Shaowu a week. It was not severe. "But," he complained, "I have to rest, and that has delayed our getting settled." The situation was not improved when, without warning, the ceiling in their bedroom collapsed. Fortunately, they were not underneath! Edward blamed this on the haste with which the plastering had been done following the Boxer trouble. After plasterers made a new ceiling, U Chin, the loyal coolie, whitewashed the whole apartment. Edward felt an attachment for this man he hired when he first went to China and who asked to be rehired when he returned. Although U Chin was a proud man—"He has to be handled like delicate china"—May got along with him. She got off to a good start by showing him how to run the sewing machine. She complimented him, claiming he was the only man in Shaowu who could do it.

The whitewash was hardly dry before the Reverend Willard Beard arrived from Fuzhou on an evangelical tour. Walker was no longer up to the rigors of touring, but Beard, who had been a sprinter at Oberlin College, had good, strong legs for the work. He made the newlyweds' home his headquarters for three weeks. Then, just as he left, a Lutheran missionary appeared from nowhere on his way to the next province and stayed through Christmas week. On New Year's Day, Edward wrote, "We have enjoyed having these guests, but somehow it seems cozy to have just our two selves alone together again. We haven't been married very long, you know."

The first year they were married, Edward, who had never taken a music lesson in his life, suddenly appeared with a cornet. It was a beautiful, silver-plated instrument, one of the few items of luxury he permitted himself, and he pursed his lips and blew on it and made noises and persevered until one day he played a small tune and then laid it away.

Years later, the subject of the cornet came up when Edward was asked if he ever played a musical instrument.

"Yes," he said. "I played a cornet."

"When you were a boy?" a daughter asked.

"No, in China."

"In China?" It was impossible. None of his children had ever seen a musical instrument in his hands.

"Yes." It sounded like a confession.

"Oh," said May, "he knew I was musical, so he thought it would be a nice thing to do. He never played it."

"Why, I certainly did!" he protested. "I practiced and played tunes."

"Where?"

"Around," he said, and it is to May's credit that she let the subject drop.

After their visitors left, the newlyweds were as busy as ever, but whatever free time they had was their own. Wedding presents were unpacked. The gifts from America had not started arriving, but vases, rugs, pictures, and assorted Chinese brassware given them by Fuzhou missionaries were taken out of their boxes and distributed about the house to best effect. In his letters, Edward spoke specifically of a hanging parlor lamp given them by the Beards and a double rattan chair, which was a present from the Bements. "So you see," he said, "with the other things we received we have the making of a pretty parlor." May planted a packet of columbine seeds from the States and bought four pots of yellow chrysanthemums. Taking turns reading, they finished *Jane Eyre*. And, at long last, they drew up a list of people who should receive wedding announcements. Because of difficulty finding a Chinese engraver, they had given the order to a firm in Philadelphia.

The order went out about the same time they received the formal announcement of Charles's marriage. Edward wrote home, "I was glad to receive the announcement from Charles. We rejoice in his happiness."

Now We Are Three

THE SIX YEARS between marriage and furlough in 1908 were their happiest years in China. In 1903 Edward wrote, "We have three kinds of pairs in the station now—a father and daughter, two sisters and a husband and wife. May and I agree that our kind is the best."

From the day she sailed for China, May had been doctor-prone. Dr. Lucy Bement had gone out with her on the SS *Gaelic*, and, reaching Fuzhou, she moved into the house formerly occupied by Dr. Henry Whitney. She spent her first three summers on Kuliang with Dr. Lucy Bement and Dr. Minnie Stryker, and then the fourth summer, until she married a doctor, she shared the bungalow with Dr. Emily Smith. "I seemed predestined to live with doctors," she said. "Now I am fixed happily for the rest of my life."

May was fascinated by Shaowu. Edward took her on guided tours, showing her the temple with its rows of grimacing gods; the battlements of the city; the stone bridge, built in the time of Confucius, across West Gate Creek; and, when summer came, the fine bamboo and pine-clad peaks of Nishitu.

Nothing made the little East Gate house—the parlor was only nine by fifteen feet—seem so much like home to May that first year as the arrival of the Estey organ. This was their "big" wedding present, the combined gift of Edward's family, a show of affection that overwhelmed the bride and in which she found delight all her Shaowu days. Edward was a mite more truthful than necessary in describing the condition the organ arrived in. He wrote, "May had the organ unpacked at once and set up in the parlor. The railing on the top was broken a little but not noticeably so. Some of the keys stick, as they have been made too tight by the damp weather, but it is rapidly drying out. Indeed, it is in as good condition as one could expect an organ to be after traveling so far. Its oak case makes a very fine appearance, and the tone is excellent—very rich and sweet. Nothing like it has been at Shaowu before, and I doubt if its equal is to be found at Foochow [Fuzhou]."

No one who grew up in that family would, or could, forget this noble pedal-operated instrument. During the day it stood silent, a mute thing of splendor in the parlor, its sweet reeds tuned and ready, its sheepskin bellows breathless. After supper, May would give her concerts. A favorite was the "Marseillaise." The house in the Fujian back country trembled with the anthem as May literally pulled out all stops—diapason, trumpet, forte, sub-bass, and bourdon. If anything ever went wrong with the organ, Walker would make it whole again. As a hobby, he repaired locks, cameras, typewriters, stoves, even watches. He had a workshop, and he found this tinkering, at which he was expert, a welcome change from ecclesiastical chores. Walker came to know the innermost secrets of the Estey organ, its octave couplers, reed cells, tracker pins, and mutes. And he knew that May respected him, even though in his loneliness he once had played the clumsy suitor.

For the most part, the magnificent organ was a gift from Charles, who also gave a thousand dollars for the new hospital. Charles was doing well. He soon would be cofounder of Bliss & Perry, shoe manufacturers, and later he would help rescue Towle & Company, silversmiths, when they went into bankruptcy. Charles had what they called a good business head. Edward said he had something else: heart and a total inability to pace himself. Charles was in everything—the church, the businessmen's association, the Salvation Army, the Merchants National Bank, the Moseley Foundation, the Red Cross, the health center, the Civic League, the Water Commission, and the YMCA. Edward shook his head. "If Charles goes on this way," he told May, "he can't last. The body wasn't made for it." He implored his brother to ease up. Charles's answer was to become a trustee of Anna Jaques Hospital and a director of the Oak Hill Cemetery Association.

WRITING HOME, Edward could not use Lincoln's understatement, "Nothing new here except my marrying." Besides medical emergencies—the latest had been an outbreak of bubonic plague—there were his responsibilities as station treasurer and overseer of construction. The two boarding schools were still being built, along with two mission residences. Raising a substantial edifice in Shaowu took two to four years. Edward was reminded of Kipling's lines

It is not wise for the Aryan white
To try to hustle the East,
For the white man riles, and the brown smiles,
And it weareth the white man down.

He was always trying to hustle the Chinese. And himself. He never had enough time.

The Walker house in the new compound had not gotten beyond the foundation stage. The location was ideal. The house would be only a stone's throw from Han Mei Academy, yet beyond the stench of the city in summer. A camphor tree, two centuries old, spread its gnarled arms toward the site. Violets and wild strawberries grew profusely in its shade, and birds of paradise with great tail feathers bright red, yellow, and green roosted in its branches.

Walker had suddenly become an old man. For years he had suffered from a hernia; now he was hounded by arthritis. And like every missionary at Shoawu, he was full of malaria. Still, the tall, rosy-cheeked evangelist with starched wing collar and hands that trembled administered the churches of the district and directed the work of the boys' school. Frances Bement, at North Gate, had charge of the educational program for girls. Lucy stayed busy at her dispensary. Josie Walker taught at the boys' school and conducted two Bible classes for women. She helped her father, but he could no longer tour the field.

This is how the "talent" of the mission was distributed in the spring of 1904 when *The Missionary Herald,* then the oldest monthly magazine in America, proclaimed that a new missionary "of great physical vigor, equal to this work of touring," was the crying need of the Shaowu station. "Who," it asked, "will come to this post and come at once?" The challenge was accepted by Charles Lysander Storrs, a young preacher from Hillsboro, New Hampshire. Storrs had graduated from Amherst and prepared for the ministry at Yale. He, like Edward, was descended from the first settlers of the Connecticut River Valley, and when Han Mei Academy was completed, Storrs became its first principal.

Everyone liked Charley Storrs. Edward called him "a man of kindliness and good judgment." May said, "He had a brave, gay spirit. I remember one day when he was starting off on a preaching tour. That was not an easy thing. There was no telling what he might run into—he was caught by bandits once—and he probably was to be gone for several weeks. It was a dark morning, but as he passed our window he was whistling."

Storrs came to Shaowu in 1904, and so did a daughter born to May and Edward on the twenty-first of November. By that time Lucy and Frances Bement had gone home on furlough, leaving May in charge of the girls' school and Edward again the only practitioner of Western medicine in the region. Ruth was born in a little room above the women's dispensary, since they had moved to North Gate so May would be closer to her work. The baby arrived at three o'clock in the morning on what was, for the Chinese, the Hsia Yuen Festival. She weighed eight pounds, twelve ounces. May kept to her bed until Edward's birthday, December 10, which was also the birthday of Confucius, and when Storrs arrived on the scene eight days later, it was the first day May had gone downstairs for a meal.

There was a surprise in connection with Storrs's arrival. The new missionary was accompanied by Edward's good friend Milton Gardner, and in the week that Gardner tarried at Shaowu they had a good visit. Gardner and Storrs stayed in the apartment at East Gate. In fact, Storrs stayed with the Blisses until 1917, when he married Mary Goodwin.

Before the new Bliss baby was a month old, a Shaowu silversmith fashioned a napkin ring for her, using her father's ring as a model. May and Edward had exchanged napkin rings as gifts soon after they were married. Each ring, wrought by the same Shaowu craftsman, was ornamented with four panels showing a boy riding a water buffalo, an old man fishing, a bearded philosopher traveling by donkey, and two court ladies playing at chess. None of the embossed figures stood more than half an inch high, yet they were done in exquisite detail. Each child born to May and Edward received one of these rings, similarly adorned.

Marriage had stimulated Edward's personal correspondence. He enjoyed describing the new life. "I gave May the kiss you asked me to pass on to her, and she says it was a good one." The baby stimulated his writing even more. "We received the American Express package tonight and are very much pleased with the articles of clothing which it contained. We thank you all very much for remembering baby Ruth this way. If May had time to write, she would put in the proper adjectives."

He went on, "I find that a little babe here in China means a lot of care, and since May has her boarding school with forty girls to look after, I do my part. This with other duties keeps me hopping. However, you needn't pity me, for the life seems to agree."

After describing Ruth's eating and sleeping habits, he added, "May thinks I ought to put in the adjectives. She says the things you sent are perfectly lovely."

I Regret That We Did Not Put Up Houses Better Suited for the Chinese

THE BOARD GRANTED EDWARD an appropriation of twenty-five hundred dollars for a new house. It had title to land on both sides of the new Walker residence, and Edward chose to build on the north side, nearer his hospital. West Gate Creek separated the hospital from the building site, and women came down to it in the cool of the morning to wash their clothes. The creek had a history. It was man-made. Two thousand years earlier, when the Shao invaders pushed down from the north and erected their fortress among the aborigines, the Min River was tapped at North Gate. A huge trench was dug, bringing a dependable supply of water into the stronghold a short distance before discharging it by West Gate. From that point the creek circled the city and rejoined the river downstream. The river itself acted as a natural moat on the northern perimeter.

Edward had decided to build a substantial house because he believed in buildings of permanent value. Twenty years later, almost to the day, he was writing, "I wonder what the houses that we live in now will look like a few years after we missionaries withdraw from Shaowu, as we must eventually. For this reason, I regret that we did not put up houses better suited for the Chinese." Certainly the foreign compounds with their gatekeeper lodges and high, forbidding walls did not suggest brotherhood. But after a tiger devoured one of Edward's calves he built a higher wall, and the wall around his house was no higher than the wall around the cow pasture. The Chinese who could afford high walls built them, too. It seemed a practical precaution in the context of hungry tigers, marauding soldiers, and mobs.

They built the house together. May drew up the plans; Edward executed them. For months she had been going through the magazines, picking out this type of door, that fireplace, this recessed cupboard. Theirs was the first fireplace ever seen in Shaowu. It was made of gray brick, like the house, with a keystone that matched. The bricks were given their gray color by steaming before they were entirely burned. Doorknobs, mortise locks, coat hooks, wood screws, and hinges were shipped from America; window glass, nails, putty, and lime (from crushed oyster shells) came from Fuzhou. There was no wallpaper. Instead, they used calcimine as a paint to cover the plastering.

Love and care went into every detail. Not a single brick was laid until after the rainy season. And because Edward suspected green lumber, the laying of floors was held up almost a year. As it was, they had to settle for soft Shanmu fir. May sketched her own design for posts on the front and back stairs. Since most Chinese houses were one story, with lofts reached by ladders, she had trouble showing the carpenters how a flight of stairs should look. But actually, she said, it was all a pleasure. She and Edward varnished the wainscoting in the two dining rooms themselves. There were two dining rooms and two kitchens because Edward thought it would be more economical in the long run to build a two-family house. Hallways running the length of the house upstairs and downstairs were used by both families. Verandas were added for shade. When the project was finished in 1907, Edward moved his little family into the east side of the house. Storrs, a bachelor, took the other side, which had slightly less space. Sending his mother a snapshot of the house, Edward said, "For pity's sake, don't show it to the neighbors. I doubt that they would understand." They would see a magnificent brick residence and not understand that it cost less than three thousand dollars, that it was for two families, and that it had no central heating or running water.

Still, the house was Occidental enough to instill wonder in the Chinese, and, to satisfy their curiosity, May conducted almost daily tours. No hours were prescribed. Visitors came anytime, as long as it was daylight. Chinese would be in Shaowu visiting relatives, and the relatives would say, "While you're here, let us take you to see the foreign devils' house. We have something interesting to show you." Some sightseers expressed all manner of apologies for intruding, while others entered without knocking. "*Kan jia,* look

The two-family house occupied by Edward and May Bliss in the East Gate compound.

The East Gate compound showing the Walker house (with the five arches) in front of the Bliss house.

at house," they would explain upon being discovered in the parlor, and May would drop whatever she was doing to serve as guide.

The house was full of strange devices—magnifying glasses, fly-paper, spring beds, rocking chairs, and framed engravings on the walls. And the visitors were full of questions. A woman inquired if May made her own shoes. "What," she demanded to know, "do women in America do if they don't make shoes?" Another visitor wondered at the cruel practice of placing little children in cribs. Many of the women were poor, and occasionally, in conducting tours, May felt pangs of guilt. "They have so little in their lives to entertain them—no music, no pretty pictures, no books."

Edward wrote, "They handle everything. Yesterday May caught a woman using a toothbrush as a hairbrush—for her eyebrows!" But, he added, "It seems hard to refuse any of them, especially since we wish to mingle with the people."

In This Way I Can Multiply Myself into Several

"I HAVE THREE student assistants, bright young Chinese who help me with the surgical dressings," Edward said. It was the beginning of a training program for scores of students in basic medicine. They dispensed quinine and dressed ordinary ulcers, while Edward instructed them in *materia medica* and anatomy. "Every few minutes," he said, "I'm interrupted to pull a tooth or open an abscess, or make an application for someone's eye, but I am trying to give my students a good course, thinking it is perhaps the most valuable work I can do."

The usual "course" was two years. Afterward, some apprentices went to Nanjing for additional study. Three earned degrees of Doctor of Medicine. But most of Edward's protégés, such as Shi Xiansheng, went into business for themselves, selling drugs. While the students were learning, Edward received their services—an even swap. One day, with their help, he treated 135 patients. That was a record. Later, when the students were on their own, he sold them drugs at 10 percent above cost, and the profit—unorthodox for a missionary—went into his program, which in time included projects as diverse as reforestation and dairying. It was Yankee instinct working for the good of everyone concerned.

Occasionally the druggists overcharged. Complaints came to Edward, who would investigate. One druggist suspected of avarice did business in neighboring Guangze.

"Why is this?" Edward asked him.

"I must charge more," the man said. "Last New Year's, when accounts were supposed to be settled, many people ignored their indebtedness. Now I make up the loss."

Edward advised the druggist to conduct his business on a cash basis. The Chinese took the advice, lowered his prices, and still managed to get rich. Most druggists stayed in line. They knew if they charged too much, people would buy drugs at the hospital.

When he was a very old man, and retired, a visitor had the temerity to ask whether it might not have been a mistake to turn these Chinese loose to prescribe medicines. After all, they were not doctors. It was a sensitive subject with Edward, one that had come up before. His eyes flashed. He spoke angrily. "I didn't dignify them with a diploma or call them doctors. I called them druggists. They were mighty fine fellows, and they did lots and lots of good."

"Yes," said May loyally, "that's one of the best things done at Shaowu, sending those young men out."

This is one of the rare instances—another was the banning of rickshaws—in which Edward would find himself in agreement with Communists. Not long after taking power, Mao Zedong instituted a program for teaching the basics of medicine to men and women who would spread out across China as "barefoot doctors." The capitalistic missionary called it "just good sense."

Shi Xiansheng was the first student at the hospital, but soon after him came Zeng Jinji, who originally had been Edward's patient. The youth's right leg had been swollen twice normal size. Edward suspected gangrene; there was a large putrescent cut just above the ankle. Should he amputate? He decided to try to save the leg and succeeded. He tutored Zeng, made him his chief assistant, and loved him almost as a son.

No one he took in showed such promise. The young protégé had high intelligence—"He was a natural doctor"—and he was likable. He could be serious one instant and dazzle you with a smile the next. May remembered him as handsome, with a high forehead surmounted by unruly black hair. His bones were small, almost dainty. Edward never saw such hands for bandaging. They were a magician's hands, moving deftly with gentleness. It was like Tseng, after a year of apprenticeship, to take out his inkstone and brush and, on bright red paper, compose in Chinese a letter to the doctor's mother in faraway America. "To the Venerable Mother of My Exalted Teacher," the letter began. "Had not God's grace granted that the wonderful skill of the Exalted Teacher be displayed, my life soon would have descended into the long sleep.

126

Why am I still prolonged, alive upon the earth?" Zeng begged her to remember him in her prayers, so that he might not be ungrateful to the Lord and "in each and every way be an apt pupil."

Edward sent the flowery letter to his mother, along with an English translation by Joseph Walker. "I don't deserve this," he told her, "but I believe God used me to save his life." Zeng was one of the few Chinese whom Edward referred to affectionately by his given name. Jinji meant "golden foundation." Ironically, Jinji's sons became Edward's enemies.

They Are Highly Refined,
Educated in Convents, I Suppose

EDWARD HAD BEEN DOCTORING in Shaowu for more than a year before he mentioned that missionaries other than Protestants were on the scene. On September 10, 1894, he casually reported going inside the city to attend a Catholic priest. "I found him weak from a severe malarial fever," he wrote. "He is a fine-looking Spaniard only recently arrived."

The Catholic mission at that time was staffed by three priests of the Dominican Order. They were all Spaniards. Twenty years later, they were replaced by German priests and nuns who, with the outbreak of World War I, had been transferred from India. When antiforeign sentiment flared in 1937, resulting in the death of some missionaries in China, these Catholics appeared in less danger than the Protestants. Germany had no extraterritorial rights in China, so Germans were not molested as frequently as citizens of Great Britain and the United States. However, in the wave of Communist-Kuomintang violence that came later, a German priest near Shaowu was slain.

Edward attended the Catholic missionaries throughout his term of service, and their relationship was always cordial. They did not get in each other's way, although once Edward spoke of being delayed in obtaining brick "because the Roman Catholics here are also building and they got in their order first." Another time his pseudo-Calvinist soul led him to charge a priest for professional services rendered. The dollar went into his hospital fund. The priest could not speak English, so they communicated in Chinese. It did not occur to either of them to try Latin.

For twenty-five years, Edward was the only contact between the two missions, and the Chinese received a puzzling demonstration of how two churches can operate in the same area with almost complete disassociation. It was as though each pretended the other didn't exist. A Protestant missioner revealed this separateness when he reported in a home letter, "The Catholic fathers have acquired a church bell, and we are much more aware of their presence." The ice was broken early in the 1920s when nuns, acting boldly, exchanged visits with ladies of the Protestant mission.

Until he became physician to them, Edward had never talked to a nun. In the manner of a scientist describing creatures from another planet, he reported, "They are highly refined, educated in convents, I suppose, and all appear friendly." Encouraged by their friendliness, he soon was calling on the sisters and staying for afternoon tea. Not only tea, he said, but also bread and jam! When the mother superior, whose health was poor, returned to Germany, he missed his visits to the Catholic mission. "Those who are there now," he wrote (with chagrin?), "are a healthy bunch."

The Chinese wondered at the multiplicity of denominations, and Edward predicted China would see the elimination of these divisions sooner than the West. "Here," he said, "there isn't the sharp separation between Roman Catholics, Protestants, and Mohammedans, which we are accustomed to make. The other day a patient told me that he was Roman Catholic at times and Protestant at times. It was about the same to him." Edward rejoiced when, in 1927, several Protestant denominations, led by Chinese, united to become the Church of Christ in China. It was the most comprehensive church union achieved anywhere in the world up to that time.

In August 1930, Edward invited two priests to dinner. "One," he said, "was Father Mai, a German of about thirty who lives regularly at Shaowu; the other, Father Cassidy, whose native state is Indiana. Father Cassidy's station is up on the mountains several days' journey from here to the east, where he has been the only foreigner for about three years. He is a sociable man and had been counting fondly on the treat of talking with other foreigners after his long isolation. He joked about his beard, reckoning how long it would grow before time for furlough."

There was a postscript to the letter. "I didn't tell you what I gave them to eat. We had vegetable soup from a tin, then Pot Roast of Beef with steamed rice, bean sprouts, white cornmeal muffins (because the wheat flour was soured), Pumpkin Pie from tinned pumpkin, and tea. I had to cook the meal myself because the woman who does this work has been sick, although she did come in time to serve." His pride showed in the capitalization of Pot Roast of Beef and Pumpkin Pie. This was, for him in that distant place, a very great spread.

He did not say why he invited the Catholic fathers to this feast. Perhaps it was to still a conscience plagued by the silver dollar charged a very long time ago.

Come See the Clouds!

✠

IN THE EARLY YEARS, the wife of a missionary was listed in the official records as Female Assistant. Quite by coincidence—Edward took no credit for it—the appellation was discarded by the patriarchs in Boston in the very year May Bortz became a bride. Henceforth, all women married to missionaries would be known, unimaginatively, as Wives. It was one of the changes that took place shortly after the turn of the century, along with the assassination of President McKinley and the Iroquois Theatre fire.

They had a good life together, May and Edward, although in her heart, no matter what facade she raised, a question haunted: Why had he chosen her? On their fiftieth wedding anniversary she was reminded how love pervaded the letters Edward wrote at the time of their engagement.

"I wish," she said, "I had been more worthy."

The statement was greeted with some surprise, for she was not given to humility. But she was not finished. "Perhaps," she said, with a flash of her old spunk, "I was as worthy as a good many others would have been."

That was more like her. For example, she might not be the equal of Edward, but she had no doubt her college was the equal of Yale. Did not Yale come to Doane for its teachers? If Edward should suggest, delicately, that not *all* Yale professors came from Doane College, May would counter, "Doane was founded by a Yale man. You can't deny that."

The argument went on, illogically, for years. During their first furlough Edward made the tactical error of showing his bride about the Yale campus. Outside a classroom—the door was ajar— May caught a glimpse of Professor Fred Fairchild lecturing on economics. Fairchild had taught at Doane. He was, for her, living proof that her school was every bit as good as Edward's. It was something—about the only thing—on which she would stand up to Edward every time. Edward never did say Yale was superior. It was just that May seemed to be saying *Doane* was superior; this he could not buy.

Theirs was a bittersweet relationship. One summer, in retirement, they flew from Boston to Dayton to visit a daughter. After Edward died in 1960, May made the flight alone. Attendants on the plane were wonderful, she said, but the clouds, the great dazzling masses of cumulus, made her sad. Edward had so enjoyed the grandeur of them when they made the trip together. She rarely wept, but when the daughter inquired about the trip, and whether she had seen any scenery, tears filled her eyes. She spoke of the clouds. She said, "It came back to me. The summer we met he asked me to come with him and look at the clouds. It was on Kuliang. I was in back of my cottage, working in the garden. I don't remember what I was doing, but it seemed important. He came from the top of the mountain and called to me, 'Come see the clouds!' He was standing on the path above me. He looked happy. 'The clouds are beautiful!' he shouted. 'Don't you want to see them?' I told him that I had better finish whatever I was doing. I remember he seemed disappointed."

The old woman crinkled up her face, fighting the tears. "I wish I had gone with him," she said. "You know what I was doing wasn't as important as that."

It was all wrong because she loved beauty. At Shaowu she filled the compound with flowers—once she grew twenty-seven varieties of roses. A letter written one November speaks of the house being decked with "armfuls" of white chrysanthemums. And thanks to her, surrounding the family as it grew, were Titian's *Assumption of the Virgin,* Rosa Bonheur's *Horse Fair,* Millet's *Angelus,* Reni's *Aurora,* Watt's *Sir Galahad and His Horse,* and other reproductions from the great masters, all tastefully framed. At Nishitu the summer cottage was similarly decorated, but those pictures were unframed. Snipped from old *National Geographic* magazines and fastened to the wall with straight pins, they covered the world from temples in Bangkok to St. Basil's Cathedral in Moscow. The children received geography lessons unaware.

Thirty years after she left China, when May was ancient, she was asked what she remembered most about that faraway land. She pondered on the question a surprisingly long time.

"I believe," she said, "I think most of our home."

Her descendants were shocked. She was *supposed* to have said that she remembered the Chinese, at least something relating to them. But it was the home—her home, her husband, her children—her thoughts went back to, and the fact that the home was in China only made it more precious and now more remote.

I Am Growing Stronger
All the Time for My Work

❉

ALTHOUGH MAY BECAME eligible for furlough in 1904, she stayed with Edward. It meant not seeing her parents for another four years. But it also meant a new home, and settling in it, and having another baby. Beth was born as the cannon sounded curfew on February 2, 1908. Edward's letter proclaiming the event has been lost, but we have his mother's response. "We received your welcome letter announcing the arrival of another dear little granddaughter. What does Ruth say to her little sister? What nice companions they will be for each other!"

Now, in 1908, Edward was due for furlough. After a visit with May's people in Nebraska, they would come East. "May," he reported, "finds it hard to leave this home, having worked so hard to make it what it is." The last night before taking the riverboat, after her babies were asleep, she walked alone from room to room in the twilight, her heart aching. If only she could *show* her parents what her new life was like; if only she could be two places at once.

They spent that whole summer on the Bortz farm. Beth, a dimpled baby, squiggled in her buggy and got brown in the sun. Ruth, who was three and a half, discovered a new world. Grandfather Bortz showed her apple trees, fields of sweet corn, and a hen that had adopted five orphaned ducks. The cows were white and black, not yellow, as they were in China. And such horses! They were twice the size of any she had seen at Shaowu. May helped with the housework. That, in addition to making missionary talks and caring for two lively children, left little time for anything else. Edward did take her to hear William Jennings Bryan, and that oration, in Omaha, was perhaps the high-water mark of May's "political life." In her ninety-third year, her dark eyes smoldered in anger as she read a columnist's description of her silver-tongued idol as a "tedious windbag." The blasphemy of it! "What does that man know about it?" she spluttered. "I'll wager Bryan died a good twenty years before *he* was born!"

Simon Bortz was not well. He had a crippling hernia, and Edward did the heavy chores. This was his first real farm experience. He had visited farms—Newburyport was surrounded by farms—but this was the first time he had done farm work. In assuring his sister Clara he was in good health, he boasted, "Yesterday forenoon I did a washing and in the afternoon went into the hayfield and pitched three loads of hay. After that, I walked a half-mile to the pasture and pumped water for thirty-two head of thirsty cattle, and, after they had drunk enough, filled the trough up again for them to drink next morning. I do this twice a day, so you see I don't need Indian clubs for exercise. I am growing stronger all the time for my work."

In September they came on to Massachusetts. The house on Allen Street could not accommodate another family, so they stayed at the missionary home in Auburndale, in the Boston suburbs. Edward and May made frequent trips to Newburyport, and May lost her heart to Edward's mother. It was different with the sisters; she never got over being overawed by them. Part of it was their Boston accent and her knowledge that they had graduated from the best eastern schools. She was a farm girl. The fact should not have bothered her, but it did.

That winter, Edward went to Bangor, Maine, as a scout for the American Board. The board wanted new blood in Shaowu. What he should look for, it said, was a man who could act in an administrative capacity, organize the twenty-three parishes of the Shaowu district, and teach in the boys' school. It went without saying that the candidate also must have high scholarship, an agreeable personality, and robust health. Edward was given no leads except to look over the senior class at Bangor Theological Seminary.

In Bangor, Edward stayed in the house of a Congregationalist minister who said if he were choosing anyone, unquestionably it would be Ned Kellogg. He didn't think Kellogg planned to be a missionary; he had never joined the Student Volunteers. But Kellogg was well trained. He already had served two small churches, built up their congregations, and pulled them out of debt. He was able, and he was well liked. Edward called on the prospect that same afternoon.

"How soon would I have to leave?" Kellogg asked. For Edward the question was encouraging. The young minister sounded as though he could be persuaded.

"It was hoped someone would go out with me in October."

"If they want me," Kellogg said, "I'll go."

That night Kellogg wrote a letter to his banker father in Orange, Massachusetts, reporting what had happened. "There have been bolts before out of a clear sky," the letter began, "but I suppose none surpassing the one I shall now propound, i.e. in my own life. I am today sending to the American Board an application for appointment as missionary to China." Farther on in the letter he explained, "I couldn't get away from it. When he asked to see me, I knew what was coming. And I knew there was no other answer I could make."

Kellogg had been dating the daughter of a professor at the theological seminary. Her name was Alice Ropes, and they married at once so they could go to China together. She was a fair, blue-eyed girl. Kellogg's own features were deceptively dour. One time, when he sent home a snapshot of himself, his father complained that he had "a stern look." Kellogg answered, "I really do not mean to have such a forbidding countenance. It's a sad case for anybody when cheerfulness leaves them and they forget how to laugh."

Once they reached Shaowu, the Kelloggs settled in the old house on East Gate Street. May and Edward, and their two girls, returned to find everything in their new home just as they had left it. May had been seasick all the way across the Pacific. "She seems happy," wrote Edward, "to be at the journey's end and back in our nest. Shaowu has really come to be a spot close to our hearts, and it will be a real sorrow when at last we have to leave it forever."

The Protestant missionaries assigned to Shaowu now totaled ten. Edward returned from furlough to find a new "single lady" teaching at the girls' boarding school. Her name was Grace Funk, a tall, stately woman in her late twenties. Her brown eyes seemed full of the delight of living, and when she went home on furlough, Edward gave her the address of his mother in Newburyport. But it was not his mother he was thinking of. "Miss Funk," he wrote, "has an unusually fine mind, is warm-hearted, dresses well, and is popular. I wish George had a better chance to become acquainted with women like her."

George, it so happened, needed no help. He married the pretty sister of the girl who married Charles.

IN PEKING, the dowager empress was dead. As her last act, she proclaimed her grandnephew as successor. The boy's name was Pu Yi. Because his father, the regent, underestimated the desire for self-government, the Great Pure Dynasty of the Manchus also died.

The year of the Revolution was 1911.

There Are a Good Many Things Indicative of a Change

ON TUESDAY, October 31, 1911, Ned Kellogg and Charles Storrs set out in fine autumn weather on a church tour that would take them from Shaowu for fifteen days. The most remote village they would visit was Li Xin, which meant Mile of Hearts. Li Xin was a full hundred miles from Shaowu to the southwest, and no American had ever been there before except Storrs. It was about the only place Walker in his rambles through the back country of Fujian had missed. Kellogg was glad to have Storrs along, not merely because of his wider experience but also because he liked the man. "A royal fellow" is how he described Storrs in one of his letters. When Storrs ultimately found a wife for himself it was Kellogg who married them, the first union of foreign devils Shaowu had ever seen.

The purpose of the tour, says Kellogg in one of his letters, was to hold what he calls Bible institutes. He speaks of stopping at Yangkou, "where is located one of our most flourishing churches. Here for three days we discussed with its members the letter of Paul to the Ephesians and also some of the great passages in the Gospel of Luke." Although they traveled mostly by riverboat, they walked a lot, "all the way," says Kellogg, "from an easy walk of eight miles to an all-day tramp of twenty-eight miles."

The two theologues set out despite signs of political upheaval. Agitation against the Manchus was widespread, but missionaries took comfort in rebel warnings that anyone caught meddling with foreigners, or their possessions, would be beheaded. Two days after Kellogg and Storrs began their tour, the main force of imperial troops stationed at Shaowu was dispatched downriver to bolster the Fuzhou garrison. Edward received this news with mixed feelings. "Whatever protection was afforded by these soldiers," he remarked, "has been lost. On the other hand, their leaving could be a good thing. If they had stayed and mutinied, as was quite likely, considerable blood might have been shed." Now that Shaowu was undefended, a battle for the city seemed unlikely. Perhaps they would be allowed to sit this one out.

Certainly it was quiet enough in Shaowu that last day of October. Most members of the mission, like Edward and May, had only recently returned from a summer on Kuliang Mountain. The trip had taken seventeen days. The children were out of sorts due to cramped quarters on the riverboat, and Edward caught a severe cold. "We were glad," he wrote, "that the trip wasn't a day longer." As for the uprising, he asked his mother not to worry. He told her—how often through the years he was to say this sort of thing—that there was no cause to be concerned for their safety. "Everything here," he said, "is very quiet. Besides, this is simply a revolt against the Emperor and his government. None of the action is directed against us." He ended by saying that as far as Fukien (Fujian) Province was concerned, the decisive factor was Fuzhou.

The exodus from Fuzhou began that very day, October 31, and lasted until the gates of the city closed on the evening of November 8. Everyone who stayed was to be witness, willing or not, to one of the bloodiest battles in the port's history. Women and children of the American Board mission had been hustled to the relative safety of the foreign settlement outside the city wall and close to the U.S. consulate. The men stayed in the mission compound and were joined by six bluejackets from the USS *Bainbridge*. Some revolutionary soldiers also showed up in the compound, claiming they were sent to guard the premises. Everyone was closer to the scene of battle than they supposed. Rebel artillery was hauled up Temple Hill, near the compound, during the night of November 8, and at twenty minutes past four on the morning of November 9 began shelling the Manchu quarter of the city. Imperial troops tried to storm the hill. They were repulsed, and the battle, waged a scant three hundred yards from the mission property, ended in victory for the rebel forces in late afternoon.

In this affair, the mission's new operating pavilion received a baptism in blood. The missionaries organized rescue teams, and soon a double stream of wounded was flowing into the hospital from the rebel and Manchu lines. Doctors attached to the Anglican, Methodist, and Congregationalist missions worked at four operating tables all that day and the next night.

Thanks to a new telegraph line running upriver from Fuzhou to Nanping, word of the fall of Fuzhou soon reached Shaowu, which feared that, in the absence of any real government, the lawless element might go on a rampage. Brigands already had seized control twenty-five miles below Shaowu, bringing traffic on the river to a standstill. Boatmen loitered in East Gate Street, many of them big, tough Jiangxi men who, deprived of their livelihood, were ready to join any mob that held out the prospect of plunder. And there were renegades with their own special scores to settle with the mission. Several servants had been discharged because of petty thievery or incompetence. Chu Chien, who had entertained harlots on the Kellogg premises while they were away, was one of these. And just that summer a local man who had worked for Storrs was caught breaking into mission property. The missionaries' peace of mind was not enhanced when on Sunday, November 12, Lucy Bement received warning from an informant in the post office that her residence was to be set on fire.

Some kind of outbreak appeared imminent, but it was impossible to sort out the rumors and make sense. Edward, in walking to the hospital, noted a peculiar air of excitement. An inordinate number of people—not just the idle boatmen—seemed to be going nowhere, simply waiting for something. Shops were being shuttered as though before a storm. Certain persons were reported plotting together in one of the towers on the city wall, over by the East Gate, and the chief magistrate, hearing this, promptly assigned the few soldiers left in Shaowu to his own personal protection. As tension increased, local societies erected barricades in the streets, and all doors opening onto side streets were locked at night to help keep agitators from assembling secretly after dark.

"The rabble had no firearms," wrote Walker afterward, in language of the French Revolution. "But the soldiers were well armed with breech-loading rifles." He made no mention of the .22 Winchester Edward suddenly produced out of nowhere and began making a great display of in his backyard. He would emerge from the kitchen door, walk with great solemnity over to the asparagus patch, stop, take careful aim at any one of a dozen sunflowers, fire one, two, three through the center of the blossom, and repair whence he came, never looking to right or left or taking the least note of the small crowd of Chinese that watched. When Walker asked the meaning of the performance, Edward said it was simply a matter of being prepared.

"Must you practice? They say you never miss."

"Oh," said Edward, "that's the whole point. I have to *show* them I don't miss."

The evangelist asked Edward if he could actually bring himself to shoot anyone. "No," he said slowly, "I don't think so, unless . . ." He must have been thinking what he would do if anyone tried to harm his family. What he said was, "Perhaps if they know I have a gun, I won't have to make that decision. That's why I put on this fool act."

Black Monday

WHEN WORD CAME that Fuzhou had fallen, the Shaowu prefect said nothing remained but for him to kill himself. A delegation of leading citizens called at his official residence, begging him to reconsider. If he did away with himself, they said, disorder surely would ensue. They asked him, for the sake of the people, to declare his allegiance to the revolution. The prefect did not reply immediately, but there were others, the conspirators in the tower, who decided that if he did not "pluck the flower of life," they would pluck it for him. They were reported to have reached this grim decision on Sunday, November 12.

The next day, November 13, has gone down in the annals of the Shaowu mission, somewhat melodramatically, as Black Monday. It began with Edward calling on Walker to discuss strategy. The people of Shaowu, as a whole, had always been friendly. Nevertheless, with Storrs and Kellogg away, and with an almost complete breakdown in law enforcement, the safety of the women and children had become their responsibility. They agreed that if the Chinese populace was alarmed enough to set up street barricades, it behooved them to draw up some kind of defense. An inventory showed that they had within the compound eleven kerosene lanterns, which they placed at intervals along the top of the wall to discourage trespassers. They established two watches, lasting from six in the evening to midnight and from midnight to six in the morning, with Edward taking the first tour. Helping them in this business would be three Chinese servants. Both Edward and Walker would be armed, and when Storrs and Kellogg returned— they were due back on November 15—they would have a defense force of seven men with a combined armament of one rifle and four revolvers. Missionaries traveling in remote country often carried firearms as protection against wild animals. Twelve tigers were killed in one season on the outskirts of Fuzhou.

Alice Kellogg and her baby were transferred from the house outside the compound; until the danger was past, they would stay in the Walker house. The women at North Gate were relatively safe. Not only were they surrounded by a higher wall, but also they were close by the Yamen, the magistrate's headquarters, and the small body of imperial troops. Even when the touring missionaries returned, none of the men residing at East Gate was spared for the protection of single ladies on the other side of the city. Half a century later, Grace Funk was asked if this had struck her as ungallant. She was astonished at the suggestion. "Why, no," she said, "the married men had their families to look out for. They naturally came first." Her eyes twinkled. "And as for a single man coming and spending the night with us, *that* just wouldn't do!"

As Walker and Edward discussed security measures, a teacher from the boys' middle school came to them with a report that the prefect, together with his principal subordinates, were about to be assassinated. They would be wiped out by the tower clique that afternoon while attending a feast. And just after hearing this, they received notice from the U.S. consul that all Americans in the interior of Fujian Province were to proceed at once to Fuzhou, where they would be safe. This was a new complication. How were they to reach the coast when upper reaches of the river were controlled by brigands? Would they not face greater danger on the river? Besides, here at Shaowu they had many Chinese friends. It was decided that, in any case, they would make no move until the evangelists returned from their tour.

That night, Mrs. Kellogg and her baby stayed at the Walkers'. Josie welcomed their company. Edward, feeling slightly ridiculous, kept the first watch as scheduled; when Walker came to relieve him at midnight there was nothing of a suspicious nature to report. Nor had anyone heard of an assassination. U Chin, who had gone into the city, learned only that the feast had been canceled. No member of the mission undressed that night, not even their shoes. Ruth and Beth lay on top of their beds, tingling with excitement. May sat beside them singing the Peter Pan song they loved and her own favorite hymns. But it was no use. They refused to shut their eyes until Papa came in, which meant that Beth did not get to sleep until five hours past her usual bedtime. But grown-up little Ruth lay with her eyes wide open all night. The girl was terrified, and fascinated, by the strange sounds in the yard and the unknown. When her mother explained that Walker was down there, seeing that no harm came to her, she said, "I felt safer when it was Papa."

Not until the night began graying into dawn did Ruth fall asleep. Looking at her, May had to smile. It was a wistful smile. For months Ruth had tacked onto her now-I-lay-me a prayer for a baby brother. May wanted to confide the news of the new life that was in her. But she dared not. Edward had enough to worry about; her secret would keep. Outside the window she could hear Walker saying something in Chinese, probably to U Chin. Walker's voice sounded perfectly calm.

It was like that for two nights. Nothing changed in the city as regards either the prefect or the barricades, and nothing changed in the routine in the East Gate compound. Everyone continued to sleep in their clothes. Mrs. Kellogg spent her nights at the Walkers', and the two men patrolled the premises.

When Storrs and Kellogg returned on the fifteenth, after a day's journey of twenty-seven miles on foot, the night was broken into three watches instead of two—Walker was relieved because of his age—and a plan was devised for spiriting away the women and children in case of attack. In such an eventuality, Kellogg was to lead them out the seldom-used back gate of the compound into a bamboo thicket, where they could hide. They debated at length the request of the U.S. consul that they withdraw to Fuzhou. Kellogg and Storrs had found everything quiet during their fifteen-day tour, which had taken them 275 miles. There was no sign, they said, of antiforeign feeling in any of the nine towns they visited. Their religious and educational programs for the year were just getting started. They hated to abandon them.

Edward felt the same about his medical work, and Walker was of the belief, based on thirty years' experience, that Shaowu was much preferable to the river. They were of one mind but did not want to flout the authority of the State Department, so they asked the consul that they either be allowed to stay in Shaowu at their discretion or be provided a suitable military escort to take them out. They congratulated themselves on devising this message. Not only was it unlikely that an escort would be sent, but also, with this reply, they had bought time. They felt sure that in a few days the situation at Shaowu would be demonstrably safe.

As it turned out, the only member of the mission who came near being killed was Edward—at the hands of Storrs. On guard duty, Edward heard a suspicious sound outside the wall. When he climbed a ladder to investigate, Storrs let go at him with his eight-shooter. Fortunately the same shadows that caused Edward to be mistaken for a marauder made him a difficult target. It was farcical yet serious. Had it not been for the still-fresh memory of the Boxer Rebellion—fifteen missionaries of the American Board had been slain at Paotingfu—the Shaowu missioners probably would not have gone to such extremes. They felt foolish promenading about with their revolvers, and they imagined that the Chinese must be amused. On the other hand, they remembered Paotingfu.

On Thursday, November 16, the nightmare ended. The prefect issued a proclamation declaring that Shaowu henceforth was aligned with the Revolution; all male citizens were to cut off their queues, symbol of inferiority to the Manchus, and go peacefully about their business. Edward never learned what went on behind the scenes, except that on Tuesday one of the humbler city officials had gone to the tower to negotiate. A deal was worked out, and two days later came the proclamation.

The barricades were removed from the streets. Shops reopened. A detachment of ten revolutionary soldiers appeared at the East Gate compound. The military escort, which the missionaries felt confident wouldn't be sent, had arrived to deliver them safely to Fuzhou!

Marco Polo Climbed Here

A DIZZINESS FILLED his head despite the sun helmet, and Edward sat on the roof to rest. He had not reckoned with the humidity, nor had he foreseen how the rough edges of the tiles would cut his hands, or how the mere ascending and descending of a ladder can drain the energy from legs unused to such labor.

It had been a frustrating season. He belonged at Shaowu, but they had been at Fuzhou now for seven months. He had helped at the mission hospital—there were still wounded left over from the battle for Fuzhou—but, compared to the workload at Shaowu, it was a vacation. Because of the consul's order summoning all foreigners to the coastal city, the mission was, for the first time in history, overstaffed.

Edward had decided in his spare time to relay the tiles of their three-room bungalow on Kuliang Mountain. Although good-sized rocks had been set on the tiles to keep them intact in a typhoon, many of the tiles had slipped, causing a good deal of leakage. He could have hired Chinese to do the work, as May suggested, but it was something he wanted to accomplish himself.

He had brought her to Kuliang, with its pleasant elevation of two thousand feet, so she could have her new baby away from the malaria-ridden heat of the city. It was a three-hour trip by sedan chair on the same rising path Marco Polo was said to have traveled in the late thirteenth century. May, already in her ninth month, was carried in a sedan chair by three bearers. The two girls rode in a second chair, but their father walked. Three other coolies carried supplies. Tiger lilies grew in profusion beside the path. Once they passed a wayside inn from which came the familiar smell of frying peppers. No one ate along the way, but four times the bearers stopped to rest. Each time the doctor would poke his head inside May's chair and ask how she was feeling. "Fine," she would say, and then everyone in the family would drink tea from a thermos. The tea was warm, but it was refreshing.

Sitting now on the roof of the cottage, with his knees pulled up so they almost touched his goateed chin, Edward looked down at the teeming, black-tiled city in the valley and then, by long habit, eastward to where the yellow-silted river between picturesque mountain peaks emptied into the sea. It was a scene he loved and that, at the same time, made him sad. Here was China—an exciting fragment of it, anyway—and here again was that strange beauty, rugged yet delicate, with which Chinese artists down through the dynasties imbued their landscapes, creating fairyland scenes of scudding sampans, storybook bridges, and mist-clad mountains. He looked beyond Pagoda Anchorage and watched a single-stacked coastal steamer slip past Matsu island, trailing a long, low-hanging veil of smoke. Edward wondered if it was a troopship. For weeks after arriving in Fuzhou they had seen soldiers rallying for defense of the new provisional government. Two of his medical students had joined the thousands who came from all parts of the province to enlist. Three hundred boys quit the Shaowu middle school, and the school, which the missionaries hoped would continue without the presence of foreigners, closed only a few days before graduation.

It was a fever. Young girls were joining the "Dare to Die" societies and marching off with the men. Edward scarcely recognized his two students, who overnight became medical officers in the new Revolutionary Army. The day before leaving for Shanghai they looked him up in Fuzhou to say good-bye. May served them tea. "It makes one very sad," she wrote, "to think what their future may be. They seemed so young." Yet she could add, "Here in China, everything points toward a great change for better things." The Manchus had abdicated. China had possessed two presidents: Sun Yat-sen, the idealist, quickly succeeded by Yuan Shikai, the practical politician. There had been assassinations and mutinies, and national capitals in Shanghai, Nanjing, and Beijing. "It seems impossible," wrote Edward, "that a nation can be born in a day."

The missionary, resting from his labor, pondered on the fact that far off, over the horizon and touched by the same ocean, lay America. He did not miss America because of its body comforts, or its finely balanced freedoms, but because it was home. It was the land where he had spun his first top, belly-slammed his first sled, and donned his first pair of long pants. The first Christmas he could remember, a most wonderful cozy Christmas, had been there in that New England town within sight of the sea, and it was where he had seen his first circus and gone to school. It was where his parents had raised him sternly and with affection. But here in China he had found the Nebraska girl who was now his wife, and here, as he tried to demonstrate Christianity in combating disease, he was raising a family. Here, surprisingly, he would be content to die. Edward worked another hour with the tiles and then joined May and the girls for supper. They noticed, just before sundown, that the whole sky was illumined by a greenish-yellow light.

The next morning everyone on Kuliang knew of the approaching *tai fung*. Kellogg came over from next door and offered his help. "After all," he said, "I've got a roof and you haven't." The offer was accepted. Almost half the tiles were still on the ground and had to be brought up and set in place. The sky was overcast, but it got inhumanly hot. The thermometer on the north side of the cottage, in the shade, rose to ninety-six degrees, and the stagnant air became so humid that the expectant mother, reading on the veranda, found the pages of her magazine stuck together. On the roof, the two men did little talking. They were dead serious. The black dust from tiles made paste with their perspiration, so that their faces were the faces of coal diggers. Overhead, the sky was an inverted bowl of porcelain, shimmering hot.

Toward evening, as the first breeze rustled in the bamboo, May called to him. Edward shouted he was coming and scrambled down the ladder to where she was sitting, the magazine on the floor and her face drained of color. He had just gotten her into bed when Ruth and Beth came running in.

"Did the baby come?" cried Ruth, looking quickly about the room.

"The baby?" asked Beth, who was four. In her hands she held some pretty bugs she wanted to show her parents.

"No," Edward said, "but soon. Now I want you to do something for me. Stay with your mother. If she wants anything, let me know. I must go back on the roof."

The Bliss children, Ruth, Edward, and Beth.

May held out her hand to them. They rushed to her side. By the time Beth remembered to show her bugs, they were all dead. She had forgotten and squeezed too hard.

After putting water on the stove, Edward rejoined Kellogg on the roof. The wind was picking up. It sang a shrill tune among the bamboo, and it kept singing in a higher pitch. It sang through the bamboo and over the top of the typhoon wall and across the roof. It shoved the two stooping figures with a steady pressure, then sang off in the distance like a phantom note hurrying to elude the rain.

The baby and the typhoon arrived together. Kellogg had gone back to his cottage, while Edward worked on to the last. Just as he got off the ladder, the wind caught it and tossed it end over end down the mountain. In the light of two kerosene lamps, while the girls waited in the other room, he delivered his son. The son bawled, and the wife slept after her ordeal. The typhoon stripped the roof of every last tile. Yet it didn't matter. All else had gone well.

She was awake now. Her face was wan, but her eyes were alert, following him as he took an oilcloth and rigged it over her bed to ward off the rain. The oilcloth had a pattern of dikes and windmills, which struck Edward as ironic.

I Am Preoccupied with Cows

WHEN HE DIED, newspapers spoke of Edward as "a pioneer in the immunization of cattle against rinderpest." Nine words summed up twenty years of personal struggle against the most costly animal disease in Africa and Asia. To those who knew Edward, the phrase was antiseptic. It told nothing of the manure on his shoes, or the blood on his rumpled suit, or the peculiar stench of the disease, or his defeats. Nothing about leading a bull sixty miles over mountain passes by a ring in its nose, or being gored, or feeding baby goats from bottles.

Rinderpest is an acute, highly infectious disease that inflicts on ruminants what virulent malaria inflicts on humans. Rinderpest has been called many other names. Among the civil terms are cattle plague, steppe murrain, and bovine typhus. The French call it *peste bovine*. An ultravisible virus, rinderpest attacks ruminants in almost every organ, permeating the tissue and literally rotting the animal apart in ten to fourteen days. The first symptom is a slight increase in temperature, followed in quick succession by the symptoms that accompany diphtheria, influenza, typhoid fever, cholera, pneumonia, and dysentery. It is as though the devil distilled "all the ills that men endure" and bestowed the supreme contagion on dumb beasts.

His private war on rinderpest began with the need for milk. As a doctor and as a human being, Edward was haunted by the terrible mortality of babies, and the cause in most instances was malnutrition. The mothers, undernourished and anemic, often were unable to nurse. They could not order from a dairy. No dairy existed. There were no baby foods, no formulas. So they chewed vegetables in their mouths and transferred the partially digested food to the mouths of their infants. They began this primitive, unhygienic type of feeding as early as the first month, and half the babies, racked by digestive disorders, died within the first year. In that time and place, if a woman gave birth to ten children, she could hope for only two or three to reach maturity. Sometimes none survived.

The Chinese did not raise milk cattle. Their small yellow cows were for plowing. Moreover, to drink a liquid produced by animals was regarded by many as disgusting. A patient for whom Edward had prescribed cow's milk begged to be allowed, instead, to take milk from his married daughter. "She has been favored," he said, "and has milk to spare." As Chinese learned the value of cow's milk, a few dairies were started. But the price of milk was prohibitive. One quart cost the equivalent of a worker's daily wage. It was as though a quart of milk in the United States cost a hundred dollars. Since the cows were bred as plow animals, they gave pitiably little milk, and then only if kept with their calves. After a hungry calf started the milk to flow, a proficient milker was lucky to get a quart a day; often he got less than a pint. It distressed Edward to see mothers taken from their calves in the midst of nursing to be milked. The calves were half starved. And if they died, their mothers dried up. Another negative was that the milk had to be boiled, making it less digestible for small babies. Not to boil the milk was unthinkable, as Chinese dairies in the beginning were highly unsanitary. Cows, covered with flies, stood hock-deep in manure, and had teats so ridiculously small that milking consisted of stripping, which meant milk spilled over the milker's hands on its way to the pail.

In desperation Edward imported sweetened condensed milk from America. He bought the sweetened variety because refrigeration was nonexistent in Shaowu, and in hot weather a can of unsweetened milk spoiled as quickly as it was opened. It was, he knew, an improvisation. Although he sold the condensed milk at below cost, thanks to contributions from home, it was still beyond the reach of the vast majority of Chinese. And the high sugar content made it less than ideal for infants.

His next step was to buy fresh milk from a wealthy Chinese named Liang. Liang rented out cows for fieldwork, but he had them brought into the city at calving time, when a fresh cow might provide milk for several months. But this supply was dribbling compared to demand, and its availability was uncertain. In winter, milk produced by the entire herd dwindled to a trickle, and during an epidemic of rinderpest, which swept China on the average of once every two years, the milk gave out entirely.

151

When the plague struck Shaowu in February 1913, the mortality rate among Liang's herd was better than 80 percent. Five cows had been sent up to Nishitu so that milk would be available for the missionaries staying there that summer, but these animals, too, were stricken. Then Edward made a fateful decision. "I have made up my mind," he wrote, "to buy some first-class cows and see what good care will do. It doesn't seem as though there was any good reason for the calves dying so, and I have small doubt that the plague is caused by filthy conditions in the stables. I hate to take the time for it, but it is important that not only our babies but Chinese babies, too, have milk."

Edward had not yet read any of the literature on rinderpest. He did not know what he was getting into. If he had known, he might have reconsidered, though it is doubtful that the final decision would have been different. So now, underestimating his adversary, he stepped into the arena. Almost casually he took on what was then the worst, most invidious cattle scourge on the face of the earth.

It was not his first experiment with livestock. In a small way, three years before, he had raised sheep. This had been at Nishitu where the chief industry of the mountain folk, the manufacture of paper from bamboo, was threatened by competition from other parts of China and from Japan. It seemed to Edward that the mountaineers might improve their economy with sheep. All mutton purchased in the vicinity came from Jiangxi, and he didn't see why sheep couldn't be raised on the mountainsides and sold in local markets. To this end he bought a ram and a ewe. But nothing happened. The ram seemed more fond of the doctor than the ewe, following him everywhere he went. Once it followed him to church. Kellogg chronicled the event in a poem:

> The doctor had a butting ram
> Its fleece was white as snow,
> And everywhere the doctor went
> The ram was sure to go,
> It followed him to church one day,
> Though rams but seldom do,
> And when they tried to put him out,
> In came the bleating ewe!

No baby lamb appeared until the spring of 1911, and then only one. Edward watched the little fellow frolicking and took heart. But that same day a dog mauled the lamb to death. He planned to take up the project again in 1912, but was thwarted by the Revolution. He gave the ram and its ewe to the Chinese girl who had looked after them when he was in Shaowu.

What was needed, Edward decided, was a strain of Western cattle that would give at least ten times more milk than the Chinese breed. It would be a service, he believed, more valuable than pouring medicine down people's throats. After seeing an advertisement for blooded Ayrshire stock at a place in North China called Tamingfu, he wrote for particulars. These reached him at Nishitu on September 11, 1913. That night he and Kellogg, who had been raised on a farm, debated what action to take. The cost was sobering. The bull Edward wanted was priced at $175, and that was just the beginning. They also needed a foreign cow, for even if Willomoor Farmer, the young bull they had their eye on, was put to service at once, it still would be five years before cows of three-fourths and seven-eighths pure stock could be obtained. But if they began with a foreign bull and a foreign cow, not only would they be in milk right away, but also they could start immediately to raise blooded stock.

Edward made a proposition. If Kellogg would put up the money for a cow—$285—Edward would pay for the bull, take care of the feeding, and see to the building of barns. Maybe his colleague's banker father could be enticed into footing the bill for a fine heifer. Kellogg said he would write home at once but that, whatever his father's reaction, he was assuming responsibility for the purchase. "Now," he said, "seems the accepted time."

As they talked, exploring the possibilities, they could almost see their dream come true, cows with big, fat, well-veined bags giving forth such a flow of rich Ayrshire milk that it could be sold to Chinese parents for a pittance. Who knew? As the calves came new herds might be established and dairies owned by Chinese scattered over the whole province. And Kellogg, father of two small girls, and Edward, who had his own new baby, could be sure they would have fresh milk on hand.

It became apparent after further study that the expedition into North China should be led by Kellogg and that Edward should remain behind. Since the earliest practical time for setting out was late October, the animals' arrival at Shaowu would coincide with the start of winter rains. This meant that a suitable barn would have to be ready, and Edward, who had done so much contracting, seemed right for the job. Also he had more dealings with local farmers than Kellogg and so was better fitted to make the arrangements for feed. He did not know how to milk—Kellogg did—and the cow would have to be milked throughout the long journey. But the prime consideration was that Edward was physician to the mission. It would be patently unwise to leave the mission without a doctor for as long as six weeks.

Kellogg got off according to schedule on October 22, in company with a Chinese assistant and two coolies who would carry their loads. Edward bade them good-bye with envious heart, then plunged into the task of preparing for their return. He first negotiated with carpenters for construction of a dairy barn, something that became at once a subject for great speculation among the Chinese. A building specially designed for cattle! The Chinese turned their cows loose in pens, which were cleaned out once or twice a year. This low, one-story structure for cows possessed not only a tile roof but also had a concrete floor and stanchions to keep the animals turned in one direction and feed boxes and even a gutter for the manure. It was an incredible thing this foreign devil was doing, and so they came from throughout the *xian* to behold the barn, since seeing was believing.

Edward had a wall built about the property, for neither tigers nor contagion were forgotten. An adjacent field was walled in for pasture. Weeds were rooted out and ruins of old foundations removed to encourage the growth of good grass. Not content with a supply of straw from the early rice crop, or soybean vines, the doctor planted wheat and sent a rush order to Shanghai for five hundred pounds of rock salt and bran. He began visiting the cattle fairs. Here native cows could be purchased for fifteen dollars, and he bought sixteen of the best-looking for mating, along with their calves. These, too, required an enclosure. Up went other walls. And all during this time, with the help of one medical student, he was treating an average of sixty patients a day.

"I am no longer troubled with insomnia," he wrote his mother. "I sleep as though I were dead."

Kellogg had written from Tamingfu that he hoped to be back at Shaowu on December 6. As it turned out, he started home with Willomoor Farmer and his consort on November 11 and reached Shaowu on the exact date anticipated, a remarkable piece of timing

Several of Edward's cattle. Note the newly born half-breed calf, lower left.

considering that in twenty-six days, in all kinds of weather, they had traveled 450 miles by freight car, 300 miles by boat, and 150 miles on foot. Since neither animal was accustomed to being driven, they had to be led the whole distance they walked. And the cow, in a public ritual, had to be milked every morning and night. Willomoor Farmer fell into a river along the way and was terrified, although he landed in only two feet of water. But there was no real mishap. Kellogg had carried out a difficult mission; the first stage was a success.

How wonderful the animals looked in their new barn, munching on soybean vines and cabbages! Indeed, the bull was nicely set up, solid red in color and mighty in girth. The cow was half Ayrshire and half Guernsey, so that she had about as much white on her as red. Her well-proportioned bag showed good milk veins, and she had what Edward called a lovable face. Her name was Daisy. The bull, which came affectionately to be called Farmer Boy, had a face that was almost ugly—it *was* ugly—but to both missionaries, and to all other members of the mission, he was one of the most beautiful of God's creatures.

A month earlier, when Edward was assembling his native herd, he had no trouble finding men to care for it. There were always patients who came from a long distance and who, while recovered enough to work, still needed treatment. They could not go home; nor could they afford, economically, to remain idle. For years Edward had racked his brain for odd jobs for them so they could stay and be completely cured. Now the problem was solved to mutual advantage. The patients became herdsmen, milked the native cows, and grew the soybeans, Kaffir corn, and wheat. Some stayed on permanently. Years later, Edward said, "They were not mere hired men. They were the most satisfactory helpers to be had."

Yet he and Kellogg never allowed anyone to tend their precious Ayrshires but themselves. Edward, who had been getting up at six o'clock in the morning, now got up at five. So did Kellogg, who milked Daisy that first year. But later, after Kellogg taught him the art of milking, Edward took over that chore along with the feeding, and May saw even less of him than before. His letters became infrequent. "The reason I'm so pressed for time," he wrote home, "is cows. Beside the feeding and milking, I have consumed a lot of time buying more land, and then of course there is the medical work at the hospital. Twenty-four thousand patients in the past year. So from early morning until late at night I am on the jump." Then he added, "There is a satisfaction in it. If a success can be made of this cow business, it will be such a boon for these people, especially the babies."

For this he would throw in all he had.

We Aren't Supposed
to Solicit ... but ...

※

NONE OF THE DAIRYING was according to the book. It appeared nowhere in the formal program; the mission board made no appropriation for it. Today, of course, all this has changed. Peace Corps–type projects long since have become a recognized part of missionary enterprise. But in the early years there was no place in the budget for cows, which meant Edward had to use his Yankee ingenuity. It explains in part why he went into the wholesale drug business and why the dairy, as much as possible, had to pay its own way. Occasionally he received personal contributions. "We aren't supposed to solicit money for our own particular work," Edward wrote his family, "but for pity's sake don't turn it down!" These gifts and the income from unorthodox enterprises gave him a degree of independence that at times must have annoyed the hierarchy in Boston but without which he could not have progressed in his purpose.

For almost a year the dairy was run according to Kellogg's boyhood recollection of such things. Information bulletins from the U.S. Department of Agriculture that Edward sent for did not arrive until November 1914. Yet their venture prospered. Every day Daisy gave eleven quarts of rich milk that could be drunk without boiling—the entire native herd produced only ten quarts— and although this was literally drops in the bucket compared to what was needed, Edward saw no cause for discouragement. It was a time to lay foundations. He bought an abandoned rice field outside South Gate and planted it in alfalfa, a crop unheard of in that part of China. A new barn for the native stock was finished. That certainly was a step forward. And because Farmer Boy had been dutiful, the mission now had eight half-breed calves. But the really big event came on September 11, 1914, when at eleven-thirty in the morning, at Nishitu, Daisy gave birth to a full-blooded heifer calf. It was a fine little animal weighing fifty pounds and eminently deserving of the name Ruth gave her, which was Beauty.

EDWARD'S FIRST REAL ILLNESS in China had occurred in July 1893. There was no particular name for it. It was whatever someone suffers who is beset by malarial parasites and dysentery and trespasses the limits of endurance. The second illness occurred this summer of 1914. He had left Nishitu for a few days to attend patients at Shaowu and look at his alfalfa. As he recalled, "There were many things to do and all too little time to do them in." Still, he was able to start back to Nishitu in time to be with his family on the Fourth of July. Along the trail he felt faint. He was alone. His legs buckled, and he barely managed the last ascent, climbing as a stepladder the broad stone steps to the ridge. When May helped him into bed—nobody ever *put* him to bed—he was suffering a chill. He diagnosed his trouble as malaria complicated by grippe.

He meant to stay in bed the next day, but patients began calling for him, so he went downstairs to the dispensary. Two hours later, he was back in bed and did not get up again for a month. He wrote his mother, when he was back on his feet, "I got over-tired and took the grippe. I took it good, as though I was trying to make up for all the years I have been free from colds." He told how hard it had been to get the dairy going—barns to be built, pastures provided, crops planted and cared for, and stock to be fed. "Everything had to be done at once," he said, "with little money to do it."

May had to finish the letter for him. "Dear Mother Bliss," she wrote. "I'm very sorry Edward didn't get this off before his relapse. I just happened to come on to it. He has been worse than before, with constant headaches, but thanks to quinine is now somewhat better. He had looked forward to this summer. We planned to go out with the children every afternoon, but we went only twice."

Three days earlier, Kellogg, writing to his father in America, had confessed to some concern about the doctor because, he said, "he is so slow to spare himself." But Edward, who was grateful that his illness, if it had to be, had come in the slow season, was up and about again by the time Daisy presented them with her calf. Just to prove he was fit, he hiked eight miles into the next valley and returned proudly with another native cow "to raise half-breeds from."

It was quite a procession they made coming down from Nishitu that year. Beauty, the newborn calf, rode down like a sultana in a huge, swaying bamboo basket borne by two coolies, a contraption especially designed by Edward so that the animal could stand up at her convenience or, if she chose, lie down. The baby heifer took to the palanquin with perfect aplomb, looking about at the scenery aloofly when standing, as though this were how all little calves traveled and saw the world; whenever she lay down in the basket she was either listening dreamily to the strident song of cicadas or was fast asleep. A most forlorn-looking native calf, which was sick, was being carried in a galvanized washtub, balanced on a coolie's shoulder by a basketful of rock salt. But an older calf walked and, of course, so did Daisy and Farmer Boy and the native cow, making a parade of four animals hoofing it, two who were being carried, and five men, all moving together down the mountain trail.

This was the cattle train. Another "train" made up of women and children who had spent the summer at Nishitu would follow in three days, giving the men time to see their cows settled at Shaowu and get back up the mountain for the final trip with a day of rest, which happened to be a Sunday, in between. But although they had waited to leave Nishitu until they thought Daisy was recovered from calving, she tired before noon. Consequently they were obliged to spend the night at a farmhouse along the way. The disruption the next day was caused by Farmer Boy, who, though of sweet disposition, seemed bent on proving himself a real blunderhead. He already had demonstrated a propensity for falling into rivers. Besides the incident in Jiangxi, where he fell into a rapids, he had tumbled off a bridge on the way up to Nishitu. If the water had not been deep at that point, he might have broken a leg.

Now as they entered a deep ravine, not ten minutes after setting out from the farmhouse, Farmer Boy, true to form, stepped over the edge of the trail and fell crashing toward the mountain stream a hundred feet below. Edward could not have felt greater fear if he had been falling himself. He scarcely dared look. Fortunately the fall was broken by dense underbrush, and the animal suffered no more than loss of dignity and a few scratches. The problem now was to get him out of the ravine. A few yards downstream a path led up to the road, but Farmer Boy made himself totally oblivious to this exit, insisting instead on trying to scramble up the same way he had come down, which was impossible. After half an hour of much shouting and threshing through thickets, and some cursing by coolies, the bull finally allowed himself to be led away from the scene of his embarrassment.

The rest of the trip was fairly uneventful. Toward noon, Daisy's strength again gave out, and the procession had to stop at frequent intervals so she could rest. It took four and a half hours to cover the last five miles to Shaowu. But a week later, when Daisy was completely recovered and two new half-breed calves were born, Edward expressed confidence. He wrote home, "I think this should be a profitable year, if we are spared the plague. The groundwork has at last been laid."

Sometimes in a Certain Sense Discouraged

THE PLAGUE CAME in January. It appeared first among a few cattle belonging to farmers in the region and quickly spread. The average Chinese had no knowledge of germs. Since nothing was allowed to go to waste, dying animals were slaughtered and sold for food, and the raw meat, carried from village to village, spread the infection. A farmer who saw his cow coming down with the plague rushed it to market in hope that it might be sold before its condition became obvious. If the cow died, and he had no money to buy another, how would he plow his field? How would he live?

This abiding fear was dramatized in the experience of an early Shaowu Christian named He. One day, while discussing his new faith, he was dared to violate a roadside shrine. Ho reached into the shrine, stood the small idol on its head, and threw dust in its face. Soon afterward the cattle plague visited his village and the little god was quoted as saying, "Standing me on my head confused my mind. Throwing dust in my eyes blinded me, and in my confusion and blindness I fumbled onto the cattle and killed them." On the strength of the god's testimony, villagers beat He to within an inch of his life.

As soon as he learned of the contagion, Edward took preventive measures. Daisy and the bull were placed in isolation, along with their calf, and the native herd was divided in two sections so that if cows in one section became infected, the others might escape. One group was sent a few miles downriver to Tung-sang, while the rest stayed at East Gate. Neither herd was taken out to graze, and their care was turned over completely to the Chinese. Edward did not go near the native cattle for fear he might carry the contagion to Farmer Boy and his family. The Ayrshires were kept in the barn by themselves, literally under lock and key.

The first infestation reported among the herd at Tung-sang was on the third of January, and in two weeks six native cows died. Kellogg wrote on January 19, "The foreign cattle are thus far all right, although Dr. Bliss has some fears regarding Farmer Boy and the heifer. They have been a little off their feed, and he has deemed it safer to separate them. So the heifer came over and is living at our house now, and the bull is living in a newly built shed in the small pasture across the road. It has been a time of great anxiety for the doctor. A good deal of the strength he gained after his long illness has now been lost."

On January 26, Kellogg had sad news. "Flags are at half-mast today, for Farmer Boy succumbed to the plague at an early hour this morning. For eleven days he and the doctor have battled against it, and while the odds on the whole grew stronger for the enemy, yet there was to the last ditch some hope that he might be saved. Usually the disease runs its course quickly, but he stood it longer, owing doubtless to the doctor's strenuous efforts. He has doctored him as he would a person, has kept his place warm on cold nights and usually has been out to see him during the night. But with Paul the doctor would say, I think, 'cast down but not destroyed.' "

Kellogg wrote that if Farmer Boy had recovered, he would have been worth a great deal more than other cattle because he would be immune. Then he added, "But there are other bulls and probably, if the cow business is to be carried on, there will be another [to] take his place. He had grown since he came to be a fine, big fellow, and to the last he was very good tempered. I am glad to say that Daisy is in excellent health at this writing, and the heifer is about normal."

The Kellogg letter is quoted at length because it says things missing from the doctor's writings. In a letter home, dated January 28, Edward said the thing that had been keeping him busy was the cattle plague. He dismissed his effort to save Farmer Boy in one sentence: "In some way, the foreign bull contracted the disease and has died." Of the whole experience he said, "I exerted myself to the utmost." And since that is all a man can do, he turned to the future. "Of course," he said, "this is a great disappointment, but if we keep the cattle we have, especially the foreign cow and calf, we may well be thankful. Perhaps the loss is a blessing in disguise. It has taught me many things which I should probably not have learned in any other way."

How often in the years to come he would equate disaster with instruction! In closing, he apologized for running on so. "Well, this letter has been all cows, but I think of and do other things. Still, no one can know what this thing means to me, to teach this people how they may have one of the greatest necessities of a healthful life."

The plague, indeed, had taken a heavy toll. Of thirty-six head comprising the native herd, only five cows, two heifers, and four calves survived. Only one animal, a heifer, took the disease and recovered. During the year, Edward had given Lucy Bement, for her women's medical work, two half-breed heifers sired by Farmer Boy, and both survived. The milk herd at Tamingfu in North China, where Kellogg got Daisy and Farmer Boy, numbered sixty head. In April, word reached Shaowu that of the sixty animals, six were left.

I Must Admit I'm Tired

THEN AN AMAZING thing happened: Edward almost ran away. In 1913, he had removed a "sort of wart" from one of May's fingers. Nothing more was thought of it until that summer, at Nishitu, when a new growth appeared around the old scar. He again operated, cutting deeper this time, and wider, in the hope of removing all roots. It was instinctive to fear cancer; her father had recently died of that disease. As it turned out, the second operation was successful; the growth never reappeared. But Edward could not know this, and soon after the plague he asked permission to send May and the children home to America. It was important, he said, that May see a specialist and that the children, who had been suffering from malaria, return to a more temperate climate. He also asked leave to accompany his family as far as Shanghai. The mission voted unanimously to grant both requests.

They left Shaowu on April 20, 1915, and reached Fuzhou without mishap. Edward's letter reporting their arrival was, logistically speaking, one of the most curious he ever wrote. The letter, addressed to his mother, was begun in Fuzhou on April 25, finished in Shanghai on May 8, and mailed in San Francisco on June 1. "May," he explained, "will take this along with her on the steamer and mail it in San Francisco, so when you receive it, even if she does not find time to write, you will know that they have crossed the Pacific in safety." Then, remembering May's aversion to ocean travel, he added, "I hope they have pleasant weather and a smooth passage."

For May, getting ready to return home after four more years in Shaowu was more than a matter of packing. She was a woman, and she had pride. She wanted to look right in America, and she wanted her children to look right, and so in both Fuzhou and Shanghai she was busy with Chinese tailors. "Dressmaking," reported Edward with a certain note of disapproval, "has her tired, too." He was glad she was going because it was best for her, but there was another reason: they had received word that her mother was failing. It would be good if May could see her again. He remembered how he had written letters to his father two months after he died, and with May's father it had been the same.

Edward saw them off on the SS *Mongolia* on May 9. It had been his first choice in writing for accommodations because the Kelloggs, who were due for furlough, also were sailing on that ship and because it was one of the largest, most comfortable steamers on the Pacific run. As he watched the hawsers cast off and the ship move slowly out into the murky waters of the Whangpoo, he felt terribly lonely. A light drizzle fell on his face. For some reason, probably because of something having to do with the children, May was nowhere in sight. The Kelloggs, too, seemed to be down in their cabin. To catch a glimpse of one of them waving would have meant a lot to him. The whole scene was depressing, shrouded in the grayness of all harbors on rainy days.

He did not linger on the pier. Tugs were still jockeying the liner into position when he walked across the Bund, past clamoring rickshaw men, to the telegraph office, for he had a premonition—a fear—and there was nothing to do but send a cable to meet the ship at Nagasaki, its first port of call. The cablegram he sent May consisted of three words: BETTER TETHER EDWARD. Unrestrained, his lively son of twenty-two months might topple overboard. And how natural that he, physician turned cowman, should say *tether*!

That night, writing to his mother, he said, "I must admit I'm tired. I've been working steadily for five years." The full effect was hitting him, now that pressures were removed. But when he went to bed he could not sleep. He was staying at a place called the Evans Home, a boardinghouse for missionaries. His room, on the third floor, overlooked one of Shanghai's busiest streets, and the traffic noises came up and swarmed inside him. For months he had suffered insomnia. His body craved sleep, but his mind worried the body. During his first term, Marian had implored him to tell more about himself in his letters because, she said, it was hard to read between the lines. In reply, he had said, "I am sure I don't know what to write about myself. Of course I have my ups and downs, my hopes and disappointments. Sometimes enthusiastic, sometimes in a certain sense discouraged; sometimes looking at the

Chinese Christian in a certain light and thinking that they average a good deal better than Christians at home, and then the light changes and they seem a good deal weighted down."

Now he was looking at himself. Had he "had" it? He did not question the rightness of what God had called him to do. But Shaowu had a hospital now—two hospitals, in fact—and the people had come to know Western medicine and accept it. China was producing its own doctors. Why not call it a day? His brother George was in Idaho. Why not retire to a farm in Idaho, far from the roundworm and anopheles mosquito, and grow Winesap apples and carry on a country practice? Then the family could be together. It would not be necessary within two years to leave Ruth alone in America so she could attend high school. And it would not be necessary after that to leave Beth and then his son, who was named after him. After all, the pioneer work was done. Shaowu no longer needed him; it needed a young doctor trained in surgery.

He had often wished for a surgeon's skill. The course in eye surgery, taken during his first furlough, had been rewarding, but there were other kinds of operations crying to be performed. A surgeon could have saved the coolie with the strangulated hernia, instead of opening him up and then, confronted with the black, gangrenous bowel, sewing him up again just as he was, without hope. And, worst of all, without having really tried. But what nonsense! A surgeon's hands, and brain, must keep in practice. What practice could he have? You do not prepare yourself for an intestinal resection by swabbing throats, dispensing quinine, or pulling teeth. Perhaps if he had considered himself more of a surgeon he would have rebelled at the lack of facilities. Heaven knows, he chafed enough. Or did he? And if he kept on, would his strength be equal to the task? *Could* he keep on? He lay awake torturing himself with these questions.

He went to Shanghai to stay four or five days and stayed seven weeks. It was, for him, a retreat, a time for finding himself again, for repairing himself, for rededicating himself and testing the recuperative power of prayer. He was withdrawing himself into a city so big he could be lost among its millions and be alone and take stock, for he had been used up, in Keats's phrase, by the "weariness, the fever, and the fret." He wrote Charles that in another year he would retire. And writing to May with a hand that trembled like an old man's, though he was forty-nine, he said he might come home in another month.

But all the time he was talking about quitting, he was trying, because he could not help himself, to find out all he could about rinderpest control.

Something May Turn Up to Keep Me Here for Some Time

IT WAS NOT in Edward's nature to take hold of a thing and then let go. The references when he applied for appointment as a missionary all spoke of his persistence. "I think," said a former teacher, "that he inherits this from his father, who is one of those men who always get there when they start." So at the same time Edward was searching for an escape, he kept wondering how dairymen in Shanghai coped with rinderpest. And after wondering for so long, he had to find out.

A good place to start, he thought, would be the city's largest dairy, in the French Concession. To the very end of his life Edward enjoyed telling how he met Culty, the proprietor of the dairy. He had taken a streetcar in what he thought was the right direction when another foreigner boarded and took a seat directly across from him. "We were the only passengers. He seemed pleasant, and after a few minutes I asked him whether I was on the streetcar that would take me to the Culty Dairy. Yes, he said, it would, and he should know because he was Culty! Well, we talked for three hours. He took me on a tour of his barns. His whole herd, Ayrshires mostly, had been inoculated, and he gave me the names of other people to see."

The "other people" were the municipal veterinarians Keylock and Pratt, who began inoculating cattle against rinderpest in 1912. As it turned out, Keylock was in England, but Edward had no trouble buttonholing Pratt. The veterinarian said they used a serum prepared from cattle that had recovered from the disease. The protection lasted only a few days, nor was immunity absolute. But the serum did cut down losses, since injections could be repeated as long as there was danger of contagion. Pratt not only explained the procedure but also took Edward to a barn and demonstrated it by injecting a calf.

Out of all keeping with a person bent on retirement, Edward asked where he could buy a good breeding animal. The result was that twenty-four hours later, upon payment of two hundred dollars, he came into possession of the bull Willmore Explorer, a half-grown Ayrshire "immunized" by the veterinarians Keylock and Pratt. At the same time, Edward wrote two letters. One was to his colleague Storrs, asking him to buy a duck boat, hire a crew, and get them down to Fuzhou to await his arrival, for he had bought a fine new bull to take the place of Farmer Boy. The second letter was to May, suggesting that she continue writing to him in China. "Something," he said, "may turn up to keep me here for some time." He did not identify the "something" as a quadruped, but seeing all those beautiful milch cattle of Culty's, and then finding a bull of good milking ancestry such as Explorer, what else could he do?

His letter to Storrs was dated May 22. More than a month later, on June 28, Storrs found himself in a quandary. He wrote Kellogg in America, "Dr. Bliss is not yet back from Shanghai. The fact is I don't know where in the world he is. One letter only from him has come to hand, informing us that he had bought a young bull and that the Shanghai dairymen all believe in inoculation against rinderpest."

Edward was too busy to write. Culty had presented living proof that rinderpest could at least be curbed. Pratt had demonstrated the immunization technique. Still, Edward was not satisfied. How could he be? The serum could be purchased, but for Shaowu its cost—twenty dollars a pint—was prohibitive. And even if he could afford to buy the serum, how could he preserve it without refrigeration? It was impossible to keep a fresh supply on hand, making it continuously. If he tried that in Shaowu, he would have to abandon all his other work.

The same exigencies, he realized, faced dairymen throughout most of China, for they, like him, had no way of maintaining a supply of serum, let alone the means of securing it in the first place. And a serum bank was necessary. He remembered Pratt's warning that as long as danger of exposure lasted, injections had to be repeated at least every two weeks. They might be making headway in Shanghai, but in the hinterlands of China the problem was far from solved. The problem was pressing in India. And in the Philippines more than half of all its carabao had died of rinderpest. There, the U.S. Health Service, working with army veterinarians, was embarking on a primitive immunization program.

In those days, Professor William Bailie of Nanjing University probably was in touch with more people interested in animal husbandry than any other man in China. Edward wrote a long letter to Bailie, requesting information on rinderpest control. He mailed the letter in time for it to catch the night train to Nanjing. In the morning, when he went down to breakfast, he had a pleasant surprise. He heard someone say, "Hello, Dr. Bailie." The professor was sitting at the next table.

Edward introduced himself, and they saw a great deal of each other during the next three days. It was the culmination of a series of coincidences that caused Edward to write Charles, his brother-confidant, "It would be difficult, perhaps impossible, for me to make plain to you how it seems perfectly evident to me that God has been leading me, sometimes blindfolded you might say. Even some things that seemed mistakes have turned out to be profitable and necessary. Money from the sale of medicines has been accumulating, not because we couldn't use it, but because we couldn't decide the best use to put it to. The men needed for this cow business, the best men we have had, came to me as patients. Then the farm at South Gate, a fine piece of land in an excellent location for our purpose, was offered to us at a low price just when we needed it, and without our seeking it. And finally the rinderpest, with its loss of cattle, especially the bull, seemed very hard, but the experience taught me lessons which I could never have learned otherwise and which, if I am allowed to follow out, ought to prove a great thing for our work and for China. May's being obliged to return to America also seemed pretty hard, but this rest in Shanghai has been a great thing for my health, and I am growing younger again. I grew old pretty fast the last year!"

Professor Bailie was the kind of man Edward liked—quiet, unpresuming, capable. When Bailie listened, his mind was alert to implications. He possessed only a general knowledge of rinderpest; his chief interest was land reclamation. But he saw the plague as a national catastrophe. While certain parts of China suffered severely from drought or flood, rinderpest was a scourge throughout China. It struck North and South, afflicted rich and poor.

Edward told Bailie all he had learned and took him to see the inoculated cattle. He also related, in detail, the problem he faced at Shaowu. Bailie was so impressed that he immediately wrote to the Chinese minister of agriculture and to the Rockefeller Foundation in China, urging them to recognize the vital importance of rinderpest control. And when he asked Edward to come to Nanjing to visit the agricultural college, the invitation was readily accepted. Bailie's perpetual activity reminded Edward of himself. "He is a very busy man," he wrote, "with lots of irons in the fire and many people coming to him at all hours." Still, Bailie found time to show his guest about the university campus and introduce him to members of the faculty. Edward noticed with some awe that the same Taiping rebels who razed so much of Shaowu had demolished most of the wall surrounding Nanjing. Thirty feet thick at the base and seventy feet high, the towering wall was reduced to remnants. Bailie's family, too, was in the States, and Edward frequently ate with him in his home. But most of the visitor's time was spent with cows. Three of the Nanjing missionaries maintained herds, and Edward told them everything he learned at Shanghai. He spread the gospel.

He toyed with the idea of bringing the bull to Nanjing and returning to Shaowu by the back door, through Jiangxi, as Kellogg had done with Farmer Boy. He wanted to see more of the Yangzi (Yangtze). By taking a river steamer to Jiujiang and then cutting overland to Shaowu, he would be traveling a five-hundred-mile stretch of the Yangzi, and he would be going through that most picturesque part of China where mountains rise like daggers into the sky. Perhaps, too, he wanted to duplicate something of Kellogg's experience. But this was not the time or the bull. Edward discarded the plan and, after a week in Nanjing, started back to Shanghai by the morning train.

The train seemed to stop at every inhabited place. The sun had not dissipated the coolness of the night, and it was chilly enough for Edward, seated by an open window, to wish for a topcoat. He felt attuned to the June morning. He had in Nanjing, even more than in Shanghai, been able to repair his spirit. Everyone had been cordial; there were no crises to meet, no remittent fevers, no financial reports to make out, no babies to deliver in the middle of the night. Looking out the train window, he realized that he was seeing the countryside for the first time, that on the trip up to Nanjing he had been so preoccupied with thoughts of rinderpest that he had scarcely noticed.

At one stop, a well-dressed Chinese entered and sat down across from Edward. No one else was in the compartment. The man appeared to be about thirty. He wore a Western-style suit, and Edward noticed that his black oxfords were highly polished. He looked deathly ill. His face was like a face in a coffin, and after a few minutes he lay down on the seat and closed his eyes. Edward found himself staring at the face.

Outside the train window, the scene changed. The hills leveled down into a plain rippling with wheat. Earthen-walled farmhouses dotted the fertile bottomland. The train was traveling along the bank of the Grand Canal, dug in the thirteenth century to link the port of Hangzhou with Beijing, nearly a thousand miles away. Barges and passenger boats plied the ancient waterway. Many of the boats, Edward noticed, were being sculled. Along the roads were many donkeys. Some carried large wicker panniers full of vegetables for market. The donkeys, Edward thought, looked very small and the loads very large. He wondered whatever became of Jacqueline.

The train was leaving Suzhou when two British businessmen entered the compartment. One of them nodded to Edward and took the vacant seat beside him; the other asked the Chinese to sit up and make room. When the sick man did not move at once, the foreigner gave him a resounding slap. "Imagine the nerve of him," he muttered after the Chinese, without a word, went away. It was an incident Edward recalled, with some anger, more than once.

He had been back in Shanghai a week, and was preparing to ship his newly acquired bull to Fuzhou, when he received word that rinderpest had broken out among the herd owned by Dr. John Williams, one of the missionaries he met at Nanjing. At once Edward turned from observer to combatant. This was his fight. He went to the veterinarian Pratt, obtained a supply of serum, and hurried to Nanjing by the first train. He arrived to find the disease so far advanced among the Williams herd as to make inoculation futile. It had to be written off. Although the other two herds had not come down with the plague, they had been exposed, having used the same pasture. Since Edward did not have enough serum to inoculate every animal in the two exposed herds, and as cattle that had survived epidemics were supposed to be immune, he injected only calves and yearlings. The results were revealing. Almost every untreated cow died, but all that received the serum lived. He knew now that, contrary to general belief, recovery from an attack of rinderpest did not necessarily confer immunity; it was a discovery upon which, back at Shaowu, he planned to build.

A footnote is in order. Dr. Williams later became president of Nanjing University. On March 24, 1927, he was killed by a Chinese soldier who did not like foreigners. Edward was grieved by this news, which reached him at Shaowu. At the same time, he remembered the Chinese who was slapped.

Now I Am Back Home Again

BY THE TIME Edward returned to Shaowu, Storrs had left for Kuliang. But the evangelist had seen to it that when Edward and his charge reached Fuzhou, a riverboat would be waiting for them. The boatmen may never have witnessed such togetherness between man and beast as they did on that river trip. Willmore Explorer, a bull of fierce countenance, a prodigious animal worthy of any Spanish arena, *slept* with his master. Edward had no choice in this. The crew certainly would not accept Explorer in their quarters, and there was nowhere else for this young bull to go.

"Did you sleep right alongside him?" he was once asked.

"Certainly," Edward said. "His feed trough was up front. And behind him there were—certain disadvantages."

"Weren't you afraid he might step on you?"

"We lay down together."

It was the beginning of a beautiful friendship. They were three weeks on the boat. At least once a day, usually in early afternoon, Edward took the fellow for a stroll on the riverbank. He found a great deal more Ferdinand than terrible *taurus* in Explorer's character, and the great Ayrshire found in the physician a true friend and provider. Edward's only fear was that Explorer, unmindful of his strength, would stomp a hole in the boat. This would have placed a considerable strain on their friendship, but it never happened.

A story Edward told, rather proudly, concerned an incident that occurred two years later. He wanted to transfer thirty head of cattle, including Willmore Explorer, to a new dairy farm he had set up across the river from Tung-sang. In the beginning, all went smoothly. The animals had been driven down to the fording point without incident the previous day. Explorer seemed to sense adventure and departed willingly enough from his corral at East Gate. But when the time came to make the crossing, and the herdsmen led him into the water, the bull lowered his head and, no matter how hard they tugged at the ring in his nose, refused to take another step. No amount of coaxing, pleading, pulling, or pushing availed. There he stood in water no higher than his fetlocks and, rolling his sad brown eyes, refused to budge. For some unknown reason he was not leaving the south bank of the river. There he stood and there, come high water, he would stay.

Edward got word of Explorer's recalcitrance and hurried to the scene. Chan, the chief herdsman, demonstrated the animal's obstinacy. The current was slow. The two half-breed bulls, sons of Farmer Boy, had crossed without hesitation. Why was the big, bold foreign bull so stubborn? Could he be afraid? A coward? Perhaps the solution was to hire a raft. Then Explorer—what a travesty he was making of that name!—could cross without getting his precious hoofs wet. That was the simple answer, but it meant delaying the operation until the next day. And Edward could be stubborn, too.

"Bring two of the cows," he ordered.

Explorer was to be enticed into fording the river with bovine bait. He had not been impervious to such charms in the past. It took less than a minute to bring up two heifers.

"Now drive them in."

Chan slapped the cows' rumps, and they trotted dutifully, not in the least flirtatiously, past Explorer into the river. Herdsmen shouted, wading out after them, and soon the bait was scrambling, dripping, up the opposite bank. Edward was applying a switch to Explorer, who remained immobile and, turning his head just enough, gave his master an almighty injured look. Edward told Chan to stop tugging the bull by his nose ring. Explorer had won round two.

Round three began with Edward getting into a small boat and taking the lead rope.

"All right," he said as Chan prepared to row. "C'mon, boy! Got to get you to the other side. *Come on!*"

Then the miracle happened. Explorer let go a long, loud, reverberating bull sound like the deep-throated trumpeting of an ocean liner about to sail and, with a great splash, struck out for the opposite shore. Chan grinned from his position at the oars. "I think," he said, "the honorable bull was loath to leave without the honorable Fu Xiansheng. I think the bull was not afraid."

Edward felt highly complimented. Explorer cared. And a few minutes later, rowing back to Tung-sang, deserting the bull that would not leave without him, the honorable Fu Xiansheng felt ashamed. Looking back, he saw Chan lead the bull over the first ridge and disappear from sight.

"Well, my friend," he thought, "at least now you will be safe."

Neither the bull nor his consort was safe. Edward hoped that by setting up a farm on high ground across the river, well separated from native herds and human habitation, he might preserve them. Indeed, they did survive the next epidemic, but when the plague came a second time, the "immune" bull succumbed, even as Farmer Boy. After two weeks, only a remnant of the select herd was left.

The doctor never spoke ill of Willmore Explorer—or brooked criticism of him—though the bull once broke three of his ribs. The stud animal had been placed in a pen with a native cow. Edward was walking across the pen to pick up a bucketful of bran when Explorer rushed him, caught him on the brass-knobbed horns, and tossed him. The crumpled amateur breeder, lying on the ground, found it hurt to breathe. He withdrew painfully to the house, taped up his chest, rested for a half hour on the bed, lying perfectly still, then went out and led a very docile Explorer to his stall.

A member of the mission, hearing what happened, later remarked in Edward's presence that all bulls must have a streak of meanness in them. "No such thing," Edward said, as though he had just heard someone desecrate the memory of a dear friend. "It was my fault. I came between him and the cow."

We Must Help Them
Extricate Themselves

器

IT WAS AUGUST 1915. "I am alone as far as foreigners are concerned," Edward wrote, "but though I miss them, I am not as lonesome as you might imagine for I am at home with the Chinese." And he had a new dream. "Much of the disease," he told Charles in an excited, almost impassioned letter, "is attributable to poverty. I think there is a way to raise the living standards of these people. I must give it a try."

The challenge that possessed him so he felt neither loneliness nor heat was nothing less than a program for resuscitating the economy of the region. He would start with the basic industry, agriculture. The people had enjoyed comparative prosperity, thanks to the tea trade. Their Oolong, or Black Dragon, tea was famous. But now this income was gone because of competition from Ceylon and India, where tea was produced more cheaply by modern labor-saving methods. As a result, the hillsides once covered with tea plantations lay barren, inviting erosion and floods.

Edward wrote, "The Chinese Government wants the people to put such land to use, but around here no start has been made. So I have suggested to several prominent Christians that they start an association to buy this neglected land, plant trees and whatever else the soil is suitable for and get out some foreign tools and agricultural implements. In a word, to start an agricultural experiment station to teach the people the possibilities."

They would set up a cooperative. He saw no end to the possibilities.

"I should think the region would be good for grape culture, and certainly it ought to raise a lot of cotton. . . .

"It is my idea to turn the dairy over to the association and also introduce milch goats and poultry. . . .

"There is very little fruit grown here. In this climate, fruit is a valuable food, and the region is adapted to produce a lot of good fruit. . . .

"We can set out fir trees. . . .

"Water power is running to waste in the rapids, waiting to be turned into electricity."

The possibilities, the neglected opportunities, tumbled over each other on their way from mind to paper. He acknowledged the Chinese genius for farming, but surely they had fallen into a rut. The climate was favorable for the production of three crops a year; it hurt him to see farmers, struggling for subsistence, growing one crop—rice—when they could also be raising soybeans and winter wheat. This question of use of land was crucial. "One great reason for China's poverty," he wrote, "is that she has too many people for the area of soil under cultivation. She lacks diversity of food products."

He spoke of the discontent of the have-nots. "As we live among the Chinese they see the difference in our way of life. They naturally wish more of the good things we have." His answer: "We who have so much more of everything must help them extricate themselves from their condition."

He reported that the Chinese liked his idea of a cooperative and that already "a number" of them were looking around for land. He said, "I have proposed they go into it, not as a money-making scheme, but as something they can do to make the community more prosperous." He asked them to demonstrate this by allocating one-tenth of the profits to civic improvement and one-tenth to the church. It was to be a Christian enterprise.

Edward pressed the American Board to send out an agricultural expert. At the same time, he published a pamphlet describing the pilot program and sent it to potential contributors in America. He assured them that after three years the project would be self-supporting—shares were being sold and profits would accrue—but in the meantime it needed help. He itemized as follows:

Additional land and buildings	$2,000.00
Additional stock (cattle, goats, poultry)	1,000.00
Equipment for inoculating cattle	1,000.00
Tools and implements	500.00
Maintenance for three years	$1,500.00
	$6,000.00

Six thousand dollars for revival of a region. It seemed so little to ask. Contributions, he said, could be sent to the American Board of Commissioners for Foreign Missions, 14 Beacon Street, Boston. And he added discreetly, "They should be in addition to your usual contribution to missions."

Agriculture was the key. He was sure of it, and history was to prove him right, for in the end it was failure to carry out agrarian reform that gave communism its opportunity in China. He was firm in his belief that to fight poverty was both good medicine and good religion. The last page of the pamphlet carried this quotation from the Bible: "If a brother or sister be naked and in lack of daily food and one of you say unto them, 'Go in peace, be ye warmed and filled,' and yet not give them the things needful for the body, what doth it profit?"

He did not wait for contributions from America before acting. Boldly he organized the cooperative and persuaded it to buy several square miles of hills for reforestation. These trees were his joy, comparable to Chinese babies and foreign bulls. His notes give this account:

> Where a fir is cut down, shoots sprout out from the stump. When these shoots are two years old, they can be cut and planted with a fair chance of taking root. As the season for planting (three or four weeks) was so limited, not many shoots could be set out in a single year. But by continuing a number of years our hills at length were covered by thousands of young trees. In one section, they grew to a height of thirty feet only ten years after planting, but this was due to unusual depth of good soil.

Purchased at this same time was the site of an abandoned leper colony—cheap. These idle acres were converted into a grazing range.

More than a year had passed since Edward had seen his family sail from Shanghai. So in June 1916, when his furlough came due, he placed Zeng Jinji, the man he saved from gangrene, in charge of his work and went home to New England. He trusted Zeng. The man was highly resourceful. His drug business had thrived. He had married well and been favored with sons. Edward had only one cause for uneasiness. "I know he can run the dairy," he said. "The great trouble is that he may want to profiteer."

Edward was reunited with May and the children in a small frame house next to his mother's in Newburyport and almost at once became immersed in the study of animal husbandry. A German submarine sank the *Lusitania*, and Congress declared war, but he hardly noticed. Instead, he lived agriculture, reading all the literature he could lay his hands on, brushing up on everything from poultry management to what had been done most recently in rinderpest research. Late at night May would find him perusing mail order catalogs for such nonmedical equipment as hand cultivators, incubators, galvanized steel netting—"Three twists in every mesh"—feeding troughs, and plows. Then from 14 Beacon Street came the news he wanted most to hear: "The American Board has recognized the opportunity for service and widespread influence offered by such an enterprise and has appointed a keen-minded, highly trained agricultural expert to the Shaowu station."

The expert was Charles Riggs, a recent graduate of Ohio State University. He was supposed to have gone to Turkey, where his father and grandfather were missionaries before him, but because Turkey had come into the war on the side of Germany, the young agronomist, freshly married, was being reassigned to the mission station in western Fujian.

Now I Sleep Soundly at Night

EDWARD LEFT San Francisco with his assemblage of five goats, twelve chickens, wife, and two younger children aboard the SS *Siberia Maru* in late August. (Ruth remained behind to attend school.) In a letter written two days before reaching Yokohama he reported that the ocean had been unusually calm. "I am especially glad," he said, "because of the goats." No mention of May, who dreaded rough weather and was made ill by the slightest sea.

The goats, of pure Swiss lineage, had been purchased on the West Coast with money donated by the men's Bible class of his church in Newburyport and were confined to wooden crates near the stern. Edward feared the havoc a storm might wreak on his animals, unprotected on open deck, and they were located where the pitching of the vessel would be most pronounced. He tried to secure better accommodations, but the captain was adamant. The animals belonged aft; no barnyard odors were to be wafted about *his* ship.

"This providentially fair weather," said Edward, "has helped the goats through what is at best a very trying trip." Then he went down the roster of animals, describing their condition. "The two doe kids are in a crate so large that they get considerable exercise playing together, and they in consequence have kept better appetites than the others. The older doe has had a dainty appetite from the first, but hasn't been sick at all and is eating today perhaps a little more heartily than at any time. The little buck seemed sick half a day, but with a pint of warm milk from a bottle morning and evening he soon got very vigorous, though he is still thin. The older buck had a poor appetite several days and seemed to be unhappy, but he is naturally strong. Today I had him on deck, and he has been through a good many gymnastic exercises. How they all enjoy themselves jumping and skipping!"

Poor May, she was so proud to have married a doctor, and everyone on board knew him as a keeper of goats. He spent more time with the goats than with the poultry because he enjoyed them and because they needed him. The Leghorns and Barred Rocks, in their two coops, seemed completely at home and, aside from their feeding, self-sufficient. In his letter mailed in Japan he gave them one sentence: "All twelve chickens seem in first-class condition."

At Yokohama, the ship was delayed three days while an army of dockers, working day and night, unloaded steel plates to be used in Japan's wartime industry. Simultaneously, the ship disgorged scores of boxes filled with twenty-dollar gold pieces, leading Edward to speculate that the *Siberia Maru* may have carried the most valuable cargo ever to cross the Pacific Ocean. The goats felt the heat in port. Panting, they refused to eat. But once the ship put out to sea, bound for Shanghai, their appetites returned.

By mid-November Edward had brought his small menagerie to Shaowu without the loss of so much as a single hen. He wrote, "Of course, the goats and poultry getting here before there were any facilities provided for them has made a great deal of extra trouble, but suitable quarters are nearing completion and we can begin to see smoother sailing ahead." In one respect, the goats were an immediate success. "The children," he reported, "have found a good deal of entertainment in the Swiss goats. They are natural pets."

In the goats, Edward's medical, dairy, and agricultural pursuits met. Native goats gave little milk, and by mixing breeds of goats, as he mixed breeds of cattle, he hoped to increase their yield, for he remained a great believer in milk. Peasants who could not afford a cow might be able to keep a goat. The high grasslands around Shaowu seemed ideal for raising these animals; he wanted to demonstrate the feasibility of this to the new cooperative and to anyone else it might help.

Above all, he wanted to perform an experiment in his vendetta with rinderpest. If he could not keep serum on hand because of lack of refrigeration, why not inoculate goats and use them as walking laboratories? With the return of the cattle plague in 1919, he carried out the test with good results. He knew now that when need arose he would have serum from the goats, fresh and unspoiled. And he discovered that the goats produced a safer serum.

182

Edward and two of his Swiss goats. The crumpled khaki suit was his uniform.

By passing through their bodies, the virus was attenuated; a cow inoculated with serum extracted from goat's blood was less apt to contract the disease.

The foreign poultry he introduced were for purely economic reasons. His hens were better layers than the native hens, and eggs were expensive in Shaowu. For that matter, so were hens. Hens cost ten to fifteen cents a pound liveweight, and a skilled laborer had to work a whole day to earn ten cents. If the supply could be increased, the price might be brought down.

On December 16, 1917, he wrote to Ruth in America, giving her a progress report couched in language that, to his mind, befitted a thirteen-year-old. He told her: "We have made a fine building for the hens back of our house. It is twenty feet long and ten feet wide, and Mr. Riggs had made some nice roosts and nests. Beth likes to go in and hunt for eggs. She has written about the five little chickens which are, we hope, the first of a large flock. Most of the Leghorns are pullets which have not begun to lay yet, but they are growing rapidly. The only Barred Rock hen we have has malaria and has stopped laying. Queer, isn't it, that hens should have malaria, but birds do as well as people."

Edward doused the foreign hens with quinine and turned their care over to Riggs. After an absence of a year and a half there were, as he said, "so many snarls to be straightened out, so many lines of work to be got into running order." Zeng had done a creditable job managing the dairy, though it was apparent from the leanness of the cattle that he had done a good deal of economizing on feed in the hope of showing greater profit. Albeit, the herd had grown: three pretty half-breed heifers had been born in his absence. The association, marked by mutual respect and no little affection between Tseng and the foreign doctor, now came to a tragic end, for soon after this, when Tseng set out for Fuzhou on personal business, his boat foundered in one of the rapids. The able Chinese drowned, leaving a widow and four sons.

Despite the arrival of a trained agronomist from America, Edward remained manager of the dairy, for he regarded the dairy as an adjunct to his hospital. "What I am trying to do," he said, "is preventive medicine." The cows, the bulls, and the goats were his personal charges. Although ultimately he had three herds totaling more than two hundred head, he appeared to know each animal—its age, pedigree, and whether it had survived a plague. He could not conceive of any Chinese taking such interest. Nor could he conceive, perhaps mistakenly, of the newly arrived expert ever coming to know the problem, with all its ramifications, as well as he did. And so he still supervised the milking and feeding, the building of stockades, the inoculation for rinderpest, the bookkeeping, and the hiring and firing of herders, whom Beth and son Edward called cowboys.

At the same time, he was removing cataracts, putting up prescriptions, lancing boils, dehorning calves, buying land, and supervising the final stages of construction of a women's hospital at North Gate. This was the time in which his hands were transformed from those of a doctor to those of a farmer. He handled feed, rock salt, and earth with his bare hands. Kids were weaned to bottles by sucking his forefinger, babies were delivered with those two strong hands; so were calves. In winter he never wore gloves. His hands became so chapped and the skin so broken, and creases so deep, so filled with grime, that they never appeared clean again to the end of his days. Turpentine and calcimine and iodine all made their mark on them; so did charcoal and kerosene, which was good for getting rid of ticks. It was not the dairy and rinderpest alone to blame, but all the rough things he did, in his phrase, to get the job done. He wrote his mother, "I thought I was busy when I first came, but every year seems to be busier than the one before. Still, giving a good deal of my time to outside work is less tiring on me than a stream of uninterrupted medical work. Now I sleep soundly at night, while I used to be much troubled by insomnia."

As early as 1915, Edward had appealed for the appointment of another doctor. Lucy Bement had her hands full at North Gate, and when either of them went home on furlough, or to Nishitu in summer, the situation became impossible. Even when both physicians were at their post, the service, Edward felt, was inadequate. He wrote, "We ought to be doing more. They say the people at Shaowu 'enjoy great blessedness' with foreign doctors to care for them, but people at a distance fall sick and die without medical attention. With two medical men we could do something. As it is, there is always so much on hand here that it is next to impossible to get away."

Care required by the missionaries themselves helped tie him down, and as their family physician he had special appeal. "It was not only that we trusted him," one missionary recalled. "We liked him. If someone was sick, he'd bring little surprises. Once he brought me some lettuce he'd babied along in his garden. In Shaowu, *that* was a treat!"

His workload increased steadily until 1917, when, while on furlough, he was able to go before the mission board and, in person, plead his case for another doctor. Again he lost. No one questioned his facts, but while the need for another medical man was unquestioned, Shaowu was not the only mission on the board's map. Other hospitals in China, India, and Japan were understaffed, and it was the duty of the board, with its overall view, to decide where the greatest need lay. After all, Shaowu was getting the agricultural expert he wanted. For the time being that would have to suffice.

Two years later—in 1919—Edward was still writing, "I hope there will be another doctor appointed soon." But in the same letter he conceded that the new doctor might never be assigned. He had heard reports of a new mission to be opened at Jianning

(Kienning), four days' journey to the southwest. "If so, the first doctor appointed may be sent there."

The report of a new mission station, and Edward's premonition about the appointment of a doctor, proved accurate. But the sex of the new appointee—Josephine Kennedy, M.D.—came as a surprise. Another female to practice medicine in the back country of Fujian! He was not against woman doctors. His sister Marian was one. Still, he doubted that a woman was right for such an isolated place. It was a disappointment, but one searches vainly in his letters for resentment. He went on with his work.

The Need Is Beyond Belief

THESE WERE the vintage years. Since 1892, when Edward arrived, the mission force had increased threefold. The latest recruits were Leona Burr, whose sweet violin added a whole new dimension to prayer meetings, and Robert McClure, a product of Colby College and Bangor Theological Seminary, and Jeannie, his bride. Just as Woodrow Wilson preached lasting peace, so the missionaries of Shaowu looked to a future of infinite promise. Each year saw records broken in baptisms, student enrollment, and patients treated. Instead of praying for patients to come to him so he might demonstrate his medicine, Edward now prayed for strength to attend the sick who filled his hospital. It was not uncommon for him, with his helpers, to treat a hundred patients a day. He told his mother, "They come in never-ending streams. The need is beyond belief."

Again the physical plant was expanding. Besides the new women's hospital, a residence for the McClure family was rising at East Gate, and Riggs was putting up a house near the new farm at South Gate. New earthen-walled corrals for half-breed cattle were rising at North Gate and East Gate and across the river. As usual, because of his Yankee trader instincts, Edward doubled as purchasing agent and overseer of construction. With its growth, Shaowu no longer functioned as an outstation of the Fuzhou (Foochow) mission but qualified as a mission in its own right, making independent decisions in all but the most crucial matters. And because it enjoyed autonomy, more time was spent discussing policy. How much emphasis should be placed on evangelism? How much on education? Chinese pastors were to have a freer rein in administering their churches. How free a rein? How self-supporting? Edward regarded many of these business meetings as a waste of time. It was the long-windedness of the discussions that annoyed him.

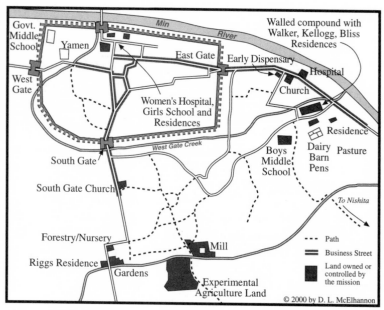

Shaowu in about 1920.

"Talk, talk, talk," he grumbled. "This everlasting beating about the bush."

A member of the mission, recalling those meetings, said, "You know, we had our differences. But we had to live together, so there was a reluctance to speak out. We were palavering once and getting nowhere, I remember, when finally the doctor said, 'Why don't we all say what we really mean? Then maybe we can decide.' It worked. Everyone said what was on his mind, nobody's feelings were hurt too badly, and a decision was reached."

The mission was feeling its oats. It published a small magazine, *The Bulletin,* which appeared three times a year and printed everything from annual reports to vignettes of Chinese history to original poetry. Two tennis courts were built, one at East Gate and another on the mountainside at Nishitu. Periodically socials were held, at which parlor games were played. The mission even blossomed out with its own stationery, the letterhead proclaiming the establishment of 33 churches, 60 regular preaching stations,

Building the earthen walls for one of Edward's pens.

2 hospitals, an agricultural experiment station, a theological training school, 2 boarding schools with 193 students, and 36 primary schools with 780 students, all staffed by "a force of 15 foreign missionaries and 125 native workers covering a field the size of Massachusetts." Such a letterhead, crammed with statistics, quickly became outdated. For this reason, and because of evil days that descended, the boastful letterhead soon disappeared.

But in the halcyon days, strange, marvelous things were happening. Then it was, thanks to the cooperative, that a water system was inaugurated, water gurgling down in hundreds of lengths of bamboo pipe from springs at the base of Crystal Hill, three miles distant. No one had faucets, only pegs, which, pulled out of holes

The boys of Shaowu Middle School in about 1916. The Americans on the top steps, left to right, are: May Bliss, Josephine Walker, Dr. Walker, and Edwin Kellogg.

in the bamboo, produced a stream of cool, clean water. It was then, too, that a small Delco generator purchased by a local merchant enabled Shaowu to see its first electric light—and its first movie. The film, shown at the East Gate church, was a one-reeler in which a Mack Sennett character, carrying a full market basket, took a pratfall down some stairs. The picture, projected on one of May's bedsheets, was jerky, the comedy low, but for all who crowded into the church that night it was a delight.

More important was the arrival of the John Deere plow. Two coolies brought it up from the quai at about four o'clock in the afternoon, and the excitement it generated rivaled the excitement of the first picture show. Edward had come from the hospital just in time to see the precious, steel-banded pine box from America set down in the backyard. No heed was paid to the rest of the river shipment. Years later, no one remembered what else came off the sparrow boat that day, or recalled any crate except the long, sweet-smelling box containing the Deere plow.

Quickly there was a crowd. First, He Kuan emerged from the kitchen, wiping his hands on his apron, looking puzzled. A missionary child, playing coal miner, climbed out of his small trench by the kitchen steps. Three herders, including Chan, came over from the barns on an errand and stayed to see this huge new tool that had been sent to Shaowu from across the sea. Charlie Storrs heard the news from a student at Han Mei. By the time Storrs arrived, Edward already was going at the nails with his largest claw hammer, wrenching them squealing out of the wood. Then Amah came hobbling onto the scene, her wise almond eyes intent on the glint of polished steel, for the plowshare now showed, and it was a mighty bright, impressive sight compared to the rough, iron-shod wooden ones used by hundreds of generations of the sons of Han. May, who had been sewing on a new dress for Beth, looked down from the upstairs veranda and could not see the plow because of the crowd. She hurried down to Edward, who was on his knees, unfastening a packet of nuts and bolts wired onto the plow handle.

"Your plow came!"

"Yes," he said, "and in jig time. No more than seven weeks."

"What are you going to do?" she asked.

He said, "I'm going to put it in the ground," a question so innocent, an answer so artless, so matter-of-fact, that they became part of family lore.

Edward and Storrs assembled the plow in the field across the road. It went together snugly, each part—handle, moldboard, share, clevis, and brace—bolted until it stood complete, altogether beautiful, ready to cleave China's good earth. The earth at Shaowu had never known such a plow. By comparison, the wooden Chinese plow, so light a peasant could carry it home over his shoulder, barely scratched the surface. The honor of pulling the new plow fell to a cow commanded by Chan. The tall, handsome chief herder gave the order. The plow cut deep, laying bare to cultivation soil that may never have been exposed to sunlight by man before, slicing a furrow that ended, so great was Chan's enthusiasm, only when he reached the far end of the field.

IT WAS IN THIS TIME, at the peak of mission activity, that old Dr. Walker died. Edward had gone with him to Fuzhou for China's first national conference of Christian leaders when, shortly before returning, Walker lapsed into his final illness. For years he had suffered from the hernia, and now, after a severe attack of influenza, he became alarmingly weak. Edward reported in a letter dated June 6, 1922, that Walker had to "be tended to like a baby." Three weeks later, very quietly, the grand old man of the Shaowu mission died. He was seventy-eight and in the fiftieth year of his service in China. An entry in Walker's 1904 diary illustrates the universality of his interests:

> Killed a snake 52 1/2 inches long. After prayers, pupils came in and took a look. Put it in a glass jar in 2 lbs. of alcohol. Read a detective story.

Rather Young to Send on Such a Long Journey

THERE WAS Farmer Boy, a rather tragic figure, and then Explorer, the affectionate one, and finally Gilman Improver. The story of the last bull began fifty years earlier in Newburyport, where Edward's mother and Sarah Hurd were close friends. Of the same age, they had an abundance of children, delighted in sharing new recipes, and attended the same church. The Hurds' elm-shaded house with the granite doorstep at Fair and Temple Streets was five blocks from maple-shaded Allen Street, but the distance did not discourage the young mothers from visiting back and forth.

Among the Hurd children was Mary Elizabeth, who was called Mabeth. A playmate of Edward's sisters, she grew up, married a lawyer, and moved to Chicago, where she became an intimate of Harriet Hammond McCormick, wife of Cyrus Hall McCormick, whose father invented the reaper and founded the International Harvester Company. Mabeth spoke to the McCormicks of Edward's work in China. She told how his herds had suffered, and the Chicago tycoon promised that as his contribution Shaowu would have the finest cow to be found.

This conversation took place sometime in 1921. On January 15, 1922, Edward wrote his mother, "In your last letter you spoke of how Mabeth had interested Mr. Cyrus McCormick in our dairy project so that he offered to give us a cow. She wrote me, and at the same time I received a letter from him."

McCormick had put his offer in writing. Edward thanked him and made a counterproposal. Because foreign cows fared poorly in the region and half-breeds had proved hardy, would he donate a bull calf instead? McCormick replied that if it was a bull Edward wanted, a bull he would have. It would be a thoroughbred of good milking ancestry; he could rest assured of that. Thereupon

McCormick turned the problem over to his aide, C. S. Stilwell, who promptly sent money to the American Board for purchase of a likely animal. The board, unaccustomed to purchasing bulls, nevertheless acquitted itself with dispatch, as demonstrated by the letter signed by Henry H. Kelsey, the American Board agent in San Francisco. The letter is dated April 1, 1922:

> My dear Mr. Stilwell:
>
> Will you pardon me for not acknowledging immediately your letter of March 20, in which you enclosed a check for $250 for use in behalf of Dr. Bliss? I delayed until I had some information about the possibility of making the purchase and shipping the bull.
>
> I have found candidates abundant and am just arranging for the purchase of a high-bred animal very near San Francisco for $100, which will enable me to cover all expenses, I hope, through to Foochow [Fuzhou]. We shall ship the calf by the steamer sailing April 19, due to arrive in Shanghai May 11.

The letter closed on a note of gratitude to McCormick.

Stilwell sent a copy of Kelsey's letter to Mabeth Hurd, promising, "I shall undertake to keep you informed from time to time of such news as I may receive regarding this most unusual missionary." Three weeks later he was able to report that the young bull, Gilman Improver, late of Gilman's Ayrshire Farm, Woodside, California, had indeed sailed out the Golden Gate, bound for Shanghai.

Pacific Rural Press, reporting the sailing, identified the voyager as no less than a grandson of that great milker Willmoor Vesta IV, which was champion three-year-old at the Panama-Pacific International Exposition in San Francisco in 1915. The paper described the havoc inflicted by rinderpest and said, "Dr. Bliss thinks he has found a serum which is a perfect cure." This was an exaggeration. Edward never imagined he had a perfect cure for anything. He had discovered new techniques, and they held promise. That was all. Yet he was grateful for the article. It told people about his sworn enemy rinderpest, and it told him things about his wet-nosed helpmate that he otherwise would not have known.

The lonely calf, bewildered by dockers' shouts and blasts of the ship's horn, sailed for China as scheduled on the SS *Empire*

State. Consigned with him for provision were 200 pounds of powdered milk, 175 pounds of feed grain, and 2 bales of alfalfa. Little is known of the voyage except that like the goats that went before him, he occupied a special place on the ship. Also like some of the goats, he refused to eat the first two days. He reached Shanghai on May 10, a day earlier than expected.

Edward was already in Shanghai attending an all-China conference of Protestant churches. It was an important meeting. John R. Mott, a future Nobel Peace Prize winner, had spoken. So had the eminent churchman Sherwood Eddy. It is reasonable to speculate that, listening to these speakers, Edward's thoughts often strayed to the remarkable bull that, God willing, would help him rebuild.

It was love at first sight when Edward went aboard the steamer and saw what a fine bull he had been sent. "He was in the pen when I first saw him," he wrote, "a chunky little fellow, rather young to send on such a long journey, handsome and as docile as can be." This docility would stand the doctor in good stead, for they were about to set out, man and beast, on a new journey covering almost a thousand miles. Together they would travel by river steamer into the heart of China, to Jiujiang, then south by narrow-gauge railway to Nanchang, east by flat-bottom boat to the head of navigation on the Fu River, overland on foot across the Jiangxi divide to the headwaters of the Min, and finally a day's sail to Shaowu. This was the route Kellogg had taken in bringing down the first bull from North China. Now, after nine years, it was Edward's turn. He chose this long, circuitous route in order to avoid the Min's rapids, which, flooded by spring rains, had become doubly treacherous.

When the doctor went on board the *Empire State* in Shanghai, he found Improver lying in his stall, watched over by the deckhand who had tended him during the three-week voyage. Because it was too late to catch the evening steamer for Jiujiang, and since Edward knew of no suitable place to stable the bull, Improver spent another night aboard ship. In the morning, Edward presented his papers of ownership and, with the deckhand's help, conducted his prize bull onto Chinese soil.

Then he had to get the animal through Customs. "It was quite a problem," he recalled. "The river steamer wasn't in yet, and I had to go to the Customs House. So I did something, looking

195

back, I can't imagine. I tied him to a railing, there on the Bund with all that crowd, and left him while I got my business tended to. It took two hours, but when I came back with the clearance papers he was right there." Edward shook his head, telling it. "I've often thought what a chance I took. All that work and expense."

It still frightened him after those many years.

In that day, the Yangzi (Yangtse) steamer made the five-hundred-mile trip to Jiujiang in two days and two nights, even though this stretch of the mighty river, below the Three Gorges, is untroubled by rapids. Edward had no difficulty getting accommodations for Improver on the lower deck, which was reserved for cargo, and there the bull, secured by a ten-foot rope, seemed content. Now and then he would take a long look at the doctor in crumpled khaki as though wondering about him, and Edward would look at him and wonder how it would go this time.

He planned the expedition to make it as safe as possible. To familiarize himself, he had come to Shanghai by this same route in reverse—walking, sailing, traversing by train the same ground so that, returning, he would know the way. Chan's son, Timothy, had come out with him as far as Nanchang, where he had an uncle. He would rejoin the doctor there for the hazardous part of the return trip, for much of the time they would be on foot and in the mountains. In Shanghai, Edward had bought a supply of feed, selecting only the best, and on his first meeting with Improver had inoculated the calf with the refrigerated antirinderpest serum available there. The one shot cost six dollars in gold, but that was the least he could do to protect this sturdy little fellow, who looked at him so trustingly. The question was: Once they reached Shaowu, would his own improvised serum do as well?

For Edward, the two days on the Yangzi loitered in their passing. He took long spells at the rail, near his precious bull, gazing at the varied sights along the low, muddy banks of the wide river. He saw fishermen casting nets by means of long, balanced poles that reminded him of the well sweeps pictured in old New England prints and other fishermen in boats casting nets, looking much as fishermen must have looked on the Sea of Galilee. Cormorants fished from rafts with rings around their necks to keep them from swallowing their catch, and men in small boats herded flocks of ducks. All this caught his interest, but he chafed at the slowness of the voyage. Shaowu had been without a doctor for almost a month.

He reached Jiujiang on the afternoon of May 13 and spent the night as a guest of the China Inland Mission. The mission was a good mile from the wharf, and no doubt the sight of the bearded, sun-helmeted foreigner leading a bull caused people to stop and stare. The next morning they boarded the *huo che*—literally "fire cart"—for Nanchang, capital of Jiangxi Province. There were no cattle cars, so Edward arranged for the high-born animal to ride in the baggage car.

"It wasn't very clean in there anyway," he said. "The station platform was level with the door, and he just walked in."

The two slept together, one nestled against the other.

They passed Lu Mountain, celebrated in paintings for its high waterfalls, and beautiful Lake Poyang. They crossed the plains on which Zhu Yuanzhang, founder of the Ming Dynasty, overwhelmed the Mongols in the fourteenth century and where, in the twentieth century, Mao Zedong's army would administer defeat to the Nationalist forces of Jiang Jieshi, whom Edward knew as Chiang Kai-shek. Both doors of the baggage car stood open, allowing an excellent view of the scenery. The baggageman roused himself only when the train stopped. Between stations he sat on the floor, propped against a bamboo crate, head down and apparently asleep.

At Nanchang, Timothy's uncle insisted that Edward honor his house by staying overnight. Improver spent the night in an inner court, tethered to a stone lion.

In a letter home, written on his arrival at Shaowu, Edward dismisses the last leg of the journey with two sentences: "In the morning we found a large camphor boat that took us to within 180 li of Kwangtseh [Guangze today] in less than seven days. It was not the best season of the year to bring in an animal, and he might have had to endure a much longer and more trying journey had we not been granted favorable winds and cool, cloudy weather." Long afterward, it was still the propitious weather he spoke of. "All day long we had this prevailing west wind, sometimes quite strong, carrying us along."

"What about the bull?"

"We fed him wheat bran out of a bucket, and he was always hungry. Each night, when it was possible, I exercised him. We took a stroll."

When they had gone as far as they could by boat, they set out on foot. They climbed the long valley to Linchuan, then, making a right-angle turn, struck east through a whole series of mountain passes to Guangze. The "long walk" took three and a half days. Since the animal saw no reason for haste and loved, like Ferdinand, to sniff the flowers, they started each morning at daybreak and stayed on the trail until sunset. The weather, again, was generally cloudy. When sunny, Edward, taking no chances with his precious charge in the heat, had the bull travel only in early morning and late afternoon, making the trip take twice as long.

At Guangze, Edward was in familiar territory. He and his small entourage passed the night at the home of a Chinese friend and the next morning boarded another riverboat for Shaowu, arriving at their destination on the twenty-seventh of May, fifteen days after leaving Shanghai. The next time Edward wrote home, Improver got top billing. "He appears to be a very strong animal," he said. "Now if he gets through the hot summer, and escapes rinderpest, he ought to make a great addition to our herd."

"And escapes rinderpest." Always lurking offstage, to play the villain, was the plague.

On Christmas Day, as I Was Finishing My Pudding

EDWARD HAD just finished his Christmas pudding when the messenger came with a letter from Jianning.

"Excuse me," he said, tearing open the envelope.

The missionaries feasting at the Storrs' house that Christmas Day in 1923 were accustomed to messengers from the new mission station three days' journey to the southwest. Edward had been receiving frequent bulletins from Jianning on the progress of Josephine Kennedy, the young woman doctor who was recovering from a streptococcic infection that almost killed her. A soldier had come to her with a gangrenous infection in his shoulder. Although she recognized the communicable nature of the infection, she did not hesitate to operate with surgical gloves that had several small holes. She had, after all, no choice. The rubber gloves ordered from America months earlier had not arrived.

Dr. Kennedy took a larger risk than she realized. So great was her interest in treating the patient that she failed to notice a small lesion on her own right hand. She was poisoned through the almost invisible break in her skin, and by the time Edward reached her, hurrying on foot so that he made the journey in two and a half days, she was delirious. She was worn out with overwork when she became infected, so it went harder. The poison permeated her system, swelling arms and legs. The words she spoke made no sense.

Jianning, like Shaowu, is a river town where, in that time, commerce thrived and boat-builders' hammers could be heard all day. The missionaries who went to Jianning, besides Josephine Kennedy, were Grace Funk, director of the new station, and Louise Meebold, a newcomer to China who taught school. They lived with two Chinese nurses in an upstairs apartment in the church. A veranda ran along the outside of the apartment, reached by a flight of wooden steps.

Until she became delirious, Josephine told her colleagues—lucky for her that two were nurses—what medicines to administer and how to apply hot packs to her swollen arms and legs. They sterilized the dressings over a brazier on the veranda. The fire in the brazier was kept going day and night. "We suggested taking her downriver to Nanping, where the Methodists had a good hospital," Grace said afterward, "but she was afraid she would die on the boat. She wanted Dr. Bliss."

Edward had to pass alone through bandit country but was not molested. The only unpleasantness came the first night, when he sought shelter at an inn. The proprietor at first refused to open the door, fearing that Edward's insistence he was an American was a ruse. The innkeeper had not thought it possible for a foreigner to speak Chinese without an accent.

Edward reached Jianning on November 5 and stayed three weeks. No patient ever received more undivided attention. During the first week, when Josephine's condition was grave, he never left the sickroom for more than a few minutes. A cot was moved in, so at night he would be within sound of her voice. He slept little. Not once during the life-and-death battle did he remove his clothes. Then, as his patient improved, he began sleeping downstairs, in the pastor's study. And for the first time in years, he had free time. As Grace Funk remarked, "He had no cows to care for, or patients asking for him every minute. He was able to read. We had magazines he seldom saw, and he found relaxation in them. How he enjoyed the stories in *The Saturday Evening Post!*"

On November 20 he could write Marian, his doctor sister, "The original inflammations have subsided without sloughing, though the skin broke out with vesicles. Her temperature has gone down, and her mental processes are normal, but I don't need to tell you that this is the most persistent and insidious of surgical infections. So I have been staying here on watch."

Still, he was mindful of Shaowu. "As Dr. Kennedy's treatment must be kept up without much change for weeks, and since the families in Shaowu are without a physician, it seems as though I ought to be starting back." He added, "It is rather difficult for one physician to be responsible for the medical care of two stations three days' journey apart. Sickness can get a pretty good start before I could respond to a call."

He saw an approaching crisis. Dr. Lucy Bement, after serving twenty years, had left for health reasons. Edward himself was due to leave on furlough within the year. Six years had passed since he last saw Newburyport. He had been separated from May and the children for two years. Who would take his place?

"I have," he said, "been writing to the Board, telling it of the plight we are in here as regards physicians and, using rather forceful language, urging that another physician be appointed at once."

He had been back at Shaowu a month when the message came interrupting the Christmas celebration. Every few days, Grace Funk had reported how Josephine Kennedy was getting on and what medicines were needed. When the messenger appeared at Christmas, missionaries at the party assumed that Edward had received another of these routine communications. It was natural enough for him to excuse himself from the table; he would have to leave and get the medicines Dr. Kennedy needed.

As he rose to go, Polly Storrs told him, "We're so sorry. You'll miss the Christmas tree." They were about to open presents. It wouldn't be right to make the children wait.

"I'll be back shortly," Edward assured her.

He didn't reveal the contents of the message; it would have ruined the party. Fire had destroyed the Jianning church, along with the apartment occupied by the women, who had escaped with no more than the nightgowns on their backs.

"We didn't have a hairpin!" Grace Funk recalled. "I guess it was our fault, Louise's and mine. It was damp, cold weather. We were using all our bedding but still couldn't keep our feet warm. So we got the idea of warming a couple of sofa pillows over the brazier and putting them on our feet. One of the pillows got scorched. It didn't appear on fire, but the cook woke us an hour later, shouting that the church was burning. He carried Josephine out in his arms."

Edward packed a basket of bedding for the trip. By the time he got back to the Storrs house, the party was almost over. Everyone was shocked by his news.

THEY STARTED at daybreak. Edward, breaking his rule, rode in a sedan chair on the level stretches but did walk when they came to the climbs. All the second afternoon, threading the mountain passes, they were lashed by wind and rain. They reached Jianning on the forenoon of the third day.

Josephine Kennedy had been moved to a room in one of the day schools. Louise Meebold heard a commotion outside the school and ran to a window to see Edward arrive. He was a welcome sight.

"I never knew before that angels wore goatees," she exclaimed.

Grace Funk, standing beside her, said, "And I never knew they had malaria, but this angel has."

Edward was quaking. It explained why, contrary to conviction, he had allowed himself to be carried on men's shoulders. He belonged in bed.

His challenge was to get the invalided doctor to Shaowu. She had been bedridden for two months, without the strength to sit up. No ambulances existed in that part of China. There were no motor roads. Nor did Jianning have a satisfactory place for her to convalesce. She had to be moved.

"It was quite a problem," Edward wrote, "but after a lot of planning with a bamboo worker I finally got a workable contrivance, a portable bed with reinforced legs and a railing. Over it we placed a bamboo-woven *peng* to shut out the elements and prying eyes."

She would travel mandarin fashion, with four bearers. This made for less jarring, since the coolies would break step. Edward also prescribed that the bed, or palanquin, should be suspended by loosely woven bamboo ropes to serve as shock absorbers. Then he ordered a mattress made that would fit the palanquin after being folded into three thicknesses. A fresh mattress was desirable because newly fluffed cotton would be more comfortable, and warmer, than what had been slept on. Upon this triple mattress went the cotton pad on which she had been lying. To transfer the patient to the palanquin, they lifted her gently by the four corners of this pad, so she might avoid the slightest exertion. Edward took pride in these arrangements. "It was cold for this part of the world," he reported "with hard frosts in the morning. But with her thick bed and hot water bottles, and the shelter of the sedan cover, she was kept warm day and night."

It was the longest procession of sedan chairs Edward had seen. Besides Josephine's litter, there were thirteen sedan chairs for the other foreign women, a Chinese preacher's wife going as far as Taining, five teachers and three students associated with the Jianning mission school, and the two nurses whose homes were near Shaowu. Twelve load carriers, in addition to forty-three chair bearers, made sixty-eight in all. Edward, recovered from his malarial attack, was the only member of the party besides the coolies who walked.

The journey, according to his plan, required three days and two nights. The most comfortable route for the uncomplaining woman in the litter would take them fifty li down the Jianning River to a place called Meikou, thence northward by land to Taining and Shaowu. In going by boat to Meikou, they approached Jiangluo, the very center of bandit activity. These same bandits only the year before had captured—then released—Storrs after holding him for three days. But Edward still favored this route, provided the party reached Meikou by noon and made the thirty li to Taining by nightfall. This would be practical if they got an early enough start. He had been warned against spending the night at Meikou. If they did not spend the night there, Chinese friends said, they should be fairly safe.

Because of the danger, Edward urged all members of the expedition to be ready to leave at daybreak. The boats and all the coolies were on hand at the prescribed hour. "The others," he wrote "did not seem to appreciate the importance of an early start, so it was nearly 10 o'clock before Dr. Kennedy's palanquin was put on the boat. I was fuming inside all this while."

As he feared, it was near sundown when they disembarked and got their procession started for Taining. The chair bearers had protested; they wanted to spend the night at Meikou. Edward exhorted them to press on because of the bandits, and with glum faces they complied. As they ascended the highlands, the procession became strung out. Seven or eight chairs moved far ahead, out of sight on the steep, twisting trail. The four-man palanquin, which was harder to handle, dropped behind. Edward stayed with it. He cautioned the bearers to step carefully. The way was rough. As darkness fell they came to a hamlet that had been pillaged only the night before. Nothing was said of this to Josephine Kennedy.

The whole long caravan had only Edward's kerosene lantern to light its path. They could not stop for the night—the danger was too great—and the coolies, understandably, were loath to travel the mountain ledges in the dark. A precious half hour was spent inducing one of the villagers to sell an iron basket that, filled with splinters of pitch pine, made an excellent torch. The lantern and improvised torch still did not give enough light, but the coolies were persuaded to stay on the trail. Soon the basket torch fizzled. The pine had not been split fine enough, and the light kept dying down. Repeatedly the procession stopped, the fire in the iron pot was roused, and the bearers picked up their loads and went on a short distance until the light again failed and the night embraced them and the men stopped in their tracks.

"After going a couple of li at this snail's pace we saw lights coming toward us," Edward wrote. "The vanguard of our party, we discovered, had reached another village and were sending back lanterns to light our way. With them we were able to go faster, and when we caught up with the others in the village we had a long parley as to what to do next." It was decided since it was getting late to make the best of the accommodations the village afforded. In his letter Edward said, "There were a number of Christian families in this village and we divided the crowd between three of them. They had all had supper long before, but they started up their cooking stoves again. The operation of boiling and then steaming the rice the way they like it takes considerable time, so it was 11 o'clock before we were ready to lie down. I had a room with several other men, but there were no beds for the load carriers. They slept in straw with a wood fire burning on the dirt floor."

EDWARD CHAFED at every delay. The longer they were on the trail, the greater the possibility of bandits discovering their presence. The village where they spent the night was only fifteen li from Taining. It was Edward's resolve to start before daylight and reach Taining for breakfast. Most of the caravan proceeded according to plan, but the palanquin bearers, coming upon a rice tavern, stopped after going only four li. "They were determined to eat before taking another step," Edward wrote, "and I was as determined that they should not. I followed them into the tavern and got them back."

So they journeyed through the mountain passes, beside rushing streams and across the valley floors, coming down from the final high divide onto the Shaowu plain on the afternoon of the fourth day. They were safe. Josephine Kennedy showed no ill effects, but Edward saw his neglected work at Shaowu and lamented, "I am so far behind in accomplishing things."

Something else was troubling him, a matter of conscience, and he could not find peace until he confessed. Thus Edward, who found it hard to speak in public on matters that were not even personal, confessed this personal thing publicly at prayer meeting. He had, he said, encountered difficulty finding bearers willing, or able, to carry the palanquin. It had been necessary, consequently, to engage four men who were opium addicts. These men did not have the means of buying enough opium for the journey. And so he, Edward, the missionary, had trafficked in narcotics. He had bought opium for the trip and rationed it out to the bearers along the way. He had used it as a club, and a carrot, to persuade them to make the forced march.

He said, "I wanted you to know."

The confession was met by absolute silence. But it was the silence of astonishment, not censure. After a few seconds, Kellogg spoke. "You need not have told us," he said. "God knows and loves you for what you did."

In the Morning I Found
Havoc Everywhere

舞

ALL EDWARD STROVE FOR can be summarized by saying he wanted to build, to lay foundations for modern medical practice, to raise up hospitals and cow barns, to show how the economy of the region might be lifted, to promote Christianity, which was to him the most constructive of all faiths. He never doubted that while he could not hope to see the whole edifice, the Chinese would finish the job. They would, themselves, become the builders. "I am getting things ready," he said.

For the first thirty years, his archenemy had been disease, epitomized by the twin scourges of rinderpest in dumb animals and malaria in humans. Superstition and poverty gave aid to these adversaries, but he and his people, the people of that remote *xian,* had been spared war and famine, and such floods as ravaged other parts of China. Now he entered a more hostile period, a decade of catastrophe—natural, political, and spiritual—that tried everything in which he believed.

His trial began on the afternoon of August 14, 1922, when Shaowu suffered the worst flood in memory. The crest, born of cloudbursts in the direction of Jiangxi, rolled down the river, a monstrous wave. Retribution, Edward wrote, for man's rapacity in leveling the forests and leaving the mountainsides bare. The angry yellow water tore at the banks of the Min, causing cave-ins. Houses, with their occupants, spilled into the river like a Doré horror. At Shaowu, the low-lying plain was submerged, drowning farmers' livestock. Mud buried rice fields ripe for harvest. The walls of the city stood, but earthen walls everywhere came crumbling down.

That morning, Edward had gone to the hospital for his regular clinic. Patients said the river was rising. "I paid little attention," he wrote, "until after the noon meal, which I take at the hospital. Then I saw that the river was dangerously high and rising. We set to work at once getting the perishable medicines and stores placed, I hoped, above the water's reach."

He had built the hospital twenty feet above normal flood stage, but by the time the three of them—Edward and two student assistants—were done transferring the drugs to higher shelves, they were sloshing about in water to their knees. Only then did Edward look to see if escape had been cut off. "Outside," he relates, "rafts were being poled along the street, moving people and goods to places of refuge. Since we could do nothing more at the hospital, there being no bed patients, I hailed a passing raft that carried me to a dry place opposite our compound."

The brook that flowed between the compound and where he stood had turned from a small, friendly stream, amicable to clothes washing and wading, into a dangerous flood bent on destruction. The doctor stripped to his underwear and entered the water. Swimming the old-fashioned breaststroke of boyhood, he strove to reach the compound's back gate, the same gate through which the missionaries planned to spirit their families to safety during the Revolution of 1911, when it appeared the compound might be attacked.

Edward, mindful of the current, did not strike out directly for the gate but aimed for a tree some forty or fifty feet upstream. The current ran stronger, deadlier, than he had thought. It seemed that no matter how hard he swam, he would be swept off target. He kept colliding with debris. A log narrowly missed his head. He fought the current as he had fought the strong Merrimack River current in his youth.

He made it. Incredibly, he was swimming, not walking, through the back gate. In a letter telling of the flood, Edward wrote, "The bamboo raft took me as far as it could, but it was necessary to swim quite a distance." Much later he gave the full story, and even then he saw nothing remarkable in what he did. "But good thing I was a swimmer," he said.

Reaching the house, he found two of his herdsmen huddled on the back steps. Rising water lapped at the foot of the steps. Edward wrote, "They thought I came in the nick of time to save their lives by letting them in."

There was little he could do except put on dry clothes. The herdsmen had rescued the Shaowu cattle by leading them out to a small knoll, the only piece of pastureland above water. But they were too late to save the poultry. "The Leghorns and Plymouth Rocks that I introduced from the United States had been frightened into flying into the flood and were being carried away by the current. Chinese in boats were picking them out of the water, legitimately theirs now by right of salvage." The only survivors among the Swiss goats were a buck and two does that had the good sense to stay on a wooden platform that floated. At least, here were the makings of a new herd. Mud lay a foot deep in the basements of the missionary houses. Few personal belongings were damaged, since the flooding never reached the first floor.

Edward camped that night in the dining room. As he lay awake, wondering what had happened to his hospital, he could hear the sound of adobe walls falling all around in the darkness. "In the morning," he wrote, "I found havoc everywhere. Large sections of the compound wall were down, along with most of the dairy enclosures. All the crops are lost, except one patch of kaffir corn. What little the flood left in the way of fodder is being destroyed by pigs, which the Chinese allow to run free during the day. Nothing can be planted until other walls are built to keep them out."

It was the scene at the hospital that broke his heart. "The high wall of a neighbor's house fell on our new operating room, reducing it to rubble. The room for storing drugs is a shambles—everything smashed—along with a corner of the brick building for private bed patients. Behind the hospital, facing the river, was a two-story addition where I had my office and rooms for student assistants. This building was constructed on 'made' ground. It stood on stone foundations, but they proved too shallow for such a soaking and the walls collapsed. The dispensary, the heart of our enterprise, still stands."

It recalled the pillaging of the Boxer Rebellion, when he had returned from furlough to find the hospital ransacked and everything wooden—floors, window frames, door frames, the doors themselves—removed. Then he had rebuilt, making improvements. Now, twenty-two years later, nature had pillaged his creation.

So be it. He would build again.

Something in the Future
Was Not Enough

MORE THAN THE HOSPITAL was in shambles. The Republic of China had practically disintegrated with the failure of President Yuan Shikai to bring order. In this period—roughly from 1916 to 1928—scores of warlords prowled the provinces, engaging each other and setting up local satrapies. *Reader's Digest* smart-alecked that it seemed like "a feud between local laundries." It was more serious than that. Soldiers, underpaid or not paid at all, plundered the populace. Banditry was rife. Generally speaking, order existed only in port cities such as Shanghai and Fuzhou. The period ended only when paramount warlord Jiang Jieshi (Chiang Kai-shek) set up his Nationalist government in Nanking.

Opposing armies occupied and withdrew from Shaowu at least a dozen times. For safety's sake, all missionaries with families were evacuated to Fuzhou. The Kellogg house became an officers' barracks, commandeered by the alternately occupying force. Many of Edward's herdsmen were conscripted. His important research in rinderpest was interrupted, and he learned to treat bullet wounds as well as boils.

A project dear to him died. Partly because of the alarms and excursions of civil strife, partly because of impatience, his cooperative failed. Potential investors shied from it because of the uncertain future; others who had invested wanted their money back. No dividends had been paid, they said. Edward argued to no avail that it was a long-term investment, that time as well as capital were required for new crops to be introduced, for sewage systems to be built, for seedlings to grow. He had stressed from the start that the cooperative was not a get-rich-quick scheme but a long-range project for making the community more prosperous. "It was the lack of immediate results," he said later. "Something in the future was not enough." He did not think identification of the program with Christianity played an important negative role. Most of the leading families of Shaowu, he pointed out, were Christian anyway. In any case, if the cooperative was doomed because of its Christian character, so be it. He could not disassociate himself from his mission.

But he planted no more trees.

The people of Shaowu, he kept saying, thought well of America. They had never been fired on by an American gunboat, and if they saw no reason to forsake Confucius, at least they benefited from the hospitals founded by American missionaries. And from what they heard, America must be a land of indescribably healing and learning and loving one another. Their phrase for America, literally translated, was "Great, Beautiful Country." The envelopes addressed by Edward were so inscribed. Even during the Korean War, Communist demonstrators in Beijing—perhaps with unwitting sarcasm—used the "beautiful" character in naming the United States. T. Howard Somerville, the British mountaineer turned missionary, once remarked that one of the tragicomedies a missionary had to face in India was the almost universal way in which an Indian mistook what was British for Christian. Somerville cited the Christian engineer on the Madras railway who, desiring to give his son a Christian name, named him Engine Oil. Undoubtedly, Shaowu's missionaries contributed to a similar misunderstanding. They loved and missed America. Its faults faded in time and distance, and they were infused with a kind of superpatriotism. No small group anywhere—in Wichita Falls, Peoria, or Sacramento— ever sang "America the Beautiful" with more fervor than this band of missionaries on the Fourth of July.

Now, in the twenties, America to the Chinese no longer appeared so far away, so beautiful, or so Christian. Each year, more of them enrolled in American universities. One of these was the Chinese schoolboy who, long ago, had accompanied Edward on his first, unforgettable trip up the Min. After a few years of teaching, the youth decided to attend the University of Chicago. He returned with a master's degree and stories of ugly slaughterhouses, houses of prostitution, political subterfuges, and slums. He had acquired knowledge in his special field, which was government. He had also learned, he said, that Americans regarded the Chinese as an inferior race.

Edward had taken pride in his Chinese friend's career, confident he would become a leader of the New China. When the scholar returned from the States disillusioned—anti-American and anti-Christian—Edward understood it because they had a long talk together. But it was a severe blow. Young, idealistic Chinese had found in Wilson's Fourteen Points a new, revolutionary creed of self-determination and redress for injustices inflicted by foreign powers. But instead of settling old grievances, new grievances were added.

The United States seemed to support Japan's grab for Chinese territory and, at Versailles, actually joined in giving Japan the Kiaochow Peninsula. Student demonstrations charging betrayal were followed by new, widespread agitation against the extraterritorial privileges enjoyed by foreigners. A wave of antiforeign feeling engulfed China, and brigands as well as politicians rode the tide. Two Englishwomen serving an Anglican mission near Shaowu were taken for ransom. The abductors sent back two severed fingers to show they meant business, but the ransom failed to arrive in time and the two women were executed.

Edward went to the dairy barn one morning and found one of his prized cows mutilated. The animal was about to calve, and someone had slipped over the wall and aborted it clumsily with a knife. Soon another cow was aborted in the same fashion. Edward posted a guard, and there were no more knifings. Then, six months later, when rinderpest struck, so did the plotters against Edward's herd. They smeared his best milkers with the blood of diseased cattle, knowing they would lick themselves. McClure talked to Edward soon after these incidents. "He suspected who did it," McClure said. "You know how mild-mannered he was, but he was in a mood to kill the man. I never saw such anger. I kept him talking until he cooled off."

The suspect was none other than the eldest son of Zeng Jinji, whom, years before, Edward had saved from death by gangrene, the same Zeng Jinji he had tutored in medicine and who had written to Edward's mother of his gratitude and who had died later in the river accident. Now the sons of Zeng Jinji were operating a dairy. Edward believed they resented the mission dairy, which

211

sold milk cheaply; nor did they like foreigners. Still, the suspicions never were proved. Oddly, when Zhu De approached Shaowu with his Communist army, it was the wealthy, opportunist sons of Zeng, with the most to lose in a Marxist society, who went out to meet the general and show him the way into the city.

So That He Would Know There Was Something Here Worthwhile

IT HAPPENED when he had almost given up hope. Fifteen years after his first appeal for another doctor, and two years after telling the board that the need precluded further delay, and long after the withdrawal of both Josephine Kennedy and Lucy Bement, making him the lone medical missionary among a million or more Chinese, the news came. He was going to be joined by a young Nebraska surgeon, Dr. Walter H. Judd.

A natural public speaker, Walter Judd was destined to become the most active missionary in American politics. Besides serving in the U.S. House of Representatives, where he rounded up votes for the Marshall Plan and helped found the Peace Corps, Judd served as a delegate to the United Nations and, in 1960, delivered the keynote address at the Republican National Convention. He was a powerful member of the China lobby, supporting Jiang Jieshi, and some people, including Dwight Eisenhower, said he would make a good president. But in 1925, when Judd went to China, he had no thought of politics. His purpose was simply, through surgery, to minister to the physical needs of the Chinese and to bear witness.

While Judd spent a year at Nanjing University, learning the language, Edward redoubled his efforts at Shaowu. Probably he overdid, because he succumbed to a particularly severe case of grippe, which kept him in bed the whole week before Judd arrived. His absence caused attendance at the daily clinics to drop off, and he wrote, "I am especially sorry as I wished to have a good volume of work to show Dr. Judd when he came, so that he would know that there was something here worthwhile." Still, in that year, he rebuilt the operating pavilion the flood had destroyed and, in his own lonely house, personally revarnished the floors in the four rooms set aside for Judd.

Edward in the late 1920s, after warlords, malaria, plague, and flood.

His new colleague came to Shaowu by the back way, through Jiangxi, because the old bandit Lu Hengpang had a stranglehold on the Min and was holding up traffic by demanding unacceptable tolls. Traveling with him were Leona Burr, Jeanne and Robert McClure, and a new missionary couple, George and Clara Shepherd, temporarily assigned to Shaowu. Judd describes what happened: "We had reached the Fu River and had two little rice boats that were rowed in deep water and poled or pulled in the shallows. The first night on the river we could hear cannonading in the distance. A Nationalist army had come up from Canton and was fighting the Northerners for Nanchang.

"The Northern forces were defeated, beaten by the red hot, souped-up Communist-dominated Nationalist troops, and some of the fleeing Northerners who had thrown down their arms—all except their side arms—held us up. They weren't regular bandits, just soldiers who were demobilized, demoralized and trying to escape. They demanded our watches and things like that, anything they could carry, including my glasses. But when it came to Jeannie McClure's wedding ring, she put her hand down and sat on it and said, 'No, I just can't give you that.' Well, that set them back a bit, and while they were deciding what to do, somebody else came along so they fled." A postscript: Before they left, Judd, with his deft surgeon's fingers, retrieved his glasses by picking the soldier's pocket.

Judd was soon to learn how ubiquitous and overwhelming were the people's medical needs. At the next town he treated the postmaster, who had a leg ulcer, and for hours was in need of police protection from being trampled by the curious and pleading sick. It was the same for the rest of the journey, people of all stations presenting themselves for treatment by a Western doctor. When Judd reached Shaowu he wrote in the mission newsletter, "All this did not happen by accident. It is a tribute to the work Dr. Bliss has done these many years."

It was the beginning of a remarkable partnership. Judd, the trained surgeon, took the cases requiring operative care, leaving Bliss, the general practitioner, to run the dispensary and conduct rinderpest research. Often, because of the dangerous military situation, they were alone in the mission, the two Phi Beta Kappas, one of them young, talkative, a surgeon to his fingertips, knowledgeable in the latest medical techniques; the other aging, sparse with words, woefully in arrears in his reading of the medical literature, already wondering who would take his place, but both convinced of the rightness of what they were doing, working, planning together, treating each other's ills.

Judd was more susceptible to malaria than Edward, who soon was giving him daily quinine injections. The injections shriveled the large deltoid muscle of Judd's left arm and, said Judd, "Then he went for my buttocks." Malaria ravaged Judd for five years until, in 1931, after almost dying of the disease, he left Shaowu for North China, where he found himself removing Japanese shrapnel

215

from the torn bodies of Chinese. Much of the shrapnel came from America as scrap iron, and so in 1938 he went home to urge an economic boycott of Japan. He foresaw war. "You have a choice," he warned American mothers, "between your silks and your sons." It was a warning he gave in forty-six states and was giving in a church in Minneapolis the day Pearl Harbor was attacked.

But it was the Chinese who came closest to killing Judd. In 1927, not far from Shaowu, a foreign missionary had arranged a truce between northern and southern forces. The missionary acted in good faith, but he was betrayed by the Northerners, who during the night pounced on the enemy and butchered a great number. The southern revolutionists blamed the missionary, whom they summarily executed. Then they marched on Shaowu.

Judd was taken into custody almost at once and stood against a wall to be shot. The order to fire was about to be given when a middle-aged man, a former patient, burst from the crowd and began pleading for Judd's life. When the soldiers ignored him, the man beat his head against the wall, screaming as blood poured over his face that the foreigner was no spy but a performer of good deeds, and that if they put this benefactor of the Chinese to death, they must kill him, too. Others in the crowd began murmuring that what the man said was true. The soldiers listened, and Judd was set free.

That same afternoon, walking near the hospital, Edward fell into the hands of another detachment of southern troops. "They seized me roughly and started to haul me off," he reported, "but some local merchants interceded and engineered my release." He had a closer call at the hospital, where all the wounded happened to belong to a northern regiment. A southern officer, flanked by two subordinates, strode in and announced, matter-of-factly, that all enemy patients would be shot.

"Why?" Edward demanded.

The officer spoke English. It was to make room, he said, for Cantonese wounded.

"I will attend to them," Edward said. "Where are they?"

The officer would have none of that. "I must have these beds," he said. "These beds. Now!"

"But you see that is impossible."

"And you do not seem to realize I am in command here. I can shoot you."

"Yes," Edward said, "but you also require my services. You would make a mistake."

The Cantonese drew his revolver. He released the safety catch and, from less than five feet away, took deliberate aim at the head of the man who challenged him. Edward waited. He knew he should say something, yet all he could do was stand there and be stubborn. "You are being foolish," he told himself, "very foolish. And your foolishness may cost you your life."

The officer was not saying anything either. Or doing anything. Conflicting thoughts, like cloud patterns, passed across his face. "All right," he said finally, "return to your work. We are moving in beds." The doctor went back to his patients. Suddenly his legs were very weak. It had been, as he said afterward, "quite a scare."

Early in 1928, Edward fell desperately ill. "He had a high fever," Judd recalled. "I didn't know how high until eventually he let me take his temperature—it was 105. He was sick unto death, but he wouldn't use a bedpan. When he tried to walk, he toppled over. When he toppled over, he crawled. This went on for three weeks. When the fever went down I noticed he was not entirely rational. Some things he said didn't make sense, and I thought of encephalitis, inflammation of the brain.

"He had to leave Shaowu, but he couldn't go by himself, so I decided to go with him. Well, there were bandits on the river, we knew that, but we had to take the chance. I was worried. These bandits, we were told, were a particularly rough lot, and I knew they were bound to stop us at Rooster Fight, that bottleneck where the Min narrows down between those great rocks.

"Then a lucky thing happened. I was ashore a few miles above Rooster Fight, buying something we needed—I think it was kerosene—and I saw a man on the street I knew was a bandit, a man I had treated for a leg wound a couple months before, so I threw myself on the mercy of this man. 'Gee,' I said, 'I'm glad to see you! Dr. Bliss is very sick and I have him down there in a boat. If I don't get him out of here and down the river to Foochow [Fuzhou] as soon as possible, he will die.' I didn't tell the fellow he was a bandit—that gave him face. I just said perhaps the bandits would listen to him. He said he would try.

"The next morning we waited to allow time for the man to send runners down to Rooster Fight and deliver the message. It was a gamble. I had no right to think it would work. But as we approached Rooster Fight the bandits put a man on our boat. He stood in the bow as a sign to the others, and no one stopped us. No one wanted harm to befall Dr. Bliss. They knew his good works."

Edward failed to respond to treatment at Fuzhou, and Judd, who had business to attend to in America, went earlier than planned so he could accompany his colleague, a virtual invalid, to the States for further tests. No record has been found telling how Edward's illness was diagnosed or how he finally was treated. One reason is that Edward was with his family and not writing letters.

In November 1928 Edward, fully recovered, returned to his post. Because it was relatively safe—Jiang's southern forces had won their revolution—and because the children were old enough to be left in the States, May was back at his side. The Kelloggs, the Riggses, and the McClures were back, too. So was Judd, working furiously in defiance of Edward's counsel to ease up because of the malaria that racked him. It seemed almost normal, almost as though the new hospital at North Gate would be finished and that Edward would find the rinderpest vaccine that, more than any other scientific discovery in the field of veterinary medicine, would help the Chinese farmer.

The "normal" situation was short-lived. Within two years it became apparent that Jiang could not control the distant provinces, where warlords held power, and that the Communists, who once supported him, were in reality his enemies. In 1930 Jiang, with the help of an elite German-trained officer corps, succeeded in forcing some warlords to their knees. Not so the Communist rebels. They not only defied him with impunity, seizing large sections of Hunan and Anhui Provinces, but also established their own people's state, or soviet, in Jiangxi. Because of rumors that they would strike next into Fujian, the women and children of the Shaowu mission again withdrew to Fuzhou. May returned to America with an aching heart, never to return. And a few months later, after Judd left for North China, Edward once more became the lone physician practicing Western medicine in the region.

In the years that followed—both men lived well into their nineties—Edward spoke respectfully of Judd, and there is no question that this respect was mutual. Judd said he had difficulty treating patients because there were so many ailments the texts he studied said nothing about. "But Dr. Bliss," he said, "he knew about them. I'm sure he put up with my inexperience, thinking to himself, 'He'll find out after a while that some things aren't in the textbooks.' For example, he knew there are strains of malaria and that there is such a thing as immunity to malaria. But you never would find that in any book published at that time. Now they know."

Judd was amazed at Edward's stamina. "I remember a picnic on Lotus Mountain. We were starting down afterward, and he began to run. And, golly, he ran most of the way." If the astonished young doctor had known that Edward ran hare and hounds (cross-country) at Yale, he might have been less surprised.

Edward lived to see Judd serve ten terms in Congress and become the Republican Party's expert on China. When Edward died, Judd said that to have known him, and worked with him, had been a privilege. He told Ruth, Edward's older daughter, "He was like a father to me, too."

But Judd had hurt Edward. Grievously. In his biography, *Missionary for Freedom: The Life and Times of Walter Judd*, Lee Edwards quotes Judd as saying that "although Dr. Bliss was one of the finest, most benevolent, loving men who ever lived, from my point of view he was a failure as a missionary." This, Judd said, was because he "did things *for* people, always *for* people." It was Judd's belief that a big part of the missionary role was to show people—in this case, the Chinese—how to help themselves. They should be in charge.

"I didn't try to argue with him," Judd said, "because he was too saintly a man, but I did with the Mission Board."

Edward learned of Judd's report to the board, and it devastated him. A failure! In his colleague's view, a failure in his life's work! The judgment hurt because of the respect, even affection, he held for Judd and because he regarded the charge unfair. He *had* worked to help the Chinese help themselves. That had been the whole purpose of the cooperative. The project died, but it had been of and for the Chinese. Judd told his biographer that Edward also failed in that in all his years at Shaowu "not a single boy or girl had gone away from there to medical school." But Edward, taking a different approach, had instructed dozens of students in *materia medica* so that many of them had their own drugstores. And how about the bright young men he taught to treat everything from leg sores to malaria and who became "barefoot doctors"? And some of his students *had* gone to medical school.

It was to set an example for Chinese to follow that he had planted fir trees in barren places, introduced alfalfa, established a dairy. Didn't Shaowu now have a Chinese dairy copied after his own? And he had this dream, the big dream that one day there would be a serum the Chinese could use for combating rinderpest. Production of the serum, making the dream real, was his goal.

I Hope You Have Not Formed an Exaggerated Idea of the Importance of My Contribution

EDWARD'S PECULIAR CONTRIBUTION was his rinderpest research.

Two months before he died, he wrote his children: "I hope that from my letters home you have not formed an exaggerated idea of the importance of my contribution to the whole matter of rinderpest prevention." The major contribution, he said, was made by U.S. veterinary surgeons in the Philippines. "They used a serum prepared from the blood of cattle that had recovered from the disease. A measured quantity of this serum was injected under the skin of the animal and, at the same time, a small quantity of virulent rinderpest blood was also injected. There resulted a mild case of rinderpest that conferred lasting immunity. This anti-rinderpest serum could be purchased in Shanghai, but it was expensive—forty dollars per liter. That was too expensive for my use and far beyond the ability of the Chinese farmer to pay.

"I needed to find another method within my means. In times of rinderpest epidemics, sick cattle would be brought to the butchers for slaughter. The gall bladder of an animal having rinderpest was readily purchased from the butcher. After several days of the disease, the gall bladder became enlarged to several times its normal size and contained large quantities of bile.

"During his studies of rinderpest in Africa, Robert Koch, the German bacteriologist, learned that the bile of the rinderpest gall bladder contained the virus in virulent strength but that if this bile were diluted with an equal amount of pure glycerin, the mixture would gradually lose its virulence, so that ten days later it could be injected into the dewlap of a cow without producing active rinderpest. The injection of this rinderpest bile and glycerin would confer an immunity to rinderpest lasting several months.

"I concluded that if ten days after the cow had received the injection of rinderpest gall she was injected with a small quantity of rinderpest blood, she would develop rinderpest in only a mild form and would thereafter be immune. I tried this with a number of susceptible cattle and found my reasoning was correct. The whole procedure, viz. the preparation of rinderpest bile with glycerin and obtaining the needed rinderpest blood in times of epidemic, was a simple matter within the ability of any physician. This simplification of the method of preparing and administering the immunizing agents was my special contribution.

"The other contribution was my discovery that the calves of immune cows inherited a temporary immunity that gradually diminished. Within the first month after birth, calves from immune mothers, I found, could be injected with 2 mils [a small amount] of virulent rinderpest blood without noticeable reaction. Later they were given an injection of 5 cubic centimeters of virulent rinderpest blood without reaction, proving that lasting immunity had been conferred."

This is, beyond doubt, one of the few "scientific papers" ever written by a doctor at age ninety-four. It is deceptively simple. It is also deceptively modest. A report on rinderpest vaccines submitted to the United Nations by the Food and Agriculture Organization says that the first work with goat-attenuated virus was done in India "as far back as 1932." Edward had been experimenting with the goat-attenuated virus since 1918. On October 5, 1918, he wrote his mother, "I am inoculating goats one after the other at intervals of perhaps five days, and they stand it well. I believe that I can use these goats to produce serum. Though there is a good deal to be learned yet, as far as I know this is original work."

In March 1922 *The China Medical Journal* published a report by Edward saying: "Probably there are smaller animals which can be used for the purpose with less expense and trouble than goats. At Shaowu, experiments were started with rabbits but were interrupted before enough temperatures had been taken to warrant any positive conclusion. But," he added, "the observations made seemed to indicate that rabbits are susceptible." The first significant work with rabbits, in this connection, reportedly was done sixteen years later in Japan. Edward's experiments with lapinized virus may not have been "significant," but certainly he sensed the possibilities at an early date.

Judd praised Edward's ingenuity. "It was one of the great problems," he said, "how to keep your serum. He didn't have a refrigerator, and he didn't have an incubator, and yet he worked at that thing and faced up to discouragement. He figured it out himself." One of the things he figured out was that if he shot the virus into living animals, such as goats, he didn't need a refrigerator. The serum was inside the animal. It would not spoil.

But he was not satisfied with improvisation. He dreamed of a refrigerated bank of vaccine, set up in Jiangxi, that would be available to farmers for hundreds of miles around in time of pestilence. In 1922, when Cyrus Hall McCormick gave him the young bull Improver, Edward was emboldened to ask for ten thousand dollars so that "a centrally located laboratory can be established to provide a constant supply of reliable serum." He wrote the millionaire philanthropist, "I hope someone will see that here is a real opportunity to help China upward economically." His appeal was ignored. A quarter century later, such a laboratory was established by the Nationalist government in Nanchang, the capital of Jiangxi, just in time for Communist revolutionaries to take it over.

And so he worked, through the twenties and into the thirties. In 1932, his last year in China, he was at Shunchang with Kellogg. A middle-aged Chinese, a total stranger, introduced himself, saying that he had been delivered by Edward in 1893, near the village called Kai-tung. Incredibly, here before him, utterly fortuitously, stood the first normal Chinese baby he had delivered and heard cry for breath! How long ago it seemed—the plight that night of the mule Jacqueline, the long journey in darkness, the joy of delivering a live child, the falling asleep in exhaustion beside pigs. The name of the stranger, and what he made of his life, is not recorded. Kellogg, in a newsletter, barely mentions the incident but obviously the Chinese had been told of the spider-legged foreigner who traveled such a long distance to deliver him. Obviously, through the years, he had remembered.

By early November 1932 only Edward of the original band of Shaowu missionaries was left. Kellogg had, at last, gone home on furlough. The only other American in the area was George Shepherd. And when the Communist army finally descended on Shaowu, Shepherd was forty li away, in Jianning.

Jianning Has Fallen

※

IT WAS LATE AFTERNOON. The chief magistrate had been trying to persuade Edward to flee Shaowu before the Communist army, advancing from Jiangxi, reached the city. More than forty river-boats had been commandeered for people seeking escape. The magistrate himself was about to embark, along with other officials of the prefecture and their families. Everyone knew that no defense would be made of the city, with its useless antique cannon and vestigial walls, so for two days a stream of refugees had been going out East Gate to find sanctuary in the downriver homes of fellow clansmen and friends. These were Shaowu's people of property, the bourgeoisie. Some rode in sedan chairs. Most traveled on foot, loaded with their most treasured possessions.

Vainly the magistrate, whose first son Edward had delivered, warned of the danger. And vainly the doctor explained that he would stay until his colleague George Shepherd arrived from Jian-ning. The magistrate had first sent messengers urging Edward to go to the sparrow boat reserved for him. When their exhortations failed, the official had taken the unusual action of coming in per-son. He was grieved that the missionary saw fit to ignore his counsel, which was given in kindness. His face was a picture of anxiety. This confidence that Shepherd would appear, he felt, was ill-founded.

"How can you know?" he asked. "Jianning has fallen."

"It was his plan. He was to start back yesterday."

"*Ai,* but Jianning was taken two days ago. Have you consid-ered that your friend might be captured?"

Edward had thought of that possibility—and rejected it. Shep-herd was a man of intelligence and tough physique, a onetime mountain climber. He was not a man to sit and let himself be taken.

"Or he might be hiding," the magistrate said. "He could conceal himself in the mountains. Many Christians have gone to the mountains."

Still, Edward was impelled to wait. He *knew* Shepherd was coming. He could not explain. He thanked the magistrate for his solicitude.

The magistrate bowed, slowly and with dignity, in his fur robe. "*Ping an,*" he said. "Peace."

After the official left, Edward packed his largest suitcase. What do you pack in one suitcase on leaving a place where you have spent a lifetime? This was the house he and May had built together and cherished and called home. It was full of books and rugs and framed pictures and bed linen and boxes of well-enjoyed toys—and memories. The dining room clock ticked as comfortably as ever. The Morris chair in which Edward had rested so often, girding himself for new battles, showed no awareness of the crisis and waited with open arms. Sir Galahad remained at ease beside his white charger. The Royal typewriter stood ready for the next hospital report, or family letter, and the lovely Estey organ, so long silent, awaited May's return. These things must be left behind. Edward did not let himself think of them. He filled the suitcase with basics such as flannel pajamas and underwear, along with a pair of glasses and the silver napkin ring May gave him on their first wedding anniversary.

When he had packed these things and a full medicine bag, he prepared a simple supper of cocoa and boiled rice. He ate alone. He had lived alone for two months, but there was no time for being lonely. Throngs of patients, sometimes as many as 130 a day, had kept him busy morning to night. Now, after supper, he made sick calls at four Chinese homes. With each patient he left an extra supply of medicine.

"You do right not to stay," said one. "You must go away and then you must come back."

GEORGE SHEPHERD was making one of the most remarkable "forced marches" in the history of China missions. He was traveling with a Chinese pastor with the surname Lin. They were in open country, north of the county seat of Taining, when word came that a

Communist force led by Zhu De had broken through from Jiangxi and already held Jianning. Moreover, the Communists had cut the road leading to Shaowu. Shepherd and his Chinese colleague tried to escape to the northwest but found that route, too, swarming with troops. It appeared they were trapped.

"We have one chance," Pastor Lin said. "There is a trail leading to Shaowu over the mountains. It is very rough. It climbs the peaks and is seldom used. I am not even sure I know the way."

They picked up the trail, and in the first village a woodcutter, who was a Christian, volunteered as guide. But would they reach Shaowu ahead of the Communists? That was the gamble. Shepherd said later, "We knew we had to travel fast because the Communists made long marches. The average Chinese army traveled no more than fifteen miles a day, but the Communists could double and sometimes treble that distance. We met nothing but friendliness in the mountain villages and kept on after nightfall.

"That day we covered forty miles through the roughest country I ever traveled. We were footsore and dead tired and decided we had to sleep. Our guide selected an inn he thought would be safe. Of course, the real question was one of Communist spies being on the lookout for such a treasure as an American who could be held for ransom. But I was too tired to think much of that. I threw myself down and promptly went to sleep."

"When we were awakened, Pastor Lin told me that while I was sleeping some men at the inn had discussed the possibility of turning this foreigner over to the Communists for money. The guide overheard this discussion, so he went to the innkeeper, whom he knew, and asked him to go with us a short distance. He thought that would lessen the danger. The innkeeper did accompany us a few miles, and nothing happened, but a Roman Catholic priest, Father Geser, who worked with us at Jianning, fled in the wrong direction and was captured and shot on the spot."

The Red Army Is at the Gates

WALKING BACK to the compound after his last house call, Edward saw that evacuation of the city had not abated. Indeed, the flow of frightened humanity through East Gate appeared greater than before. Many women, he noticed, were carrying babies. Some were nursing as they walked. Everyone carried something. One boy, about seven, trudged sleepily along with a chicken in his arms. The doctor wondered where they would all find refuge. Surely there was a limit, for most of these people did not plan to travel far. They would stay with their country cousins and take on the guise of simple rural folk.

Edward got to bed at three in the morning. At four he was awakened by another messenger from the chief magistrate. "Our soldiers are retreating," he said. "The Red Army is at the gates."

"How much time have I got?" Edward was only half awake. It would be surprising, he thought, if the danger were not exaggerated. If he had taken the magistrate's first advice, he would now have been sitting stupidly in a crowded sparrow boat for two days.

"Perhaps an hour, perhaps two hours. My master begs to say that, because of this, your friend cannot possibly come here. The roads are full of the enemy."

"Please tell the magistrate I am grateful. I will go to the boat."

Torches lit the waterfront, where easily a thousand persons were milling about, hoping to board boats capable of carrying half their number. A heavy, chilling rain splattered the crowd, the thatched bamboo covering of the boats, and the rock-strewn beach and river. The people were extraordinarily quiet. All the boats had been spoken for. There was almost no chance anyone not assigned to a boat would be taken on, but still people waited to see if perhaps room for them might be found. A young officer directed Edward to a boat designed to carry six or seven persons but that already had ten on board. A good thing, he thought, he had brought only the suitcase and his bag of medicines.

The flotilla was scheduled to leave at dawn and proceed downstream under military escort. Through the early morning hours, Edward in his raincoat and paradoxical sun helmet watched for Shepherd. He still might come. The crowd on the beach melted with the daylight and the hopelessness of their situation. A few lucky ones were taken; room was made for perhaps twenty or thirty. Nationalist soldiers patrolled the waterfront; occasionally they stopped and questioned a straggler, either to help or shoo away.

Shortly after nine o'clock in the morning an officer commanded the boats farthest downstream to get under way. The boat to which Edward was assigned was drawn up in the middle of the formation. At the last moment, as it was about to set out, he asked the two Chinese families sharing the boat if they would grant him fifteen minutes, and they agreed.

The boatmen, impatient, waited sullenly. Edward kept looking at his watch. The second hand seemed to race. Minutes flew. He had no right to jeopardize the safety of either passengers or crew. And the tense situation was not improved when a former patient named Wong called from another boat and urged him to leave. Two hours later, Wong's boat struck a rock, and his wife and two-month-old granddaughter were drowned.

There was no sign of Shepherd. Edward waited fifteen minutes, and then, after another minute or two—he stole that little time—he climbed into the boat and, with heavy spirit, thanked the Chinese for their consideration. It did seem that his colleague had been trapped. He thought of staying behind, but that merely would have provided the Communists with two Western imperialists instead of one. He decided to leave. Never in the years that followed did he question the rightness of that decision, torn as he was.

As the boat left, he looked back at the city, at the conglomeration of houses, temples, and wall towers so familiar to him, and wondered what fate held in store for it. The Red Army that took Jianning was said to number thirty thousand men; other Communist armies were advancing to the west and the south. The rain and black-tiled roofs made a picture of gloom. A water buffalo, drinking at the river's edge, raised its head querulously at the sound of distant artillery fire.

The boat had put out when he heard a call from the beach. Shepherd and Pastor Lin were waving frantically. Edward shouted that they would be picked up, and with ill-concealed annoyance the crew rowed back to shore. Both Shepherd and the Chinese pastor were in a state of complete exhaustion. Their faces were torn and bleeding from brambles. Shepherd's raincoat was reduced to tatters. In retelling the story, Shepherd said, "I can still see Dr. Bliss's face as we scrambled aboard. It was a look of great thankfulness."

Shepherd lay down on the bare boards on the bottom of the boat and, exhausted, slept until late that afternoon. He had hiked eighty miles over the mountains in a little more than thirty hours.

There was no jubilation. Once more, the foreigners were being forced to abandon their work. Pastor Lin was anxious about his family in Jianning. He already was planning how to go back to them in disguise after leaving the boat downriver at Shunchang. Shepherd spoke resolutely of Lin's sacrifice in helping him, a sacrifice, he said, that he could never fittingly repay.

WHEN EDWARD looked back again, Shaowu was out of sight. He did not think of himself as sentimental, but he would have liked to catch another glimpse of it. The river was high after the rain, and the current swept their overloaded sparrow boat close—not dangerously close—to the shore where stood the arches to virtuous widows. He had a special fondness for these arches; he had walked under them the first time he came to that *xian* forty years before.

Remembering the walk along that footpath, which now had become a motor road, he knew there was something else he had seen that day on the other side of the river, high on a hilltop. And so he looked, and there it stood, the Shaowu pagoda, stark against the gray sky, guarding the southern approaches to the city and the people he loved. He could not recall ever seeing a pagoda guarding the city's approaches from the west.

Epilogue

IF EDWARD CAME HOME in defeat, he didn't know it. He could sail from Shanghai in good spirits, happy in the thought of homecoming because he really did not think he was through. The polyglot that was Shanghai, the snow-laden upper slopes of Fuji, the brown-skinned divers of Honolulu, he would see them all again, he was sure. Fuzhou, Shanghai, Yokohama, Honolulu, San Francisco. These had become commuter stops, so familiar they were part of his life. He had visited them alone and with his family, with his goats and chickens, in sickness and in health, in youth and in old age. And he had always returned.

The reason he rejected the thought of final, absolute retirement was that his work was not finished. He was confident the Communists could not hold Shaowu, that Jiang Jieshi's armies, supplied by the United States, would drive them out. When they were gone, and he had spent some time with his loved ones, he would return and take up the research where he left off. And this time he would have new, modern equipment. He would engage his old enemy with the advantage of weapons he had not possessed before, thanks to a bequest that brother Charles had made. That was his ace in the hole. He could not expect the American Board to finance his project altogether, but with Charles's gift and a supplementary appropriation from the board, he could carry on his research. With God's help, he would go the full distance.

At San Francisco, passengers proceeding to New York through the Panama Canal transferred to another liner that stopped at San Pedro, the port for Los Angeles. It was a bitter disappointment to Edward, due to the brief call at San Pedro, to be unable to visit the Gardners in Claremont, fewer than fifty miles away. It meant he would never see his old friends again. He had been poignantly reminded of the Gardners shortly before leaving Shaowu when he learned that his mother had died. It was Milton Gardner who had gently informed him of the death of his father.

Bertrand Russell said, "A man who has sufficient vitality to reach old age cannot be happy unless he is active." In "temporary" retirement in Oberlin, Ohio, Edward laid a new concrete floor in the basement, grew tomatoes, shoveled the walk in winter, mowed the lawn in summer, took up crossword puzzles, and did the shopping. And all the time he kept a wary eye on events in the Far East. The events were ominous. The Communists did leave Shaowu, only to link up with their comrades in Jiangxi and make the tortuous, six-thousand-mile "Long March" to a new lair in the Northwest. Again and again, the Nanjing government demonstrated disunity, culminating in the abduction and release of Jiang Jieshi by conspirators in his own party. Then came Japan's invasion of China and the battle for Shanghai. China was being chewed to pieces in what Japan called an "incident" but in what amounted to full-scale war.

Edward wondered if he should try to return to China when cities like Shanghai, Canton, and Fuzhou were in Japanese hands. Fukien Christian University had moved upriver from Fuzhou to Shaowu, just as other universities in the North had withdrawn farther inland, to Sichuan Province. The Japanese did not forget Shaowu; they simply didn't bother with it. Occasionally one of their reconnaissance planes would circle lazily and contemptuously over the walled city. "May," Edward would say, "can you imagine an airplane flying over our house at East Gate?" And she would say, gracious, she couldn't conceive of it.

But the city was free. Missionaries worked there, a whole new generation of them. Chinese friends had preserved remnants of the herd; there were still cattle to experiment with. And never had Shaowu, thanks to the presence of émigré professors, been so rich in scientific talent. A group of Chinese formally petitioned the mission board to make an exception and allow Edward to serve beyond the age of retirement. They argued that he was enjoying the best of health. "Furthermore," they said, "he is now like one of our own people."

What should he do?

The answer came, with finality, when May was stricken with pernicious anemia. Edward had noticed her chronic tiredness and prescribed vitamins and rest. When she failed to gain strength, he took her to the famed Cleveland Clinic, where her ailment was diagnosed. The loss of red blood cells had so ravaged her vertebrae that she had to wear a heavy steel brace. Special medicines were prescribed, including liver extract. She could not dress herself. There was no question of leaving her now.

Her illness did not frustrate Edward; it was soon apparent that he could not have completed his work anyway. War soon broke out in Europe, followed by the Japanese attack on Pearl Harbor. He would scarcely have gotten settled in Shaowu before he would have had to leave. The stark truth was: *His tour of duty in China was over.* Nothing could be done about it. Nothing. And so, philosophically, he tied on an apron and took over in the kitchen of their home, just as he had in China when he and Judd were suddenly left without a cook.

Edward bought a whole new set of heavy aluminum pots and pans, and fell to with a will, turning up great blazes under them, blackening their bottoms but producing dishes that were always tasty and in which the whole family could take pride. May, of course, would chafe at her incapacity—nor was she above giving instruction—but it helped to know that cooking was, for Edward, a source of real pleasure. He did no baking. "Nothing fancy," he would say. But his vegetables were always tender, swimming in butter, and his steaks, chops, and roasts were memorable. His only regret in cooking was that unless they had company, he could not roast a beef. A rib roast for two was impracticable.

May would make sorties into the kitchen, but it was no longer her domain. She might set the table and pour beverages, but Edward was in charge now, and sometimes her pride must have suffered. But hers was an indomitable spirit. After meeting her, Edward R. Murrow said, "I never saw so much zest for living in anyone's eyes." It was true. For her, life never lost savor. She watched the inauguration of President Johnson on television just as avidly as she had listened to the inauguration of FDR. And in her ninety-seventh year, in letters, she was still writing excitedly of bird songs, sunsets, and the flaming colors of autumn. It was an incredible thing how she lived until she died.

After World War II, with only his sister Marian surviving, Edward yearned to go back to Newburyport. He was eighty-one now. With the years claiming him, he wanted to live again in his steepled town by the sea. He knew May loved Oberlin. She enjoyed the Oberlin Conservatory concerts, and she held dear the friends she had made there while she watched over the three children in their school days. But the time had come when he must go home. So they sold the house on South Cedar Street, the only house they ever owned, and took an apartment in Newburyport. He and Marian saw much of each other for a year, and then she died.

He had loved the sea from his boyhood days when he clambered among the Plum Island dunes to the last Newburyport year when he drove to the island and sat alone, feasting his eyes on the panorama of blue water. It was a scene he had grown up with, the barely distinguishable Isles of Shoals to the north, the low silhouette of Cape Ann to the south, and the open ocean stretching three thousand miles to the coast of Portugal. He remembered how in boyhood he had studied the habits of seagulls, their setting down and taking off, and discovered the prickly sound seawater makes settling into sand.

Often at the end of the day they would take a drive and park, like lovers, and look out across the Newbury marshes at the distant, soft-contoured hills. He might recall a youthful adventure on Oldtown Hill or relive a Sunday school picnic, or tell her the story of Crane's Castle. Or they would sit without speaking and watch ducks parade Ould Newbury Green, or drive to where they could see children playing at Atkinson Park, or go to the Pines, where the sunset, mirrored in tidal waters, set their world on fire.

May played the piano that came to take the place of her beloved Shaowu organ. In midafternoon, after her nap, she would play a repertoire of hymns. She played them somewhat heavy-handedly, because she never quite remembered that she was no longer at an organ, always ending with a succession of chords that reverberated through the small apartment like doomsday. How she loved those chords! Edward liked her playing and enjoyed "good music" on the radio. His favorite program was *The Bell Telephone Hour*, and his favorite piece was "Finlandia." The fact that he and Sibelius were born the same day, he insisted, had nothing to do with it.

SO THE YEARS PASSED, and in September 1958, after more than half a century of life together, they ended their independent existence. They left Newburyport while they were able and went to

233

Edward and May in Newburyport after retirement.

live with Ruth and her surgeon husband, who gave them the large west room on the second floor of their Boston home. "The room closest to China," someone observed, and Edward smiled as though this were a happy thought.

The moving proved an ordeal. Ruth helped all she could, but even after the van came, and May went to Boston, Edward stayed a week "to straighten up." He mopped floors, washed windows, and painted the kitchen, living all the while on orange juice, peanut butter sandwiches, and milk. It was quite obvious that he was loath to leave. He loved his native city, with its long, ramshackle waterfront, stately elms, and pristine white steeples, and he knew that once he left, he would no longer be his own man. He did not tell May all he was going to do "straightening up," but later she remarked on the paint under his fingernails, and he confessed. It was a big kitchen, and painting it must have been a heavy task for someone almost ninety-three.

The next year was really quite remarkable. May and Edward began attending church in Boston, just as they had in Newburyport. Edward raked leaves that fall, and when it snowed he helped shovel the front walk. He attended his granddaughter's wedding, rode in a Thunderbird with the top down, made his first airplane flight, was visited by Murrow—minus TV cameras—and celebrated his fifty-seventh wedding anniversary, which he thought not bad for a man who married tardily at thirty-six. May shared all these experiences, except the ride in the Thunderbird. The ride up Commonwealth Avenue with the top down, she said, was bound to muss her hair.

In May 1959, May reported in a letter, "The doctors have found a growth in Father's throat. They are going to start treating it with X-rays." She did not seem to realize the seriousness of the discovery. No one had told her the tumor was malignant or that an operation would be futile. Besides, Edward was indestructible. He always came back.

Edward was not deceived. As his strength ebbed, he was increasingly at a loss to know what to do with himself. Sometimes he would want to talk. "I was busy with a lot of things," he said, looking back on his China experience. "Doctoring, farming, trying to overcome rinderpest. I enjoyed it all." Or his reminiscing would go back to college days and he would talk about old Noah Porter's lectures on morality, or about climbing East Rock—East Gate, he called it once—or recall the time when he was going door to door selling the fat volume called *The Museum of Antiquity.*

Walter Judd's critical report to the mission board rankled to the end. Edward spoke bitterly of Judd's complaint that he had not seen to the training of more Chinese doctors. One day he was sitting in the bedroom, erect in a straight chair, fully clothed, eyes angry, and he said, "I don't care. I think showing those young men how to treat the sick was one of the best things I ever did. They were a capable bunch." He was referring again to his students, the Chinese he trained to go out in the countryside as "barefoot doctors."

It was something he took pride in, one thing he believed was right. And three students did go on to earn medical degrees.

Minutes later, he turned from bitterness to recollections of youth, of seagulls and summer tide, of Yale, of East Rock and how trying to climb its face was "the most fool thing" he ever did. It was while in medical school, he said, that Yale acquired Handsome Dan, its first bulldog, as a mascot. He told how football was much rougher back then, boasting that in six years he missed not a single bruising game played at home.

But inevitably he spoke again of China. "I love the Chinese," he said. These were the last words his son remembers him saying the last time they talked.

On January 22, 1960, during the first night of the *Da Han*, or Great Cold, Edward died peacefully in his sleep. He had been granted his last wish, which was not to be a burden, for he had been confined to his bed only one day. Every morning until that day he had dressed himself in his gray worsted suit and sat in his beloved Morris chair, dozing mostly but often listening to news on the radio and sometimes, in his cracked voice, talking to May, who was never far away. Twice, when Ruth looked in to see how he was getting on, she found him kneeling in prayer.

At the time of his death, in the room where he died, Ruth discovered a dog-eared copy of *Robinson Crusoe* inscribed with Edward's name and the date "Christmas 1878." The last sentence of the book, treasured by him as a boy, reads: "And here I resolved to prepare for a longer journey than all these, having lived a life of infinite variety seventy-two years and learned sufficiently to know the value of retirement, and the blessings of ending our days in peace."

May had said, through tears, that she did not care to live after Edward died. But she lived another seven years, until she, too, died peacefully in her sleep. In the Newburyport cemetery they lie on a slope facing the sunsets. The stone bears witness:

1865 EDWARD LYDSTON BLISS, M.D. 1960
1870 MINNIE BORTZ BLISS 1967
MISSIONARIES TO CHINA
1892–1933

Edward died without seeing the emergence of China as a world power, which he foresaw, or defeat of the rinderpest virus, which he sought. After his death, a global eradication campaign was launched and gains made. A British veterinary scientist, Dr. Walter Plowright, researching in Kenya, developed a vaccine that protects cattle for at least ten years and often for a lifetime. Thanks to Dr. Plowright's achievement, the research of other scientists, and emphasis on early detection, the plague in the main has been confined to small pockets in southern Sudan, Somalia, and Pakistan. The United Nations Food and Agriculture Organization now believes that global eradication is possible by 2010. How this news would have gladdened Edward's heart!

Index

China
  beauty of, 64, 147
  Bliss's aims in, 206
  Bliss's first impressions of, 8
  Bliss's loyalty to, 34, 41, 63, 68,
    236
  foreigner-native hostilities, 34,
    68, 172, 173, 211
  harsh climate of, 57–58
  internal strife, 206, 209–12
  See also Boxer Rebellion;
    Communists; Nationalists;
    Revolution of 1911
  Japanese expansionism in, 68, 73,
    75, 211, 231
  medicine in. See medical practice
  peak mission years in, 187–92
  U.S. relations, 13, 34, 210–11,
    213
  See also specific place names
China, SS (ship), 32, 35–36, 88
China Inland Mission, 197
China lobby, 213
Chinese Exclusion Act, 34
chloroform, 71
chloroquine, 60–61
Christianity
  Bliss's deep faith in, 206
  Chinese view of, 129, 210, 211
  missionary zeal for, 95
  Shi Xiansheng's conversion, 83
  See also missionaries; specific
    denominations
Church of Christ in China, 129
City Gate Gorge, 9–10
Cleveland Clinic, 232
Cogston, Mrs. (New Haven
    boarding house), 21, 30, 97
Colombo, Ceylon, 84
colonialism, 210, 211
Columbia University, 88
Communists, 41, 126, 128, 197,
    215, 218
  "Long March," 231
  Shaowu takeover by, 212,
    223–29, 230
Confucius, 210

Congregational church, 14–16,
    26–27, 79, 94, 135
Coptic, SS (ship), 90, 91
Cowper, William, 56
Crystal Hill, 40, 57, 58, 61, 67,
    73–74, 101, 103, 189
Culty (dairyman), 168, 169
Curtis, Thomas, 24
Cushing, Caleb, 13
Custer, George, 93

dairying, 150–64, 168–76, 220
  bull importations, 153–55, 169,
    193–98
  flood damage, 207–8
  goat importations, 182–83
  infant nutrition motive, 150–51,
    182, 184
  local Chinese competition, 179,
    211–12, 220
  new corrals, 187
  plague control. See rinderpest
  as preventive medicine, 184
Daisy (cow), 155–62
Dana, Edward S., 22
dispensary (Shaowu), 60, 71–72, 114
  enlargement, 78–79
  flood damage, 208
  opening of, 54–56
  women's, 101, 119, 185
  See also hospital
Doane College, 94, 131–32
dogs, 55–56
Dominican Order, 128
druggists, Chinese, 106, 125–26,
    219–20
drugs. See pharmaceuticals
Dwight, Timothy, 13
dysentery, 87, 105

East Gate compound, 39–40, 132,
    142–44
  Bliss's new house, 122–24
  Boxer damage, 100–101
  flood effects, 208
East Gate Congregational Church,
    79–81, 83, 100, 190